SINGING HISTORIAN

SINGING HISTORIAN

A MEMOIR

EDMUND BOHAN

CANTERBURY UNIVERSITY PRESS

For Sarah, Sebastian and the grandchildren:
Frederick, George, Vanessa, Isobel, Henrietta,
Florence and William.

UNIVERSITY OF CANTERBURY
Te Whare Wānanga o Waitaha
CHRISTCHURCH NEW ZEALAND

First published in 2012 by
CANTERBURY UNIVERSITY PRESS
University of Canterbury
Private Bag 4800, Christchurch
NEW ZEALAND
www.cup.canterbury.ac.nz

ISBN 978-1-927145-31-9

eBook ISBN 978-1-927145-32-6

A catalogue record for this book is available from the National Library of New Zealand.

Cover and book design: Quentin Wilson, Christchurch
Printed in New Zealand by PrintStop, Wellington

CONTENTS

ONE

BEGINNINGS

I WAS BORN IN CHRISTCHURCH ON 5 October 1935, late on a hot Saturday during which the family cat produced kittens, a batch of chickens hatched from their eggs and my five-year-old sister became distraught when, in spite of the best efforts of her siblings to distract her, she glimpsed Mum getting into the taxi to take her to Lyndhurst Nursing Home. I'm not sure if Trish ever got over my arrival for, as she has so often reminded me, I became the bane of her childhood years.

I was named Edmund after my paternal grandfather, but known inside the family and to our friends as Ned, as was he.

Family friends and relations, as far as I know, generally welcomed my arrival but more especially were relieved that my mother survived it, for the birth was very difficult. She had suffered at least two miscarriages in the years between the birth of Patricia Therese (Trish) and my appearance, had been ill almost throughout this last pregnancy and she and my father were warned that she would be unlikely to survive any subsequent pregnancy. She took a long time to recover and throughout my childhood her health was fragile. So a heavy weight of responsibility for my care was placed on Bernadette

Mary (generally known as Gaye inside the family), who was reared, like far too many eldest daughters of her generation, to be the dutiful daughter and responsible sister. She coped lovingly and heroically and we remained especially close throughout her life.

I was from earliest childhood, as everyone in the family has so frequently reminded me, a strong-willed and talkative child who outside the family circle often hid his less adorable characteristics behind a veneer of shy diffidence. Inside that family circle, however, I was neither diffident nor shy, but often wilfully independent. My defiant cry 'I do it myself!' became notorious, and as a compulsive reader and accumulator of knowledge from my early years, I was argumentative, definite in opinion on just about everything, and always prepared to offer it whether or not it was asked for. And I inherited my father's strong belief that when I was asked for an opinion, that was exactly what the enquirer wanted to hear. It was a hopelessly naïve idea but one that has remained with me to this day. It has not always won me friends.

By the time I was eight I had decided that I wanted to become a singer and an author – preferably writing about history. It never occurred to my childish mind that there could be any conflict. Admittedly I flirted briefly and irrationally with dentistry after our indulgent dentist had rewarded me with a polished new penny for being a quiet patient; and, for rather longer, with being an archaeologist and explorer; but I never had the remotest interest in driving trains or sailing boats. Instead, I wrote and illustrated a long-lost novella, *The Ghost of Minorie,* contributed to the 'Little Southlanders' pages of the *Southland Times*, and happily sang (and went on singing until my voice began to change from childish alto into light tenor) the ghastly 'My Grandfather's Clock' and 'My Task', an even more appalling Edwardian ballad, on Invercargill's 4YZ Children's Hour.

Everyone I knew sang or, as second best, played a musical instrument, so I believed that everyone in the world had as strong a desire to sing as I had. My mother, the greatest influence in my young life, had a good and well-trained contralto voice and she played the piano well. Both my sisters had fine mezzo voices, especially Bernadette, and Trish also had the makings of a capable pianist. Desmond Bernard (Des), big in personality and a skilled impersonator of Bing Crosby, was throughout his life a popular performer at parties and other social events. Dad's singing of Irish songs and Victorian ballads was always a highlight of our musical evenings. He made a splendid tenor sound, but the intensity with which he sang sometimes pushed him sharp, so Trish and I would ritually howl and try to be funny to cover our embarrassment. Dad never minded. His sense of humour was as acute as his temper was quick, and he could always laugh at himself – a laugh as distinctive and overwhelming as his singing voice.

There were lots of records, too, stacked beside the old wind-up gramophone: Colombia and HMV pink, red and black labels of Caruso, Richard Tauber and John McCormack, Chaliapin, Peter Dawson, and Mum's special favourites, the English tenors Hubert Eisdell and Heddle Nash. As the years passed they were joined by my own idols, Tito Schipa and Jussi Björling.

A party for our family meant a gathering of friends at our place for lots of food and music, and everyone was expected to perform and invariably did; sometimes memorably, as when, during the early war years in Invercargill our friend and dentist Hans Neumann, who played the piano splendidly, brought his uncle Dr Wolf to visit us for the first time. Wolf held some position of influence in the veterinary world, came to Invercargill occasionally, and from that first visit onwards was a regular Sunday evening visitor whenever he did. They were Jewish, of course, and Hans had lived in Invercargill since some years before the war. His much younger wife, Margot, was a refugee and all her family had died, she then believed, in the concentration camp from which she had almost miraculously escaped. Mum, in her quiet and ever tactful way, 'adopted' her and provided a shoulder for her to cry on. Margot, I think, did much crying during those war years.

On Dr Wolf's memorable first visit, Hans played and they both sang Schumann's 'Two Grenadiers' in German, and I stood at the end of the piano transfixed and overwhelmed by the music and these men's passionate commitment. This, I decided, was the way I wanted to sing, and that was the music I wanted to sing, even more than the Irish and Scottish songs I already loved so much.

We had a party every Sunday evening and a lot of Saturdays as well, but Sundays were special because they almost always began badly when we argued about having to go to Mass and refought the Reformation at breakfast time. Dad would shout, Mum would be restrained and I would become increasingly shrill before settling onto the bar of Dad's bike for the ride to St Mary's Catholic Basilica, where I would continue to grumble about the discomfort and the cold until the priest appeared, when I would subside into resentful and critical silence.

Throughout Mass, and especially through the long sermons usually delivered in harsh Irish accents, often by black-gowned, frowning Redemptorists, white Dominicans or marginally less frightening brown Franciscans, I would silently dispute with them – especially when they harped on the evils and dangers of mixed marriages. Then, on the way back home, I'd argue aloud again until Dad was red-faced with a fury intensified by the sheer physical effort of pushing the old bike and my weight against a headwind. Yet by the time we were halfway through our vast and leisurely Sunday lunch we would have given up on religion and Trish and I would be arguing instead about which radio programme should be on. We didn't argue about church or religion on Christmas Eve, though. We all went to Midnight Mass in a tight and friendly family group. I loved everything about that service.

Our problem was that we were a family produced by a 'mixed marriage' – a state made much of in those days by the clannish, predominantly Irish and doctrinally intolerant New Zealand Catholic Church, which continually warned its flock to have as little social contact as possible with Protestants. Its ardour in these matters was matched, of course, by the powerful and even more intolerant non-conformist churches' warnings to *their* congregations about the dangers of Rome and too much social contact with Catholics. Battles were regularly and literally fought out on rugby fields between the

Catholic Marist rugby clubs and those dominated by Protestant values.

One of the worst social consequences of this mutual intolerance was that mixed marriage families like ours were not fully accepted in either community. We were effectively outsiders. I felt this keenly as a child and in so many ways have regarded myself as a natural outsider ever since.

Dad, born in 1897, was a New Zealand Irish Catholic and Irish nationalist, reared in a large family inside Ellesmere's tight-knit rural community and, after their original French priest died, schooled by grim Irish priests and nuns with long and unforgiving memories of famines, the agrarian upheavals of County Cork from which so many had fled, and evictions. My grandmother's Cronin family had experienced those and had come out on the *Blairgowrie* under the Vogel Immigration Scheme in 1875. Grandpa Edmund Bohan, smitten by 16-year-old Kate Cronin, had accompanied them but had paid his own fare. For their sons and daughters – and especially their youngest, my father Edward Bernard – the Elizabethan Irish Wars, Cromwell's Curse, the struggles for Home Rule and the accumulated wrongs of Ireland were combined in a bitter but cherished heritage. This was given a keener edge by the real discrimination he experienced as a young bank clerk in Poverty Bay, Taranaki and Christchurch during and after World War One from senior colleagues in the Orange and Masonic Orders and the short-lived, but long and bitterly remembered Protestant Political Association. What neither he nor his siblings inherited, though, was their parents' Gaelic. That was not an upwardly mobile language in late Victorian New Zealand and, like almost all other locally born Irish children, they were forbidden to speak it.

Mum (née Elsie Maclean – she was adamant that was how it must be spelt), was born in 1896 at Ardpatrick in Kilberry, Kintyre, near her father Archibald Maclean's birthplace of Tarbet (though *his* father, a Gaelic speaker who spoke no English and was the local ferryman, came from Mull). She had been strictly reared as a Presbyterian, in Striven Lodge on the shores of Loch Striven, where

Archie (bilingual in Gaelic and English) was a ghillie or gamekeeper. When Dad met her in Hawera after the war, however, and married her in January 1922, she was a Methodist girl and was managing the E. Dixon & Co. music shop for Edwin Dixon, who won the Patea electorate for the Reform Party in 1921.

She had been brought up to disapprove of Catholicism in general and in particular the Irish who had poured into Scotland to build the railways and work in the industrial conurbations surrounding Glasgow. Nonetheless, she converted to Catholicism on her marriage, then discovered from harsh experience and the abrasiveness of her mother-in-law, sisters-in-law, Irish priests and, especially, intolerant nuns, how difficult it was to be part of a mixed marriage; a difficulty not lessened by her own mother's continual reminder that she had only herself to blame.

Grandma Mary Maclean was a beautiful woman, but grim – at least when she stayed with us. Serious, censorious and the strictest of Presbyterians, she loathed Irish men, except, surprisingly, my father, who could always make her laugh. Sure she had suffered much during her marriage, for Grandpa Archie was a charming but feckless Highlander with a weakness for the bottle. Sometime in the early years of the new century he became head ghillie for the Earl of Haddington and the family moved to Tyninghame Lodge, Haddington, where Elsie, a bright and eager pupil according to her headmaster's report, and intended for university, went to school. Like children of the Irish Bohans in far-off New Zealand, however, neither she nor her sisters were allowed to speak their parents' Gaelic.

By 1911 there were family problems and emigration was contemplated. Grandma Mary had two brothers farming successfully in New Zealand: John Spence, near Auckland, and George Spence, near Stratford, Taranaki; and that was where they went, departing from Liverpool on 2 September 1911 on the SS *Ayrshire* and sailing via Capetown. Family tradition has it that Grandma Mary gave Archie a stark choice: if he wanted to come he had to pay his own way. If not, bad luck. He followed, but not especially humbly or with any intention of giving up whisky; and until they eventually parted for good and he moved to Wellington to live with my eldest aunt, Margaret Scoullar, and her family, he inhabited a sleep-out at the bottom of Grandma's Stratford garden. Although Grandma had brought up her daughters to abhor drink, the Irish and Catholicism, at least two ignored her warnings and married Irish Catholics. But three, including my mother, remained prohibitionists until they died.

Mum was, above all, a Maclean of Duart, as dedicated a Highland Scots nationalist as Dad was an Irish one, and determined, I think, that I should be one too – just as she was determined that I, her last child, would achieve what had been denied to her by her enforced move to New Zealand: a university education and a life of some intellectual and artistic achievement. It was also assumed, from my earliest years, that I would travel and carve out my career beyond New Zealand, preferably in Britain. Mum never regarded herself as a New Zealander.

From her I learned an inevitably romanticised history of Clan Maclean and the Highlands: of the battles of Bannockburn (before which that foolhardy knight Henry de Bohun charged Robert the Bruce and was killed before both watching armies), Flodden and especially Culloden, where Macleans were slaughtered for Bonnie Prince Charlie, and of the traditional treacheries of the Campbells, who had impinged so disastrously on Clan Maclean's history. They were blamed comprehensively for the scattering of Maclean of Duart in the late 17th and 18th centuries until, during my mother's impressionable girlhood, the clan was revived under the leadership of Sir Fitzroy Maclean and Duart Castle was finally bought back in 1912 and restored.

From the time I learned to read (long before I went to school) I was given books of all kinds about Scotland and I loved them. I was also fed with books about Ancient Greece and Rome, general history, travel and historical fiction. I consumed them avidly, and startled my Standard One teacher (and assuredly bored my classmates) by delivering morning talks on the Greek myths. I also loved the Maori myths and stories accompanied by the unforgettable illustrations that appeared regularly in the old *School Journal*. Mum bought me at least one new and one second-hand book every Friday throughout my childhood, and by the time I was 16 I had read most of Walter Scott, Robert Louis Stevenson, a miscellaneous assortment of 19th-century classics, a wide assortment of historical and travel non-fiction, and the now long forgotten Victorian and Edwardian boys' adventure books by G. A. Henty, R. M. Ballantyne, Herbert Strang and others. I had also inherited the *Boy's Own* annuals from my brother Des and had enthusiastically combed through Arthur Mee's *Children's Encyclopaedia*.

Des, after a Catholic primary education and before we moved to Invercargill in 1939, had gone to Christchurch Boys' High, where Dad's eldest brother David, a successful Wellington tea and coffee importer and racehorse owner, had also gone in the 1890s. But my sisters had attended Catholic schools, where they suffered from the educational incompetence and casual malevolence of various nuns who disapproved of Mum's Protestant origins. So, with Dad's eventual agreement, I was put into the state system from the start and sent to Middle School Invercargill, in defiance of the Church and the Bohan aunts. This technically excommunicated Dad, for the rules of our Irish-dominated Church were harshly uncompromising. He did not take communion again until I left Christchurch Boys' High at the end of 1953, though after that he made up for those long deprived years by taking communion at least twice or three times a week for the rest of his life.

We had arrived in Invercargill (a move that gave Dad a considerable promotion) in time to experience the great snow and the declaration of war. Mickey Savage's famous radio speech remains one of my most vivid childhood memories. For our first two or three years we lived on the premises of the Bank of Australasia on the gale-swept corner of Dee and Tay streets, a vast high-ceiling, three-storey place full of 19th-century furniture and wonderful hiding places, and Middle School was only a few blocks away.

There, on my first day, Miss Macdonald placed me in the care of Geoffrey Hughes, who had himself started school a mere few days before and was understandably surprised and mystified by his responsibilities. It turned out well, though. We were best friends from then on, even after my family left Invercargill in 1946. We kept in touch throughout our youth, found ourselves in the same compulsory military training (CMT) intake in January 1954 and renewed our friendship 40 years later.

I was blissfully happy at Middle School, where Miss Macdonald played us into class each morning with Percy Grainger's bouncy 'Country Gardens', after we had lustily sung the national anthems and 'Rule Britannia' – though having initially slightly misheard the words I, for some time, enthusiastically sang 'Britons never, never, never shall be saved!' I enjoyed the daily apple ration, but the equally obligatory small bottle of milk made me feel sick, as it did so many others of my generation.

Naturally the war dominated our lives. Des and his friends enlisted in the army as soon as they were able to, and from then on his regular visits home on leave were cherished and, for me, exciting events during which I could appropriate some of his equipment for my own war games with my friends. All our games were war games, but best of all were the imaginary dog fights Geoff and I were able to play out after school in the two Tiger Moths displayed in the showrooms of Vickery's Motors, where his father was the accountant.

Dad joined the hopelessly ill-equipped Home Guard, who drilled with broomsticks until they were belatedly issued with rifles. There was considerable scepticism from their families about the usefulness of their manoeuvres, but they enjoyed their camaraderie and much beer seemed to be consumed.

After Japan entered the war the mood darkened, and anxieties about possible invasion intensified. Air raid shelters were constructed, an elaborate trench system was dug through the school grounds and we carried out regular drills. These, to Trish's disgust, required the elder children to fetch their younger siblings and place them in the trenches first, after which the older ones were to protect them with their own bodies. She regarded this as grossly unfair. Why, she reasoned, should she shelter at the risk of her own life an objectionable small boy who was the bane of her and her friends' lives?

There was much debate about what should be done if the Japanese did invade. Dad favoured loading us all into our large car (a roomy Graham Page into which we could squeeze at least eight people plus picnic baskets for our Saturday jaunts to Oreti Beach) and, with his trusty .22 rifle at hand, heading for the hills. Mum briefly favoured hiding us in a vast and hitherto sealed space she had discovered between the bank premises' first and second floors – a long room where Des, Bernadette and friends subsequently played table tennis or a version of indoor basketball. Luckily, and thanks to the Americans, there was no invasion. A few American ships did visit Bluff and the community was exhorted to offer hospitality. So, on one of his leaves, Des brought home to dinner two very pleasant sailors with whom we corresponded until their ship was sunk somewhere in the Pacific. There were organised visits to other ships calling at Bluff, too, and I always enjoyed those.

Des was initially trained to be an army driver, but Mum and Dad steadfastly refused to give permission for him to go overseas before he was 21, in spite of his increasingly furious demands. So to his lifelong regret he did not join reinforcements destined for Italy but instead, and to his disgust, was transferred to the air force to become an armourer. In time he served on Green Island and later New Britain with the RNZAF alongside the Australian army and the US Seabees. From there he sent cartons of American cigarettes for Dad and chewing gum and *Captain Marvel* and *Superman* comics for me, which I shared with my more favoured friends. After we moved from the bank premises to 45 Beatrice Street my new neighbourhood friends and I established a den inside the pine plantation at the end of the street, and I purloined some of the American cigarettes too.

My time as a smoker was short. Mum and Dad dismissed Trish's report of seeing tobacco smoke rising from one of our hollow macrocarpa hedges with the sensible observation that I'd soon tire of the habit, but the climactic event that ended my smoking phase occurred one Good Friday. On returning from Mass, I discovered a fire engine dealing with a small fire in the pine plantation where, earlier, my gang and I had indulged in a cigarette or two. A policeman was making enquiries at the households overlooking the plantation and paddocks that spread down to the river about possible sightings of small boys smoking among the pines. No one admitted to seeing anything, but later the gentle old lady at whose house I had a permanent invitation to read through her complete set of Arthur Mee's encylopaedias while she fed me scones, visited our mothers and informed them that indeed she had seen us and the smoke from our cigarettes earlier that morning. No punishments were meted out, only warnings. Grateful to her and, for once, the obligation to attend Mass on Holy Days, I gave up smoking immediately. I'd not enjoyed it anyway. It couldn't compare with either going to the pictures on Saturday afternoons or starting to play rugby and cricket.

My enthusiasm for films began when I was about seven. The bank's visiting inspector, who was also a close family friend, took us all to see his favourite film, Laurel and Hardy's *Fra Diavolo*. He had seen it in every town throughout the country on this particular annual tour of inspection and was determined to share his delight with us. I'm forever grateful to him. Not even being sick from excitement and eating too many Minties marred that experience. *Fra Diavolo* (renamed *Bogus Bandits* in its latest DVD edition) remains one of my favourites. From then on, in Trish's stern care, I was allowed to go to the Saturday matinees, where I thrilled to the exploits of the Green Hornet, a host of other heroes and especially Hopalong Cassidy. I joined his fan club and had his photo on my bedroom wall. He was strong and laconic, mysterious and always victorious over evil. In comparison, that rival cowboy hero Gene Autrey was sappy and I hated his singing. I hated most of the musicals Trish liked so much too, but she was in charge of our excursions so I had to go along to them with her and her friends Ione and Anne, who found me equally tiresome. I loathed Sonja Henie, but I did find Carmen Miranda funny.

Rugby started when I was about seven too, inspired by enthusiastic teachers and family stories of Dad's playing days, when he had represented Ellesmere seniors as a 16-year-old and played club rugby with some distinction before suffering knee and back injuries that were to bother him for the rest of his life. Undeterred by that, and Mum's abhorrence of the game, I threw myself into being a forward with enthusiasm. As I've always done with whatever takes my interest, I also read everything I could find about it: in this case about the great All Blacks of 1905 and 1924. Dad had known members of both famous sides; there were large sepia photos of them covering the walls of the barber's shop; and next door to the barber's, who could we glimpse every day as we walked to and from school but the legendary Billy Stead, 1905's great first five-eighth, working away repairing shoes and smiling at us as we pressed our noses to his window.

My Invercargill childhood was a happy time for me but not quite so happy, I think, for Mum, who worried about Des away in the Solomons. Her health became so precarious that Bernadette had to abandon her training as a Karitane nurse and return home to look after her, as well as Trish and me. Wartime was equally stressful for Dad, bearing heavier responsibilities at the bank than ever before and, with so many men away on active service, making up for staff absences by working long hours – starting early and working into late evening. Money was short, too. The Labour government did not love the Australian banks and wages were frozen.

Then, in late 1945, everything seemed to change for the better. Des was demobbed and, more ebullient than ever in spite of recurrent malaria, threw himself into a prolonged bout of celebration with his similarly returning friends, though there weren't as many of them now as had gone away a few years before – not every Invercargill family could celebrate the end of the war as cheerfully as we did. And the bank offered Dad rewards at last for his service: he was, it seemed, marked out for a very senior position in Auckland. The present incumbent was nearing retirement, and in the meantime Dad was to become manager at Waverley, in Taranaki. In early 1946 he and the family furniture and effects went north to Waverley, and we, with our beloved Blue Siamese Persian cat Smokey secure in his box beside us, went up to stay at Leeston with his eldest sister, Aunty

Betty, and his two surviving brothers, Dan and Bill, until Waverley's bank premises were available.

The Leeston farmhouse had been the centre for the Bohan family since Grandad Edmund and Grandma Kate built it in 1879, enlarging it steadily to accommodate their eight surviving children and filling it with handsome antique furniture, paintings and superb steel engravings depicting a series of heroic episodes from Irish history. My favourite was the *Trial of Daniel O'Connell*, which hung above the fine mantelpiece in the dining room. I wish I had it now, but like almost everything else in that comfortable and elegant place it was lost in a fire that destroyed the house in the early 1950s. Many years later I came across another collection of those same steel engravings hanging proudly on the walls of an 18th-century Ulster country house.

We stayed in Leeston for several weeks and I enjoyed going out at dawn with Uncle Bill. He was an inveterate and comedic practical joker and the nearest the family had to a black sheep. He ran a herd of dairy cows and had a local milk round and in return for helping, I was allowed to drive Little Wonder, his former trotter now retired, to draw the milk float on our home run. Bill also often delegated to me, armed with a long whip and guided by masterful dogs, the task of bringing in the cows for the afternoon milking – and their accompanying bull.

Bill was not one of nature's farmers. Des, Bernadette and I were always entertained by him, though, and his other saving grace was his fondness for Mum. Trish did not find him amusing. Her favourite was Uncle Dan, who, like Bill and our late Grandpa Edmund, was also fond of Mum, ever her defender against our aunts' coolness. Mum was far better looking than the aunts, but even worse, she had, they suspected, instilled into us some of her Protestant outlook. Dan, a stock buyer, had been badly wounded at Passchendaele; wounds from which he never recovered. He was a generous and emotional man, but also the most hot-tempered of all this hot-tempered family. Before the German machine-guns had shattered his legs and lower body he had been a notable horseman, but since then had been unable to ride. Instead, he carried on his work from a high-wheeled gig, drawn always by a splendid horse and with his dogs sitting upright beside him. Like so many old soldiers, Dan and Bill drank heavily. They were also dedicated racing men who, with bulging wallets, went off to race meetings far and wide and usually came home with either no cash at all or a great deal less than they had set out with.

The Leeston interlude was fun. Not so our long-anticipated arrival in Waverley, where we found Dad sinking fast into clinical depression. The bank acted promptly and generously. He was granted indefinite leave, sent to a hospital in Wanganui for treatment, and we were allowed to stay in the bank manager's house until he was better.

In a vain attempt to cheer him a little I was sent to St Joseph's Catholic School. Des, footloose like so many recently demobbed young men, had applied for a job with the Department of Agriculture and was waiting for an appropriate vacancy; Bernadette continued in her role as the family's bulwark. So when Dad's course of treatment proved successful and he went off again with Mum to recuperate with his twin sister Margaret Younger in Auckland and Mum's nephew Allan McLean in New Plymouth, Bernadette and Des looked after Trish and me.

I was not a happy child in Waverley and I did not care for St Joseph's or the censorious and unfriendly nun who taught me in Standard Five and who discovered that I had neither been confirmed nor made my first communion. Those terrible errors were speedily rectified and I was put under strict instruction to be made a good Catholic child in time for Archbishop O'Shea's visit to conduct the ceremonies. That portly, bearded and benign-looking old man duly came, presided and I was confirmed, made my first confession and took my first communion, so the nuns ought to have been satisfied.

To my astonishment, however, they seemed far from pleased when I did well academically and won first prize in a Taranaki-wide essay competition. My success had offended one of their most affluent and generous local benefactors, whose son had hitherto been their favoured prize pupil, and their response was to be more unpleasant than previously, until one day I was so upset by the time I got home for lunch that Bernadette and Des would not let me return for the afternoon. Instead, Des went off in a rage to confront the nuns and deliver home truths. He was the most easy-going man in the world but he was, after all, a Bohan, and when his temper was aroused it was formidable. That day it achieved its purpose and I was not again subjected to gratuitous ill temper.

Des was less successful when he encouraged me to join the local Boy Scouts, who met weekly in their den in the local recreation grounds, the site of the Wairoa Redoubt built during the wars of the 1860s. I loathed the idea and didn't like the scoutmasters. I don't think they liked me either. I didn't like the drill, I was very bad at tying knots, and when our troop learnt that we were to go to a jamboree weekend in Hawera, I was foremost in raising rebellion. A few of us ran away into the dark evening, scattered into the trees, and I fell into a waterlogged ditch and was terrified by the squawking and violent flapping of a large sea bird that was also inhabiting my overgrown hiding place and seemed to have a broken wing. But I was determined not to be captured by the shouting scoutmaster and older scouts angrily hunting us, so I cowered in the darkness with the bird while they rounded up the others, one of whom was caught when his trousers got snared in the branches of a tree. I then crept home and informed Des and Bernadette that I didn't want to be a scout any longer. A day later the scoutmaster called and told them it would be best if I didn't go back anyway.

By the end of that year Dad was pronounced ready to resume work and the bank offered him a choice of how he should spend the remainder of his prescribed 40-year career: move to Auckland as planned, or return to Christchurch to open a series of new branches and deal with overseas transactions from the main Cashel Street premises where he had spent so many years before the war. There was really no choice. For all our fondness for Invercargill, Christchurch was our real home town.

We returned to Christchurch at the beginning of 1947, and while Mum and Dad house-hunted through the southern suburbs they knew so well and where they had friends, the bank settled us in the private residential Hotel Cecil in Manchester Street. There, among the other permanent residents, Bernadette met her future husband, Erle Duxbury from Pigeon Bay, demobbed from the RNZAF and studying pharmacy. Trish became a typist secretary at an accountancy firm, and I started at Christchurch South Intermediate. There I was put in the top Standard 6 or Form II and was confronted by a short-tempered and unwelcoming young woman teacher who deplored my less than brilliant arithmetical skills and referred to me throughout the year as 'that new boy'. When Mum subsequently proposed to enrol me at Christchurch Boys' High for 1948, she shook her head and pronounced it a mistake. I was not, she declared, likely to thrive academically. Mum, who knew my strengths and understood my shortcomings far more comprehensively, remained unmoved. I was duly enrolled in 3L for the following year, 1948, to do Latin, French, English, history and geography as major subjects – but not maths. Maths has always been an utterly unfathomable mystery to me.

If my year at intermediate was not altogether a happy one inside the classroom, there were compensations outside it: I made friends, played rugby and, in particular, became a dedicated (even fanatical) cricket enthusiast. I still am, all these years later.

The spark for this was lit on an overcast day in March when I went with a school party to the second day of the test match between New Zealand and England at Lancaster Park. The day before, Walter Hadlee had made 116, Bert Sutcliffe (in his test debut following his acclaimed 197 for Otago against the English a few days before) made 58 and early in day two New Zealand declared at 345 for 9. The great Alec Bedser took 4 for 95, but the English bowler who fascinated me was the extraordinary D. V. D. Wright, all whirling arms, bowling leg-spin at medium pace off a long leaping and bounding run. He took none for 61 and caused few problems, it seemed, but I was enthralled by the spectacle. Then England batted and got to 265 for 7, with the unforgettable Jack Cowie taking 6 for 83. While I retain no memory of Cyril Washbrook, Norman Yardley, Bill Edrich or even the immortal Denis Compton, the memory of the great Walter

Hammond, thickset and elderly to my child's eyes, marching out under lowering grey skies for his last test innings remains vivid – as does the splendour of his stroke-play as he top-scored with 79.

Throughout the next few years I doubt if I missed a single first-class or test match at Lancaster Park; I went every day I could manage, overcast or fine. Nor did I miss any Canterbury or All Black rugby game there when, with Dad, I would stand on the densely packed embankment, as one-eyed a supporter as you could find.

It did not take Mum and Dad too long to find our future home at 73 Rose Street, just round the corner from our former home at 14 Cashmere View Street; and with it came two and a half acres of what had been a poultry farm, with rows of fruit trees between the concrete bases where the henhouses had stood, all surrounded by macrocarpa hedges and a line of small pine trees. It was paradise for an 11-year-old, a world in itself. While Dad set to work to create his always cherished gardens, I practised goal-kicking over a group of apple trees, under which stood the beehives that had come to us with the property. I had unbounded confidence in my goal-kicking ability and there was never any confrontation with disturbed bees. The first time I received a bee sting was one hot English summer day, many years later, on a visit to Hampton Court Palace.

That summer of 1947–48 was scarred by the nationwide polio epidemic that closed schools and disrupted social life, and for the first weeks of the year schoolwork was carried out by correspondence. But when at last the emergency regulations were lifted my first day at Christchurch Boys' High was unforgettable.

After assembly in the brick-walled shell of the partially finished hall, presided over by towering, awe-inspiring and grim-faced Alf Caddick, whose aim was clearly to put the fear of God into us, the new 3L was marched along a corridor lined by photographs of past rugby and cricket teams and halted outside our future form room. While we waited none too silently, for there were already ominous signs that in spite of Alf's best efforts to cow his new entrants this was a 'lively' class, I studied the photo of 1921's First XI in detail.

It was, I thought, an elderly-seeming group but it included familiar names from Canterbury and New Zealand cricket's halls of fame. Its coach and master in charge – a small, dark-complexioned and remarkably gloomy-looking man resplendent in fashionable 1920s butterfly collar – seemed younger than most of his charges.

We were then called to order, marched into our form room, and there, standing behind his desk raised on a dais to command us, was Harry S. Baverstock, the man in the photograph. He was seemingly unaltered by the years that had passed since his team photo was taken in 1921, and he stared at us with the same expression of resigned gloom. He was even wearing a by now very old-fashioned butterfly collar.

At that moment I think I realised something significant about the continuity of this school's heritage, and for the next six years I was immersed in its life and traditions and totally accepting of its dominating ethos. A reaction followed after I left, of course, when I rejected sentimental 'old school tieism' and looked back with reasonably good-natured scorn on most of the colourful personalities who had taught us – largely ineffectively.

But 50 years later, when a surprisingly large number of 1948's intake gathered for our reunion, I was delighted to meet so many men after years of scarcely recalling them, and the old sense of community revived. It did again eight years later, too, when we celebrated the school's 125th anniversary. We had, after all, survived life so far and were individually and collectively relieved, I think, to have outlived many others; and despite having suffered some indifferent teaching, many had actually prospered splendidly: often those who had made little impact during their schooldays.

The troublesome 1948 class of 3L comprised 30 or so disparate souls, split academically between those of us who took Latin and those who did not, and also including a few of the school's serial villains. We behaved appallingly to any master or school monitor who showed the slightest hint of weakness, and we were the despair of diminutive Harry Baverstock. Old 'Bav', gentle, polite, artistic and almost permanently depressed, was lumbered with us as our form master for three years.

The institution the school song daily exhorted us to 'magnify' has produced vast numbers of sportsmen, soldiers, accountants, doctors, scientists, politicians and lawyers, but, deplorably, very few writers. Allen Curnow and Alan Duff would be the most famous but, to my astonishment, when I was required to write a chapter on old boy writers for the 125th anniversary celebratory book I discovered that my notoriously disorderly class had actually produced five, a distinction for any single class and unparalleled in the school's long history. No one in 1948 would ever have imagined such an outcome.

Noisy Joe had turned into cartoonist, groundbreaking playwright and novelist Joseph Musaphia. Frank William Nielsen Wright, the class intellectual and eccentric, the eldest and for the first year or two the largest of us, was eventually expelled in the upper sixth (twice, he insists with pride) for refusing to shave off a beard and shed khaki shorts for school uniform. Subsequently he became Niel Wright PhD, civil servant, poet, literary controversialist and the scourge of Wellington's literary establishment. Serious and politically ambitious Derek Round had matured into an influential international and parliamentary press correspondent and biographer. And John Broomfield, my closest friend throughout high school, varsity and young manhood, had gone on to a splendid academic career in the USA as historian and author of admired books on modern India. I was the fifth author.

Others had done resoundingly well too. John Inder (another enduring friend) became an eminent surgeon and hospital administrator, although he had been assured by our careers master that medicine was the last thing he should attempt. John Fisher, undoubtedly the quietest and most unremittingly solemn member of the class, matured into an outspoken and militant High Anglican clergyman – a truly turbulent priest and a thorn in the side for a succession of Christchurch's liberalising Anglican bishops whose 'reforms' he relentlessly excoriated in splendid, elegant and biting letters regularly published in the *Press* until the very last week of his life. John Shaw, certainly one of the most amiable and cheerfully sensible people I have ever known, went on to a distinguished career in education. And ebullient Ken Orsbourn (with Broomfield and me among the youngest in the school in that first year) became a Junior All Black, a rugby referee and official and a successful businessman. Brian Falloon's precociously remarkable piano technique, sight-reading ability and musicianship over-awed me utterly and inhibited my feeble adolescent attempts at learning the piano; and Brian, as I recall, vied with Wright to be top of the class academically. Others became businessmen and teachers, non-conformist ministers of religion, shopkeepers, tradesmen and farmers, and, sadly, a few did not live into middle age. I also have a suspicion that another tiny minority remained for life the villains they had been throughout their school careers.

It would be pleasant to praise all our teachers as paragons of teaching ability and charm; but to do so would be simple hypocrisy. Of those unfortunates who had to cope with us, only a few stood out: Fergus Murray and J. D. D. (Chops) Sinclair were the shining and outstanding men. Ferg Murray recognised and fed my love of history from the start. He was also a great believer in making copious research notes and undertaking scrupulous revision of one's essays and general writing. No one ever became a millionaire by saving paper, he would say. I took his advice. I remain a compulsive reviser and shudder to think how many forests have been felled to satisfy my demand for paper. Ferg also lent me his own books, in particular all Sir George Trevelyan's magisterial works on English history, and he guided me towards winning a Lissie Rathbone Scholarship in English and history in my last year. So did 'Chops' Sinclair, in wartime an outstanding intelligence officer with a genius for interrogation but for us an inspirational teacher of English literature. He not only encouraged my attempts at creative writing but the many long passages of Milton, Pope, Keats and Wordsworth he made us memorise have stayed in my head and inspired me ever since. We kept in touch for a few years until I left New Zealand, and much later, when he was over 90 and more or less housebound, he rang to tell me how much he had enjoyed all my books and especially the O'Rorke novels, courtesy of the Mobile Library Service. I was touched.

The gloriously eccentric Dr John Moffat, undoubtedly one of New Zealand's intellectual polymaths, naturally made an impact, as he did again later as a Division C training college lecturer. The only other who had any lasting impact – also as a teacher of English – was a lean and saturnine survivor of Hitler's prison camps and the infamous prisoners' death marches from Eastern Europe, Len Kissell. Less than two years after we met him he had to take extended sick leave of several years to regain his health, but that was Hitler's fault rather than ours for Len, like Ferg and Chops, was not a man we ever dreamt of harassing.

Len was not the only victim of war on that staff. Bav's nerves had been shot to pieces on the Western Front in 1916 or 1917, and during World War Two the deaths of so many of his past pupils exacerbated and deepened his chronic melancholia. In winter his limp was more pronounced than in summer but was merely the outward evidence of the serious physical wounds he had suffered. Alf Caddick had been severely wounded in the head during the Great War that decimated an entire generation of the school's early old boys and whose memories we solemnly celebrated before the school shrine every Anzac Day. He had a metal plate inserted in his head and suffered acutely during the hot summers, when the heat reacted on the metal and set off terrible headaches. During stifling nor'westers it wasn't only tremulous small boys who went in fear of his volcanic rages.

But those first assemblies in that unwelcoming and cheerless school hall had more significance for me than merely an awakening to the realities of school tradition, for we were immediately inspired by the Sixth Form Singers, who included almost every school monitor, leader and sporting hero from the First XV and First XI, under the frenetic direction of the young Clifton Cook.

Clifton was a small cross-eyed man of daunting energy and an astonishingly loud tenor voice who stamped and shouted while he exhorted us to bellow out the vaguely rude 19th-century student song 'Riding Down to Bangor', before demanding that we produce an ardent and soaring legato for the daily hymn. And under his impassioned direction the Sixth Form Singers stirred us with *Songs of a Roman Legion*, lamenting the loss a white-breasted lady called Lalage, and inspired us with Stanford's *Songs of the Fleet*, celebrating the Old Superb and Drake's Drum. There was nothing sissy about singing at Boys' High in those glorious years when our choirs entertained Christchurch and performed for a seemingly unending succession of visiting celebrities, from Lord Freyberg – a Wellington College pal of Alf Caddick's – to Bob Lowe, who had crucially helped Edmund Hillary conqueror Everest, and from currently idolised old boy international cricketers and All Blacks to still-serving old boy generals.

Clifton was perhaps the most disorganised, impossible and put upon music master who ever stood before a class and suffered unremitting disorder; but as an inspirer of youth with a conducting baton in his hand he was a rare being indeed. In a school of 800 or so boys dominated by a sporting ethos and military ideals, he created, year after year, a junior choir of at least 120 unbroken voices, a smaller special treble choir (whose admired soloist from 1949 on was Elric Hooper), a senior choir of over 250 assorted and mainly terrible broken adolescent voices, and the elite Sixth Form Singers of 40 or 50 seniors. He also developed an orchestra, rough but ready, that could sweep us into stamping enthusiasm with their far from note perfect but exciting attempts at the finale of Beethoven's Symphony No. 5. And for the choirs there was always the irresistible inducement of joint concerts with Girls' High.

Clifton was utterly consumed with producing music, and not all his colleagues appreciated his relentless single-mindedness, or his very high profile in Christchurch's wider music community. More than a few of the gentlemen's club that was the staffroom in those days were transparently jealous. They also resented his interruptions in the period following morning break, when the corridors reverberated to his stamping heels as he marched from room to room and flung open classroom doors to bawl out delinquents who had failed to attend the break's obligatory choir practice.

I did not join any choir in my first year, as Mum did not want me to sing until she was satisfied that my changing voice was ready to cope without damage. But in my second year I became the youngest member of the senior choir and longed for the day when I could be in the Sixth Form Singers. As I listened to the soloists during the next two or three years (especially the star tenor, Dave Plumb), I grew restless to become a soloist too. But I had to wait until I reached the Sixth Form, when, aged 16, I had developed into a clear light tenor, exactly as Mum had predicted. I was now learning the piano with old Miss Nellie Hayward up at her family mansion on the Cashmere hill, but when she heard me sing those lessons steadily became transformed into singing lessons, and very good ones that gave me an excellent start. Unfortunately I never learnt to play the piano properly, and that is a lasting regret.

Mum now urged me to seek out Clifton and persuade him to hear me sing. That was not easy. For weeks he declared himself far too busy and brushed me impatiently aside, and for weeks I persevered until he gave in out of sheer exasperation. He had also been badgered by my friend Neil Hartley, whose bass was one of the most beautiful young voices I have known, and one afternoon he at last sighed a reluctant consent and agreed to hear us both in the hall after school.

The result exceeded our expectations. Within minutes he announced that henceforth he would teach us one after the other on Saturday mornings at his home, and that next Saturday we were to meet him at Begg's Music Shop to select sheet music of suitable songs. He promised us almost immediate solos for the school concerts, and Neil was given the bass role of the Usher in the school's production of Gilbert and Sullivan's *Trial by Jury*. Although the other roles were already cast, I was drafted in to sing a few lines that were too high for the Counsel for the Defence. So we made our stage debuts in the Radiant Hall (later renamed the Repertory Theatre), with Dave Plumb as a dashing Defendant and Elric Hooper the undoubted star as the soprano Plaintiff, glamorously arrayed in bridal dress and long false eyelashes.

I achieved no academic or sporting distinction in anything except English and history until I reached the Lower Sixth, when everything improved. As already mentioned, I was a rugby and cricket fanatic, and in 1949, like so many other New Zealand boys of my generation, I was scarred forever by the Springboks' whitewash of the All Blacks. The successes of Walter Hadlee's cricket team in Britain and the deeds of Bert Sutcliffe, Martin Donnelly, Tom Burtt and the rest (about which I kept a scrapbook) had provided some balance and for most of that year I read little other than books on cricket and rugby. In 1951, though, I had my best sporting year. I was not only selected as a medium-paced bowler for the Canterbury Under 16 representative cricket team, but was also chosen as a front-row forward reserve for the Canterbury Under 16 rugby team, astonishing as that may seem in retrospect; but by the time I was 15 I was the height I am now (five feet seven and a half) and while so many of my contemporaries shot up to six feet or more in the next year, I didn't. So, though I was a better rugby player than a cricketer, my rugby ambitions were to be stalled. I was soon simply too small to remain a forward and I never really settled into the back line. During my first year at varsity, after an early season game when, as half-back, I was pummelled black and blue on a concrete-hard Hagley Park field, I finally took Mum's relentlessly repeated warnings that a broken nose might ruin my singing and gave up. I played indifferent golf instead and later took up refereeing.

As I was one of the youngest of my year, it was agreed that I should stay an extra year in the Upper Sixth. Along with John Broomfield and several others, I had by far my most enjoyable school year as monitor, tenor soloist, member of the Second XV and captain of the Third XI. I also had an agreeable social life at the Friday night parish hall dances with girls from Girls' High, St Margaret's, Rangi Ruru and Avonside Girls' High. And I was able to seriously concentrate on University Scholarship history and English. Other delights enjoyed throughout my school years included the regular groups attending the National Orchestra concerts, oratorio performances by the large rival Harmonic and Royal Christchurch Musical Societies, theatre events such as Ngaio Marsh's memorable Shakespeare productions for the University Drama Society, and touring productions at the Theatre Royal – about which I have written in *The Theatre Royal Christchurch: An illustrated history 1908–2008*.

Perhaps the most memorable school excursion during 1952 was to the extraordinary Powell and Pressburger film *The Tales of Hoffmann*. That set off a mild craze and I don't know how many times my friends and I went to see it. My love for that strange but compelling opera has remained undimmed and a minor regret is that I did not appear in it until almost the end of my singing career when, as an elderly character tenor and on the point of retiring from singing, I played the four comic roles of Spalanzani, Franz, Pitichinaccio and Andres for Canterbury Opera in 2001. That was an appropriate farewell to Canterbury Opera and one of my happiest stage experiences.

I was glad to leave school at last but not so sure of what was going to happen as we nervously entrained for Burnham Military Camp to undergo our CMT. For most of us it was the first time we'd been away from home and those of us due to enrol for the new university year would at least be getting off the last scheduled week or two. We also took some slight comfort from one of our close-knit school group's observation that at least they couldn't kill us – not intentionally anyway.

In fact it all turned out well. I enjoyed the life enormously, even having to share a hut with the pipers from the intake's highland pipe band, who practised on their chanters each morning before reveille in the baggage room. The national competitions loomed, apparently, and our pipers included some vying for the top honours.

The big event for our intake was the royal visit, and the first weeks of basic training were dominated by preparations for the Queen's appearance. Our company was required to put on a physical training display and on the great day, stripped to singlets and trousers, we marched out to our apparatus and waited for the royal cars to arrive.

And we waited: for hours, as the day got hotter and our bare arms and shoulders began to burn. We had been told repeatedly that it was a military crime to get sunburnt, so I watched in growing horror as the red-haired youth in front of me began to blister so badly that he had to be taken to hospital. Others suffered too, but, sensibly, nobody was charged. Even some of the formal guard (regular NCOs and veterans of World War Two and Korea) collapsed in the heat.

The Queen was very late, our mood soured and when she did arrive she passed in her open car with scarcely a glance, though the Duke did laughingly indicate to her one of our file over-balancing as he attempted a vaulting horse. After she vanished into the officers' mess for lunch, we scrambled for our huts, changed into our more formal and as yet unworn summer uniforms, and lined up along the camp's streets to cheer her as she did a final tour. The cheers on our street were muted. We couldn't wait for her to go because as soon as she had disappeared we were free to go off on our first weekend leave.

The best times in CMT, which I came to regard as a glorious paid holiday, were in the evenings when musicians and singers of all description would gather in the Church Army hut and entertain. Brian Falloon was always in demand at the piano and he accompanied my songs and sight-read everything the instrumentalists put before him. Out of those evenings came our revue for the whole camp, in which three or four of us, led by Elric Hooper (glamorous in drag and hugely popular), sang songs from the currently popular musicals like *Kiss Me Kate* and *Call Me Madam*.

Once basic training was over we were drafted into our specialist units and I found myself in brigade intelligence. A year or so later during our obligatory territorial training I rose to the dizzying heights of intelligence sergeant for the Canterbury Regiment's headquarters. What a mercy in every way that our territorial army never had to go to war. Our Burnham section, all students, was small – as was the headquarters clerk section – and we were all housed with a company of West Coast infantry. They were predominantly miners or timber workers who referred to us with jocular derision as the 'College Boys', yet became almost as excited as I did when Elric appeared one afternoon from HQ with a telegram informing me that I'd won the Rathbone Scholarship.

There was cheering news from the wider family, too, during these weeks. Mum underwent an apparently successful operation for cancer, Bernadette was safely delivered of a daughter, and both Trish, married and living in Auckland by now, and Des's wife Margaret (who had two children already), announced pregnancies. I liked being an uncle.

TWO

Becoming a Singing Historian

Much as I had enjoyed CMT and the brief Burnham experience, it was far more exciting to start university in March 1954, proudly armed with my scholarship and a boundless optimism when I enrolled for Stage One history, English, political science and geography – only slightly dented when I met the much-feared Neville Phillips, professor of my major subject, history.

The Neville of those days was the most intimidating man with whom I have ever had any sustained contact. Tall and saturnine, a commanding presence in the lecture room and an inhibiting, even terrifying personality in tutorials or at a one-to-one meeting in his study, there is something of Neville in my fictional Inspector O'Rorke. But, unlike my O'Rorke, Neville was painfully inept socially and generated such an aura that students and even his staff, with few exceptions, were invariably reduced to almost equal awkwardness. It required all the skill and tact that Mrs Phillips – the charming Pauline – possessed to dry the tears and soothe the bruised spirits left in his wake.

Neville had been shaped intellectually by his pre-war years at Oxford University under Sir Lewis Namier, the great political analyst of 18th-century British parliaments and politicians, and he had succeeded the adored Sir James Hight at Canterbury in controversial fashion ahead of Dunedin's Alexander McLintock, the latter fresh from his prize-winning triumph *The Establishment of Constitutional Government in Newfoundland.* McLintock, according to the version he himself later gave me, had been told he had the job, but after objections from one or two members of the appointments committee (possibly political and also perhaps because Alex was not a returned soldier) he had been asked to reapply. On leaving the second interview he had found Neville waiting to enter. The earlier decision was reversed and Neville, who *was* a returned soldier and had served in Italy (including at Cassino) with the Royal Artillery, was appointed. McLintock, a proud man, never forgot or forgave and I doubt if he and Neville exchanged many words subsequently.

Neville had embarked on his tenure in stern reforming mood, harshly critical of what he saw as the declining standards during Hight's latter years and determined to raise them and the department's reputation. He certainly succeeded. History was soon regarded as the most difficult and demanding of all arts subjects, with a fearsome failure rate at Stage I. Neville's chilling abjuration at the year's end became notorious: 'Ladies and gentlemen, look carefully at the person next to you. One of you will fail. Good luck for the exams and pray to God that you do not need it.'

He was, however, a superb teacher: a splendid prose stylist and an outstanding lecturer whose dissertations on the glories of the Italian Renaissance attracted students from other faculties and even the intellectually aware public to the always packed lecture room. He was a tutor who demanded the highest standards – mere opinion, narrow ideological fixations or prejudices were not allowed, conclusions had to emerge from facts derived from reputable and quotable sources, ideally provided by Oxford men. Woolly thinking was harshly condemned and he could, and frequently did, reduce the slovenly thinker or wilfully ignorant to tears. Some other departments' Stage III and even honours classes were soon crammed with those who had failed History I.

Neville could never have raised the standards as high as he did alone, and during my time he led a very fine staff. The senior lecturer was portly and florid John Saunders, an authority on Arab history and European Liberalism, and another remarkable lecturer – more flamboyantly histrionic in delivery than Neville but perhaps even more effective. The conspicuously brilliant David Fieldhouse from Oxford was always intellectually stimulating. His rapid-fire delivery permanently ruined my handwriting as I raced to fill page after page of notes, but he encouraged, reinforced and intensified my inherited fascination with 16th-century Ireland and Scotland.

In 1955 the young W. H. (Bill) Oliver arrived from his post-graduate years at Oxford and, hesitatingly and almost apologetically, started his lecturing career introducing us to Hobbes and Locke and, by example, to as elegant a prose style as any New Zealand historian has achieved. He also took a house for his young family down the road from our home in Rose Street, so we became neighbours and developed a friendship that has endured. When I returned to New Zealand at the end of 1987 he had a crucial impact on the way my somewhat curious career subsequently developed.

And of course there was Jim Gardner, who all those years ago delivered rousing lectures on the French Revolution and laboured in spite of Neville's scornful lack of encouragement to develop courses in New Zealand history. He too became a life-long friend, a friendship deepened by our mutual passions for music (Jim was a tenor in the Royal Christchurch Musical Society) and cricket. For a season or two we played together in the varsity social team. So did Neville, and one of the more awkward moments in our relationship was when I had to give him out LBW during my umpiring stint. It was plumb. No question. Only Neville had doubts, but he said nothing; simply glared as he walked past me back into the shade of Hagley Park's trees where Jim hid his face in his hands and pretended he hadn't been watching.

I was also lucky enough to go through to Stage III in an equally excellent English Department headed by John Garrett, with that committed Marxist and elegant scholar Winston Rhodes as associate professor, and the delightful Ray Copland and aesthetic Lawrence Baigent as memorable lecturers. Each was a splendid teacher, inspirational in the small tutorial groups that gathered in the William Morris-wallpapered rooms of Sinclaire House at 23 Cashel Street to discuss the set books, often with considerable heat. The only drawback was Charles Spear, whose rambling, feebly delivered and mind-numbing Early English and Middle English lectures achieved the astonishing feat of alienating (with some rare exceptions, I hope) a generation of students who, sadly, never learnt to fully appreciate the glories of Beowulf, the remarkable Anglo-Saxon poets, Malory and even Chaucer.

John Garrett encouraged my interest in 19th-century English literature: not only for Thomas Love Peacock, Wilkie Collins, Anthony Trollope, George Eliot and Charles Dickens, but also, oddly enough in retrospect, for that grim renegade Scots Presbyterian Thomas Carlyle. It was not Carlyle's flawed idea of the 'hero' that fascinated me, but rather his 'doctrine of work', which reinforced the strong Protestant work ethic I had already absorbed from my mother. And there was the impact of his dramatic, over-rich but powerful style that had so disastrously influenced the Victorians (especially Dickens and Meredith) and now had a similar effect on mine. My flirtation with that prose style was a harmless enough student enthusiasm, I suppose, a passing fancy mercifully more or less tamed eventually by patient tutors and, subsequently, kindly editors.

John Garrett tried to persuade me to go on to do English honours – which I was unable to do because I did not have the requisite language unit in my bachelor's degree – and he even, surprisingly, suggested I might like to be nominated for a Rhodes Scholarship. I politely declined. Apart from having no realistic likelihood of getting one, I had no ambition to attend any of Oxbridge's hallowed but ivory-towered halls. It was an irrational prejudice, I suppose, which had been fostered by my intense dislike of such literary critics as F. R. Leavis and the historian A. L. Rowse, both of whom represented for my impatient and pragmatic undergraduate mind the worst type of self-satisfied English academic intellectual snobbery and arrogance, out of touch with the real world, dictatorial and intolerant of all who dared differ from their god-like pronouncements. My dislike and distrust of literary theory and blinkered ideological bias burns as fiercely today as it did then.

One of the initial delights in returning to Christchurch many years later was to renew my friendships with Jim Gardner and with John Garrett in his last years. Yet although Garrett, Rhodes, Saunders, Oliver, Fieldhouse and Gardner influenced me intellectually in so many different ways throughout my university years, it was Neville Phillips who always loomed as an ever-present dark and threatening shadow. And I was certainly not alone in regarding him as such.

Nine of us did history honours in 1957 and we became a tight-knit group, united in our awe of 'the Prof'. Nicky Glasgow was a tall and elegant red-head; petite Doris Samlal became the first Fijian Indian woman to get an MA; Frances Finlay was a dark Irish beauty from Otago; Don Walker, indomitably cheerful except in Neville's presence, went on to have a fine career as diplomat and businessman; Bruce Davie (a steadfast drinking companion) became a headmaster; Harvey McQueen, poet and essayist, achieved influence as David Lange's education adviser; Murray Moore – vast, unforgettable, one-eyed 'Tubby' – died regrettably young but in our student days was a famously feared roisterer whose appearance at parties created havoc and often precipitated visits from the police, who would cheerfully escort him off to some other inner-city party. My Boys' High classmate John Broomfield and I made up the numbers.

Gerald Hensley, having graduated with one degree and now starting a second one in law, was also a regular presence at social occasions. Neville rated him and Marie Peters on a par with his previous star pupils, John Pocock and Patrick O'Farrell, and only Gerald and Nicky Glasgow could occasionally float above the engulfing tide of inhibition Neville created and beguile him into fleeting moments of bonhomie. Fifty years on, Bill Oliver's sense of wonder remained undimmed at the memory of Nicky presenting an unexpectedly overcome Neville with a birthday cake while our class and staff gathered respectfully round the honours room table.

Gerald's agile wit could lighten potentially embarrassing moments and did so for me during the annual ritual visit with Neville to the Carlton Beer Garden, when conversation seldom sparkled.

These always took place at exam times, and by sheer bad luck and execrable timing I was scheduled in early November 1957 – just before my last paper – to sing the tenor solos in two gala performances of Bach's Mass in B Minor with the Christchurch Harmonic Society and an augmented Alex Lindsay Orchestra (on this occasion the National Orchestra in all but name). Almost inevitably, and during an ominously lengthening lull in the stuttering small-talk, Neville turned to me, smiled in that unforgettable manner that chilled the innards, and remarked how surprised he was that I should do such a thing. As I floundered into an utterly inadequate response, Gerald cheerfully assured him that this was such an important occasion that the Governor-General, Lord Cobham, was going to attend one of the performances, which was also to be broadcast live throughout the land. Neville's smile warmed slightly. Governors-general made a difference. He glanced round our awkward circle again, laughed briefly and remarked with only a tinge of acid that perhaps Mr Bohan was going to be a popular tenor! He laughed again when Gerald explained that I was known among friends as the singing historian.

Time inevitably wrought changes even in Neville, and when I met him again 20 years later at a concert in London at New Zealand House, heart bypasses, retirement to Kent and membership of the local Conservative Party had mellowed him miraculously. Along with Kiri Te Kanawa, the London Maori Club, a number of prominent New Zealand actors, the young Michael Houston and his teacher, my long-standing accompanist friend Maurice Till, I had been asked by Brian Lynch (known to intimates as Brick), a long-time friend, Deputy High Commissioner and one of New Zealand's most distinguished diplomats, to perform at the New Zealand High Commission's first Waitangi Day concert. As a concert it was no big deal. I had chosen arias I sang practically every week somewhere around the country, there was no fee, and it was going to be a fun social evening. I was relaxed and without any pre-performance nerves as Brick welcomed London's diplomatic corps and the distinguished guests. Then came the blow: last but not least he welcomed his former professor, Neville Phillips, recently retired from the vice-chancellorship of New Zealand's Canterbury University.

My stomach froze – just as it had when I waited outside Neville's study to have my latest essay torn to shreds. All my calm fled and I was immediately reduced to the same state of nerves that I habitually suffered before Royal Festival Hall or Albert Hall concerts. When I tackled Brick later for having sprung such a horrible surprise he assured me that he had suffered exactly as I had.

But at the reception after our concert, Neville, almost miraculously avuncular and friendly, seemed a man transformed. We talked for a long time and later, as my wife Gillian and I walked to the nearest tube station, she remarked on how charming that old man was with whom I had spent so much of the evening. She hadn't caught his name in the general hubbub. Who was he? The man who had cast shadows over my student days, and about whom I had so thoroughly bored friends and family ever since, I replied. I think she decided then to take my version of those days with several pinches of salt because, as far as she was now concerned, Professor Phillips was a thoroughly delightful old fellow.

It was at the beginning of that first honours year in 1957 that I also met the strikingly vivacious Peggy. She became, and remained throughout the next five eventful and emotionally tempestuous years, the love of my young life and from time to time we contemplated marriage, or at least getting engaged. A major obstacle – apart from bouts of mutual misunderstanding and indecision – was, again, religion, for she was a Presbyterian reared to distrust Catholicism.

Kiri Te Kanawa, unquestionably New Zealand's greatest soprano, often incurred my ire by announcing to British interviewers that there was no classical music when she grew up back home. Well, there might not have been much in Auckland in the 1950s and early

1960s (though that I doubt) but there was certainly a huge amount of it happening in Christchurch, Wellington and Dunedin. By the time of the Carlton Beer Garden incident of late 1957, singing was taking up an increasing amount of my time and looming ever larger in my ambitions. The university life I enjoyed so much was never confined simply to writing essays, having my mind sharpened by inspirational teachers, taking vacation jobs at Wood's Bros flour mill or Birds Eye Frozen Foods, attending varsity dances and parties and pursuing with mixed success the succession of delightful girls who, before Peggy appeared, took my all too susceptible but regrettably inconstant fancy.

On my very first day of lectures in March 1954 I was waylaid by a couple who introduced themselves as Jennifer Barnard and Peter Zwartz and they recruited me for the University Madrigal Group, in which my school pal Neil Hartley was already singing. So began a lifelong friendship with two people who became like brother and sister to me. The Madrigal Group was in fact New Zealand's first early music vocal ensemble and at this stage was no larger than a dozen singers. Later, under William Hawkey, it grew to be more like a chamber choir. For the next few years it was more or less the centre of my social life and our reunion 40 years later renewed many of the old friendships.

It was the brainchild of Vernon Griffiths (Griff), mover and inspirer with Victor Galway of New Zealand's school music-making and a man who perhaps had a greater and longer-lasting impact on the wider community than any other university professor of his time. During a sabbatical in England in the early 1950s, and at the very start of the great and enduring revival of early music, he had seen the BBC's Northern Singers (conducted by the young John Hopkins) sitting around a table and performing Elizabethan part-songs, and he had resolved to set up something similar at Canterbury. So in late 1953 he gave the task of organising and conducting this to the most likely of his senior students, Peter Zwartz.

It was a brilliant idea, and when I joined, it was succeeding beyond anyone's expectations. This was not simply a bunch of students having a go at things, but a group that Pete, with tireless energy and limitless drive, was moulding into a thoroughly professional ensemble. We rehearsed most lunchtimes and performed somewhere almost every week: at the Music Department's lunch-hour recitals in the Great Hall, in halls large and small throughout the Canterbury region, in broadcasts for the NZBC and on mini tours for Adult Education as far as Nelson and Wellington. At most of these concerts I sang a group or two of Elizabethan lute-songs and 20th-century English art songs, usually accompanied by Jenny or, after she and Pete married and departed for studies in London, Bill Hawkey or Margaret Nielsen.

Through the Madrigal Group connection I also became closely associated with the Music Department, though I was never one of its students, and began my friendships with John Ritchie, the sadly short-lived English harpsichordist Michael Toovey and Griff himself. He not only gave me my first solo recital in the Great Hall during 1955 but he accompanied me too. I became, in effect, the department's tenor. I sang John's and Griff's songs in recitals and broadcasts from the YCs, featured in their annual festivals of English composers, worked with the first University Trio of David Stone, Beth Cook and Tom Rogers, and was tenor soloist for the big choral concerts of the University Music Society, whose combined orchestra and choir numbered up to 250 students and staff drawn from every faculty. I was its president during my last two years.

Some music honours students also wrote songs for me as part of their course requirements, and I would record these for the overseas examiners and earn an extra fee by broadcasting them. The most memorable were undoubtedly those of the young and brilliant Annea Lockwood – mercifully before she entered her glass-shattering experimental phase that produced such a (literally) explosive impact during the 1960s in London and the USA. She wrote 'Three Songs from Catulli Carmina' for me. There was also a hideously difficult setting of Matthew Arnold's *Dover Beach* for John's string orchestra and me. We can still laugh about the struggles we had with it at a special concert we gave in the Great Hall, but it wasn't so funny at the time. It was, by a very long mile, the hardest music I had so far attempted.

During these undergraduate years I was also getting paid singing work outside the university, including regular broadcasts of Elizabethan and modern English songs and lieder from 3YC, and Victorian and Edwardian ballads for the ZB's Sunday evening programmes. I had become a member of Ernest Empson's Eroica Club, whose concerts featured Ernest's best piano pupils, such as Maurice Till, Neil Hartley, soprano Anita Ritchie and baritone Winston Sharp. By now Neil and I had stopped having lessons with Clifton Cook and were studying repertoire with Ernest, who had been an accompanist on the old Australasian and Dutch East Indies international concert circuit as well as a notable solo pianist. He was a superb accompanist, a fine and knowledgeable vocal coach and in those years arguably New Zealand's only internationally celebrated piano teacher.

Ernest was leonine in appearance and surrounded by a tight court of admiring women, and by disciples rather than pupils. He was undoubtedly one of the towering figures of musical Christchurch. He was also a controversial one, though until I wrote his biographical essay for Volume Five of the *Dictionary of New Zealand Biography* almost 50 years later I was not fully aware of just how much scandal had once surrounded him and how much bitterness has lingered on among his numerous descendants. In 1905 he had married Flora Thompson, sister of his friend the painter Sydney Thompson (he had been brought up in their household), before going to study in Frankfurt and Berlin, where he became friendly with the legendary violinist Joseph Joachim, the iconic pianist Artur Schnabel, and favoured pupil of the vastly influential Leopold Godowsky and composer-pianist Ferruccio Busoni. Flora's tuberculosis brought them back to Christchurch in 1908, however, and four years later her death left Ernest alone with three young sons until, a year after that, he married Grace Prettejohns. He and Grace had another two sons and two daughters before Ernest suddenly eloped to Australia in 1922 with a married pupil, Ivy King. They did not return to Christchurch until 1941.

I got to know Ivy quite well and was always amused (without really being aware of their history) by her implacably protective manner when other women fluttered attentively around him – as they did. I often went to chamber music concerts with Ernest, and though I had been to school with one or two of his grandsons I was astonished when on one occasion we came face to face with one as we emerged from the Civic Theatre and they ignored each other.

Even before I finished my Bachelor of Arts at the end of 1956 the choral societies were starting to take an interest in me. There doesn't seem to be much awareness now about just how many active and enthusiastic choral societies there were throughout the South Island during the 1950s: from Invercargill to Nelson and from Timaru across to Greymouth. I appeared as soloist for most of them before I left New Zealand in 1962, but my oratorio debut was with the Christchurch Harmonic Society under Victor Peters in December 1956 in two performances of *Messiah*, for the grand fee of eight guineas.

This was also the first time I sang with Dunedin's contralto, Mary Pratt, for many years New Zealand's most famous and beloved resident singer and undoubtedly one of the greatest New Zealand voices I have ever heard. She was especially superb in the Bach and Handel contralto repertoire, and none of the eminent British ladies with whom I sang in later years could match her in the arias 'Have Mercy O Lord' or 'He was Despised'. Famous visiting singers such as Heddle Nash, Isobel Baillie and Richard Lewis, who all sang with her during her prime, could never understand why she didn't go abroad to find fame and fortune. The truth was she enjoyed being a very big fish in a tiny pool, she loved living in Dunedin, and when at last she did venture to Britain she was appalled to discover the realities of Britain's professional world: that even the most famous did not sing at the Albert Hall every week. Instead, as she explained to me at great length during a train journey to Dunedin when she summoned me to sit beside her and banished her husband to a seat behind us, they all had to do what she scornfully described as 'lots of little concerts in the provinces'. That wasn't Mary's ideal way of life at all. In New Zealand *all* her work was, by New Zealand standards, the 'big time'.

Mary was a very blunt woman and adept at putting young singers in their proper place and we eventually got on very well. But at our initial meeting her first remark to me was that she had sung *Messiah* with the great Heddle Nash – the implication being that I was very small fry indeed. She followed that with the crushing observation that it was all very well being admired in my home town but my real test would come when I sang outside Christchurch. I was suitably humbled.

The vast size and reputation of both the Harmonic and Robert Field-Dodgson's Royal Christchurch Musical Society is another aspect of that era's music-making that has largely slipped from the collective memory, I believe. They were fine choirs and on their best days as good as any of the major societies for whom I later sang in Britain, but the notoriety of their rivalry was equally remarkable and extended as far as London. It was the subject, indeed, of the first conversation I ever had with Sir Malcolm Sargent at a cocktail party during the 1962 Adelaide Festival.

I experienced its intensity at the very start of my career. After my first *Messiah* Victor Peters booked me for the Harmonic's 1957 performances of Haydn's *The Seasons* and Bach's Mass in B Minor. Field-Dodgson also rang me up within a week or so and not only asked me to sing the Royal's 1957 *Messiah* (the one civilised arrangement existing between the two choirs was to alternate Christchurch's annual *Messiah* performances), but also to prepare the huge role of the Evangelist for their 1958 *St Matthew Passion.* I accepted with grateful and almost indecent haste. Then, no more than two days later, a furious Vic Peters summoned me peremptorily to his Sumner home.

I was frostily received. He'd heard I'd been approached by 'another choir' to sing their solos, Vic rasped as soon as I was led into his presence. Was I aware that he did not engage soloists, apart from Mary Pratt, who appeared with 'that other choir'? He was extremely displeased and bitterly disappointed.

I explained that I had ambitions to be a professional singer, so the offers – especially of the Evangelist – were simply too good to turn down. Vic scowled horribly and there was an uncomfortable silence. Few could match Vic's scowl. He was at the best of times formidably short-tempered, but people made allowances because of the severe wounds he had received in World War One, from which he still suffered acutely. Perhaps this was one of his better days, because eventually he grunted, made a brief speech reminding me that he and the Harmonic had given me my start and that I must never forget that fact, and gave a muttered and grudging consent; not that it would have made any difference to me if he hadn't. I was then dismissed.

I continued to be a regular tenor soloist for both societies until I left for Australia in October 1962, and about 30 years after that I was a soloist for the Harmonic's last concert before they combined with the old enemy to form the Christchurch City Choir.

As it happened, and whether or not it was anything to do with the Mass in B Minor, I did not do well in my last master's exam paper in 1957 (Commonwealth and Empire), but at least I had a thesis yet to present in the hope of a good second, and almost another year in which to finish it.

Neville had originally chosen an 18th-century Namierite political study for me – some 1783 election in the English Midlands – and naturally it had not occurred to him that I might want to do something else. I did, and one afternoon in the Students' Union I sat down with David Fieldhouse, Bill Oliver and Jim Gardner to sort out some ideas.

Auckland University's history department had recently published two booklets on Sir George Grey's government of 1877–79 and his creation of a so-called 'Liberal' party. We were extremely critical of the conclusions reached postulating a clear 'conservative'–'liberal' divide in the politics of the 1870s and 1880s, and now decided that I should offer a Namierite study of the men and issues involved in the crucial 1879 election, to test the validity not just of the Auckland theory, but the entire view of the structure of our colonial politics postulated by William Pember Reeves in his classic *Land of the Long White Cloud*, which was accepted with little critical analysis by subsequent New Zealand historians, notably John Cawte Beaglehole and Keith Sinclair.

I was excited about this prospect, but Jim, David and Bill cautioned that I had to present Neville with the clearest and most precise proposal to overcome his prejudice against 'mere' New Zealand history. It was also vital that I must not, on any account, mention their part in my scheme. If I did, they warned solemnly, Neville would regard their input as a plot against his authority; so not only did my synopsis have to be a good one, but my manner of presenting it had to be tactful and suitably bland. David was going back to Oxford the following year and Bill was anxious to move to a better-paid position as soon as one became available; but Jim was a Canterbury man body and soul, and had such an uneasy relationship with Neville that he might suffer seriously if it were revealed that he had been 'plotting' with me.

Neville was, as anticipated, taken aback by my rejection of his thesis suggestion, and the knitted brow and cold silence while he read my synopsis were ominous. He then read it a second time and, fixing me with his all too familiar and hostile stare, pronounced it to be carefully thought out and impressive. But had any of his staff 'got' to me? Imperilling my immortal and still shakily Catholic soul by the barefaced lie, but saving Jim Gardner from any unpleasant repercussions, I denied any such possibility. I'm not sure he believed me, but he shrugged and remarked that at least it would be a proper Namierite exercise. But wasn't I interested in 18th-century English politics? No, I replied. He was shocked. Surely I couldn't *really* be interested in New Zealand history! I assured him I was. He seemed incredulous. Why? I muttered that it was probably because I was a New Zealander. He shook his head sadly, gave his reluctant approval and I fled in relief to celebrate at the Clarendon.

Jim, ruthless with red ink, insistent on factual accuracy and readable, grammatical prose, was appointed my tutor, and I started research almost immediately in the New Zealand Room at the old Public Library across the road from Hereford Street's sandstone colonial Police Station (regrettably demolished later and replaced by one of the city's most hideous public buildings), presided over by the mild-mannered, friendly and tirelessly helpful Robert Lamb.

From the moment I opened the old files of the *Lyttelton Times* for 1879 I entered a world I had never dreamt existed. Pilgrim Canterbury and Victorian Christchurch were revealed as being utterly different from that boring utopia of virtuous and superior Anglican beings we had been brought up to revere by our ubiquitous Pilgrims' Association. All those familiar sepia photographs of white-capped, lace-bedecked old ladies and stern, bearded patriarchs had left a very false impression. Instead, I discovered a disorderly, violent but dynamic place inhabited predominantly by young people and rent by bitter social unrest and racial divisions between Irish and English, whose denominational disputes came to a head in 1879 during the end-of-year riots between Catholic Hibernians and the militant Protestant Orange Order. There was also an astonishingly high rate of crime. Prostitution was rife in the inner city and, like drugs, was not illegal. Drink-fuelled disorders were an almost nightly occurrence, and suicide or accidental drowning in the city's rivers and open sewers disturbingly frequent.

I also quickly found that Grey's 1879 election campaign for Christchurch City was marked by increasing disorder as vast public meetings degenerated into near riots. By polling day – coinciding with a hot nor'wester – the city was at an emotional boiling point. That day's disturbances began early as a crowd, described as being made up of 'larrikins' and estimated at 1500 or so, went on the rampage, hurling flour over harmless fellow citizens, smashing shop windows in Market (Victoria) Square and fighting a running battle with the city's 35 police, still known as the Armed Constabulary. In the oppressive evening, rioters burst into Lichfield Street's Oddfellows Hall where a visiting operetta company was performing, stopped the show until they were forcibly ejected and, at the junction of High and Cashel streets, launched themselves on the battered constabulary drawn up in a military square to make a last stand. Led by their inspector on a white horse, the constabulary then charged with batons whirling, arrested the obvious ringleaders and finally dispersed the rest.

I was enthralled. Not only were the politics fascinating; here was all the material I might wish to find for a novel. But not for the moment – in fact I wouldn't get down to that for another 30-odd years, when *The Opawa Affair* took shape. For 1957 and 1958, colonial politics and real history kept me busy enough.

I settled into full-time research under Bob Lamb's avuncular eye. In the New Zealand Room there was now another occupant similarly settling in for the long summer – Keith Sinclair, researching his biography of William Pember Reeves. He had exchanged houses with the Olivers for the vacation, so we saw one another almost every day, drank an often unreasonable amount of beer, and I also became the Sinclairs' babysitter (as I was for the Olivers, the Ritchies and my siblings). I liked both Sinclairs. Keith was a great man to argue with, and although I learned much from him through our many conversations about how one should approach biography, we differed in our respectively robust ways over far more things than we ever agreed on. He took a great deal of interest in my research, as I did in his, and we often were able to help one another with odd items we came across in our respective newspapers and general archival researches. Keith, though, could be rather more selective than I was being trained to be, and he often set some things aside because, as he would put it, they 'did not fit'.

He was not at first easily persuaded by my insistence that there was an alternative to his cherished Reevesian analysis of colonial politics. However, by the time he came to write his essay 'The Significance of the Scarecrow Ministry, 1887–1891' in his 1963 tribute to Willis Airey, *Studies of a Small Democracy*, he had accepted the general validity of my conclusions and those subsequently developed by several other Canterbury theses on the 1881, 1884 and 1887 elections that had also been produced by then under Jim Gardner's direction.

Keith always expressed the heartiest contempt for Neville Phillips and most things emanating from Canterbury, and was irrationally indignant that Neville had been commissioned to write the official war history of the New Zealand Division's Italian campaign. Neville, he would fume, had served in the Royal Artillery, so what right had he to chronicle the deeds of the compatriots he had snubbed? He wasn't really a New Zealander, in spite of reportedly having been born somewhere in the Wairarapa!

Indeed, two of the major mysteries about Neville were his conspicuous reticence about his origins and his political preferences. I actually assumed from one or two conversations we had about current local politics that he was a Labour supporter. Many people imagined that he was an Englishman because of his accent, his conspicuously 'Oxford' manner and his apparent contempt for New Zealand, Australian and Pacific history. It was not until his death that his family learnt the details of his humble origins as the son of an itinerant Jewish salesman, though several of us had long since guessed he was likely to be Jewish because of his appearance and the fact that Phillips was a name often appropriated by late 19th-century Jewish refugees in London's East End.

Neville naturally had the heartiest contempt for Keith, and their open warfare intensified when Neville wrote in a widely publicised review of Keith's epoch-making *A History of New Zealand* that it might have been more aptly entitled *The Land of the Long Pink Cloud.* He had a point, of course.

What I liked most about Keith was his gleeful determination to annoy the traditionalists and stimulate debate, as he did with mordant wit when he came down a year or two later to address the Canterbury Historical Association. He made much of the vast quantities of booze that Canterbury's pilgrim fathers brewed, imported and consumed, and of the general disorder caused by the large numbers of 'loose women' who nightly staggered from bar to bar through the streets of colonial Christchurch. Many in his audience were appalled and some grew apoplectic. One who was especially enraged was my old geography teacher Len Hewland, devoted descendant (as was Mrs Hewland) of revered pilgrim fathers, and presently guide and watchdog of those of us with secondary school teaching bursaries. Anger so consumed him that during the post-lecture mingling over coffee and cream cakes he metaphorically seized me by the ear and excoriated 'your friend Sinclair' – and me by association – for being unacceptably radical, rude and vulgar. The fellow had insulted his and Mrs Hewland's forebears and was, he hissed as he gripped my arm fiercely, such a disgrace to his profession that he (Len) could not even bring himself to speak to this Auckland upstart without feeling impelled to punch him.

My tactless observation that everything Sinclair had said about Canterbury's settler society was backed up by my own research, incontrovertible statistics and the colonial newspapers merely raised Len's fury to dangerous levels. Keith was characteristically delighted at having provoked such indignation. God alone knows how Len would have reacted to my O'Rorke novels if he'd lived long enough to read them – or even my FitzGerald biography. Even 40 years later they dismayed some of the mercifully dwindling band of committed and uncritical worshippers of the 'First Four Ships' and the Canterbury Association's preposterous but mercifully never achieved reactionary social ideals.

In 1958 I also accompanied Keith, Bill and James K. Baxter as their driver when they featured during a gathering of New Zealand poets in Christchurch. There were readings at which a very drunk Denis Glover and others entertained; there was much flamboyant and very self-conscious poetical posturing, a great many parties and an inordinate amount of drinking. Many New Zealand poets of that generation seemed to think they had to behave like Dylan Thomas.

My most enduring memories of that weekend, however, are of James K. Years later, Bill Oliver recalled our initial meeting. Baxter had a 'test', it seemed, to discover whether a man was a true Kiwi or not: to tell, lugubriously, the filthiest story he could dredge up. Apparently my deliberately neutral response satisfied him enough for him to inform Bill and Keith that I *was* a Kiwi after all – like them. For my part I have seldom disliked anyone so heartily on sight. It always astonished me that at every party we went to, women, young and middle-aged, crowded around this unkempt, graceless poseur as he slumped cross-legged on the floor, and avidly drank in his mumbled inanities as though they were revelations from God. Fine poet though he could be, he remains one of the three most dislikeable people I have met. One of the others, oddly, was also a poet, but an English one. The third was a Dutch composer.

I worked hard at my thesis that year, adopting the writing routine I adhere to still, more than 50 years later: working office hours and almost never in the evening. Throughout that last university year I was also busy presiding over not only the large University Music Society but also the Literary Society and the History Society, and I was writing for the student newspaper, *Canta*, under a variety of pseudonyms. Inevitably Neville issued strict instructions about my management of the History Society: how I should introduce visiting speakers and, when an eminent Canadian historian visited, how I was to meet him at the Clarendon Hotel, transport him in my small car (having first ensured that it was, like my shoes, cleaned and polished), and above all remain deferential and polite.

My thesis had to be delivered to the Registry by a certain date, of course, and I made it, but only just, because my excellent typist had not been well. I had little time to skim through a copy in a cursory check for obvious errors. Then all I had to do was celebrate and wait for two or three months until my viva with the visiting examiner.

The day of that viva turned out to be, certainly in retrospect, the most significant of my life because by the time it ended I had decided, for better or worse, my future. It did not begin well.

I had been informed only a short time before the event that John Beaglehole from Victoria University would be my assessor, and I had been warned (obliquely) that he was neither an easy man to deal with nor particularly well disposed to our department. The moment I walked into the room where he sat behind a table with the staff ranged around him, I realised that the signs were not propitious. There was a palpable air of tension and both Beaglehole and Neville were looking angry.

Beaglehole and I all too obviously disliked one another on sight. It was a confrontation between a patently arrogant, opinionated but dauntingly celebrated middle-aged man and an equally opinionated and tactlessly quick-tempered young man. Beaglehole attacked immediately.

My thesis, he declared, glaring at me, was an interesting one and I wrote like a novelist, but it was extremely detailed and not the kind of history he liked. I was left in no doubt that Namierite objectivity was anathema to him; his own work had always been fashionably left wing and unashamedly ideological. His exact words, as he magisterially swept an arm to emphasise his point, are etched in my memory: 'You see, Mr Bohan, I prefer the broad sweep, the smooth lawn, of history.'

My reply was immediate, and because it was uttered with some emphasis, unwise: 'Before you can have a smooth lawn, sir, you have to have someone digging over the section, and that, surely, is the function of the research student.'

The entire staff – even Neville – laughed and, as each assured me subsequently, that was our tactical mistake. Beaglehole took himself extremely seriously, and he was notoriously sharp-tongued towards ideological opponents and those he considered inferior in intellect and accomplishment. He did not join in the laughter. He went red with fury and glowered at my thesis on the desk before him. The fight was then well and truly on and was waged with increasing asperity, with the occasional accompaniment of salvoes from staff members in my support. His main attack homed in on my footnotes, but I think I parried each thrust adequately until, finally, he played his trump card. I had quoted Alfred Saunders a lot, he rasped, but Saunders' 1899 *History of New Zealand* was not listed in my bibliography.

Startled, I insisted it was. I remembered entering it in my final draft because it was the last entry and I had had to get it to the typist with urgency. Find it, ordered Beaglehole, hurling the thesis across the table. I had not seen it since rushing the copies to the Registrar's office and – calamity – I had not checked the last pages of the bibliography. Saunders *had* been left out. Beaglehole was triumphant and I was dismissed from his presence, deflated, furious with my own carelessness and hurt by his aggressive and undisguised hostility. I sought refuge and solace – as ever in those days, and especially at times of youthful crises – in the Clarendon's private bar.

I was far from being drunk when I arrived at Neville's house that evening for the annual cocktail party where results were traditionally announced personally to each member of the departing class, but I had done much serious thinking. Neville opened the door to me with a rare but genuinely warm smile and a sherry glass held out hospitably. I had got a good second, he said, but I had been the most unlucky honours student he had ever had with the examiner I had got. It was the first time, he believed, that his staff and a visiting examiner had argued in front of an examinee. Professor Beaglehole, he added, would not be present at this party. He had taken the first available plane back to Wellington and perhaps that was just as well. It had been a very difficult day.

All agreed, and as the evening went on each of the staff revealed a little more of what had happened after I had left. Beaglehole wanted my original mark reduced and there had been a tremendous argument – as there already had been over other students. Finally he had issued an ultimatum: unless my mark was reduced he would fail two, or even three, borderline cases. The staff gave in. Two marks, I was led to believe, were deducted for my sin of bibliographical omission.

Neville – friendlier and more amiable than I had ever known him to be – then sugared the pill when he added that they would recommend me to do a PhD at Canberra (no one yet did doctoral degrees in New Zealand history departments). I thanked him but refused. I had no wish to spend my life in a university, I explained, and I had decided to try to become a professional singer. I detested academic politics and I did not intend to have anything to do with history again.

He tried to persuade me but I remained adamant, so he eventually accepted my decision and offered the Canberra place to John Broomfield, who accepted without hesitation and went on to have a distinguished academic career in America.

I have never regretted my decision to leave academia. Academic politics are poisonous, and academic feuds last lifetimes and are often carried on with a peculiarly vicious egotism. Egotism, of course, is also a marked characteristic of writers and musicians, but nothing I have ever encountered in the notoriously turbulent music profession can quite compare with the sheer ghastliness of academic warfare, if for no other reason than that academics are often conspicuously cleverer with words.

My vow to have nothing more to do with history was rash and absurd. Within a fortnight I had agreed to write an article based on my thesis for the *Political Science* quarterly put out by Victoria University of Wellington and an article for the *Press* on Christchurch's 1879 election day riots, and I also became a part-time research assistant for Alexander McLintock, the parliamentary historian. That invitation was made through Jim Gardner: McLintock had read my work, Jim explained, and would pay me 10 shillings an hour to research biographies of all the legislative councillors from 1854 to 1887 as part of his grand plan for a parliamentary history of New Zealand.

It was too good a financial opportunity to refuse, for I had to build up a travel fund for my intended move to England in pursuit of a singing career that I hoped would provide a basic living and enable me to write as well. Not that I was contemplating any immediate move: I had held a post-primary teaching bursary throughout my student years and was expected to work that out, so I was going to spend a year at Christchurch Teachers' Training College and then teach for a few years, or pay back the bursary bond.

I liked and admired Alex McLintock from our first meeting at his Wellington house for afternoon tea, which he served himself with considerable élan as I met his wife, chairbound and severely disabled by a stroke, and his daughter. He was a man of great charm, a notable artist and accomplished pianist and involved in music and the arts generally. He took an avuncular interest in both my singing and writing and, as a historian, became a significant mentor. Like Neville and Jim, he valued research and insisted that conclusions must rest on verifiable fact and evidence rather than ideology and prejudice;

and he wrote magisterial prose. Our shared dislike of Beaglehole, whose most cutting witticisms inside his own circle were often at McLintock's expense, was an additional bond, as was our scorn for the sniping wars between the country's university history departments. I think McLintock gloried in being an outsider from the academic establishment, though the wounds from his rejection by Canterbury never healed, and my own innate sense of being something of an outsider was perhaps further entrenched.

For almost four years we met every month, when I would take my latest research findings to Wellington, and we invariably spent some hours in Bellamy's each time, talking about books, history, politics and music while we drank Old Grouse malt whisky, never forgetting to first toast Governor-General Sir Willoughby Norrie. Bellamy's was apparently the only bar in the country where malt whisky was available in those days of draconian import restrictions. The story was that Norrie had insisted on his favourite tipple being made a minor exception to those fearsome restrictions, and in return the politicians had insisted that some should be made available to them.

As McLintock's attention turned more and more to his *Encyclopaedia of New Zealand* project and became diverted from the envisaged parliamentary history, he commissioned me to write articles for that encyclopaedia, and from time to time suggested subjects and provided research material for newspaper articles or possible stories. Above all, however, it was he who eventually, in late 1961, persuaded me to leave a stagnating country that he was convinced held nothing any more for young men like me.

THREE

Marking Time 1959–1962

In early 1959 I enrolled in Christchurch Teachers' Training College Division C for graduates intending to become secondary-school teachers. I had anticipated that my last student year would be the happiest of my life, without exams or responsibilities, and surrounded by a congenial group of friends headed, as for so many years past, by John Broomfield, at whose recent wedding I had been best man. Overshadowing it, however, was the certain awareness that Mum, already bedridden as her secondary cancer tightened its grip, would not survive very much longer.

Nor did she. She died peacefully at Mary Potter Hospice on 14 August and was grandly farewelled at a Requiem Mass at St Peter's, Beckenham, conducted with immense dignity by Monsignor Kennedy, affectionately known as 'The Mons', the one Catholic priest she admired and who, despite his advanced age and his own uncertain health, had visited to give her communion at 7am every Monday morning for almost a year. Throughout her married life he had been a sympathetic friend, confidant and comfort and had baptised Trish and me.

Div. C, with its great social life, was very relaxed, and at the end of my first teaching section at the new Shirley Boys' High, its head, the extraordinary and dynamic Charles Gallagher, offered me a job teaching English and history to what would be the school's first Sixth Form year in 1960. I accepted without hesitation. There was tremendous energy about the place and a very welcoming group of young teachers, several of whom, such as John Mullins, Ian Leggat (son of my old and admired headmaster Jim Leggat) and Tony Cooper, I knew already.

I enjoyed my next section, too, at the equally new Cashmere High, less than a block from home in Rose Street. I was offered a job there also by Terry McCombs, former Minister of Education, with whose daughter Elizabeth, a promising contralto, I often sang in both Madrigal Group and oratorio concerts. Years later in London I met him again when, as New Zealand's High Commissioner, he presented prizes to my stepson Sebastian at Emanuel Grammar School, Clapham.

Throughout that last student year I continued to receive good and increasingly frequent singing engagements and, always eager to build up the travelling fund, I also set aside many hours to carry out McLintock's excellently paid and absorbing research. A highlight, though, and on a par with our visit to play sport, debate and carouse with Auckland's Div. C (our last student fling), had to be the end-of-year revue, a rollicking concoction called *Pay As You Burn*, in which I played the lead. It was inspired by Arnold Nordmeyer's notorious 'Black Budget' of 1958, had a script by David Close and Charles Croot and lively and attractive music by the gifted Dawn Palmer. Ron James conducted and Judy Passmore, my girlfriend at the time, directed. By now Peggy was working for the Broadcasting Service in faraway Invercargill and had struck up a worrying (for me) friendship with a fellow radio announcer, so our roller-coaster relationship was going through one of its bumpiest troughs so far. Looked at now after so many years, the large list of cast and production crew (everyone in Div. C was involved) reads like a who's who of future school principals, education notables and higher civil servants. It even includes a disgraced Anglican cleric.

Dad had retired from the bank, as the law then dictated, at the ludicrously early age of 60, an event celebrated at a memorable farewell dance for staff, family and friends in the ANZ Bank's Cashel Street main chamber, cleared and decorated for the occasion. For the next few years he devoted himself to looking after Mum but, recruited by his stockbroker friend Sir Joseph Ward, he also became secretary/treasurer for the Boy Scouts, and later was to act in the same capacity until his late seventies for the Girl Guides. Joe Ward, incidentally, was the first of our friends to get a TV set and it was at his house, while he and Dad dozed over their whiskies, that I watched TV for the first time – Orson Welles' famous rendering of Shakespeare's history plays, *Chimes at Midnight*.

After Mum's death Dad and I settled into companionable bachelor life together, to the rest of the family's unceasing astonishment. Des had always proclaimed the chances of the family's two most quick-tempered and argumentative members living together in any kind of harmony to be all but impossible, and Bernadette and Trish had agreed with much head-shaking. We proved them wrong. We shared the same kind of humour, could laugh at ourselves and each other, and each of us made compromises. I accompanied him to Sunday Mass – hangovers allowing – and he, remembering his own irresponsible and heavy-drinking youth before Mum had taken him in hand, was jocularly indulgent to me and my friends. He did most of the cooking, at which, rigidly adhering to the instructions Mum had provided, he became expert, and we shared household tasks. It was about now that I began to address him banteringly by the semi-formal 'Father'. Des, Bernadette and Trish followed suit and henceforth that was what he was called. At Christmas we hired a tent and, without a single argument, enjoyed a delightful jaunt through Central Otago to Queenstown, where I saw in the new year of 1960 with a delightful girl from Auckland.

My time on the Shirley Boys' High staff from January 1960 until

October 1962 was hugely enjoyable, despite inevitably rowdy fourth and fifth formers who had to be faced and overcome during long Friday afternoons when disruptive nor'westers howled against the windows. It was a young staff and with no more than perhaps two exceptions we all got on remarkably well as, with often boisterous good humour, they welcomed the 'new' men – Mike Murtagh, Gordon Ogilvie, Denis Young, Dave Close and me. Most of us would gather at the Star and Garter after school on Fridays and stay until we were expelled in very high spirits after six. Almost all were young or about-to-be marrieds, but Mike Murtagh and I were the troublesome bachelor exceptions and on far too many occasions, I fear, we would go on with Ian Leggat and Tony Cooper for a meal and even more drinks. Barbara Leggat and Margaret Cooper were always astonishingly hospitable and tolerant, though Barbara would often darkly remind me how comprehensively and tragically it was a man's world.

Staff parties were frequent too, often ending up at our place in Rose Street, much to Father's delight and amusement. Murtagh and I often came in for trenchant and not always justified criticism from staff wives aggrieved by their husbands' hangovers, and these proliferated when Charlie Gallagher set up a staff cricket team, of which he appointed me captain. We became the social side for the newly amalgamated East-Shirley Cricket Club, playing in third grade but playing to win and from time to time doing quite well. We also had the job of delivering the club's Saturday evening beer supply, and this was a powerful incentive to see off opponents as early as possible. My style as a captain was not without its critics and could most charitably be called uncompromising. As Ward Clarke wrote in one school publication, he was glad to be on my side.

Charlie Gallagher (the country's youngest secondary school principal on appointment in 1957) read people superbly and was a brilliant organiser. He had appointed me to teach English and history to the top streams, but to keep my feet firmly on the ground he also gave me the lowest third and fourth forms, and it was with them that I developed whatever teaching skills I managed to acquire. Charlie was immeasurably aided by his deputy head, the wise and ever calmly tactful Pat Caird, and he had gathered a staff of capable and in most cases ambitious young men whom he nurtured and groomed for advancement. Everyone had some extracurricular responsibility in the school organisation and administration.

Above all, Charlie encouraged us to express ideas, and during the daily staff meetings he stimulated debate that could get heated. As he reassured me after one senior teacher had angrily attacked me for being too outspoken and even revolutionary, that was what he wanted – radical ideas and debate. He made the decisions anyway, he added, no matter what we said; I must continue to be outspoken. And I was, shocking another senior man by advocating the abolition of the Cadet Corps and startling even my closest friends by suggesting that the post-primary teachers' union (membership of which was compulsory) threaten strike action to obtain better pay and conditions. When I left, I arrived in Sydney just as the New South Wales teachers were demonstrating and striking. I immediately cut out the newspaper reports and sent them back to the staff I'd left behind me.

Outside school hours I pursued my other interests relentlessly throughout the next three years, though the parliamentary research gradually slowed and changed direction as McLintock concentrated increasingly on the three-volume *Encyclopaedia of New Zealand* that finally appeared in 1966. Most satisfyingly he commissioned essays from me on the 19th-century politicians and 'men of affairs' Edward Stevens and Edward Wakefield, whom I'd 'discovered' while writing my thesis. He also continued to encourage my writing ambitions. Indeed, when I did at last depart he presented me with a farewell gift of a list, two foolscap pages long, of possible topics for historical novels. I fear I didn't persevere with any of them, though I gave serious consideration and actually began one on the American deserter Kimble Bent, who joined Titokowaru and fought against his old regiment, the 57th Foot. I'm glad I put it into the rubbish bin. Maurice Shadbolt, in spite of his numerous historical errors, made far more effective and imaginative use of that enigmatic character.

Literary Christchurch in those days seemed to be more or less centred on John Summers' bookshop, where most of the city's would-be poets, artists and intellectual radicals would foregather whenever the inclination took them. All were welcomed by John, forthright in his humanism and radical political and social opinions, and by Connie, equally friendly (to me anyway) though even more argumentative and decidedly prickly. As her sculptor son Llew has described her, she tended to be 'dictatorial'; she was a proudly militant pacifist and cherished her reputation as the first woman imprisoned in New Zealand for being so. Their bookshop was a great place to while away the odd hour in talk and argument.

And there was much to argue about. Debate was fierce and continuous. Quarter was never given. New Zealand's small but astonishingly noisy literary world was in a ferment in those artistically and intellectually dynamic years of the 1950s and early 1960s, when we were all determined to change our New Zealand for ever – and for its own good. As A. H. & A. W. Reed, under the imaginative and dynamic direction of Ray Richards and his colleagues, developed local publishing, and fearlessly turned out very large print runs, books of every kind were appearing almost weekly and new authors were emerging in ever increasing numbers. Poets by the score, solemn and often tormented novelists, local historians, biographers, memorialists, academics and everyone with an opinion were flourishing as never before, expounding at great length their ideals and relentlessly analysing their own and other people's works, their shortcomings and their mental processes and, above all, their environment. National navel gazing was the rage. The search was on for 'trends', a literary tradition of 'high seriousness', and, especially, 'the great New Zealand novel'.

I couldn't take all this as seriously as most of my literary minded friends and acquaintances, and I was increasingly alienated by the excessive and strident nationalism, the pervading self-consciousness and – with the notable exceptions of Glover and Curnow – a paucity of genuine wit and an almost complete absence of satire. It seemed to me that there was much to satirise in God's Own. Despite the sensation created by Barry Crump's *Good Keen Man* and my own enjoyment of it, I was less and less impressed by his subsequent novels. Nor was I an admirer of some of the major literary icons. I disliked the ubiquitous 'New Zealand' short story genre and I found Frank Sargeson's mannered diction, his inherent violence and his obsession with what he saw as the 'ordinary bloke' a bore. I was not bowled over by John Mulgan's overrated *Man Alone*, and I'm afraid I did not care for Katherine Mansfield, whose ghost has so haunted our literature. I still don't. And with just about every second person I knew harbouring poetic ambitions, it seemed, there was much dross among the glimmerings of gold visible in the widening stream of New Zealand poetry. Even before I graduated I had destroyed my own feeble verse and vowed to spare the world any further outpourings. I've kept my vow. Instead, I searched ceaselessly for subjects to write about and even persevered with a few before throwing them away. It was good writing practice and I remained confident that sooner or later I would manage to produce something that someone would consider to be worth publishing.

There were also writers to admire: pre-eminently Maurice Shadbolt, Ian Cross, M. K. Joseph and Bruce Mason. I noted that Shadbolt in particular, who seemed to me to be potentially our best novelist and short story exponent, had chosen to live abroad. So had Janet Frame, though my appreciation of her very great literary gifts was tempered by my overall dislike of her obscurity. I suppose I never really came to terms with her until the appearance of her autobiographical writings.

It was singing, though, that dominated my life at this stage and Charlie was generous in allowing me days off to do engagements outside Christchurch. I wasn't an All Black like Dennis Young, a provincial representative like Mike Murtagh or a cricket rep like Gren Alabaster, so it had to be without pay and on condition that I sang to the school assemblies. I was happy to do that and often sang duets with Alec Robson, a good bass. I'm continuingly amazed at how many Shirley old boys still recall those performances.

I was lucky in that two of the best South Island tenors who had done so much oratorio work in previous years – Christchurch's Thomas E. (Eddie) West and the older Harold Prescott from the West Coast – had retired. But against that was the emergence of a formidable group of tenors nationwide who were clear rivals in an intensely competitive field. Singers like John Thompson had returned from years in England; Ramon Opie and Jon Andrew were the burgeoning New Zealand Opera Company's heroic tenors; Noel Signal and George Metcalf were emerging in lighter roles; and the versatile Robin Gordon was in constant demand with the National Orchestra and choral societies everywhere. Peter Baillie, only a year older than me, was being hailed as a future star, while Anson Austin, younger, and a small boy at Boys' High when I was in my last year, was now Clifton Cook's favourite pupil and rising fast.

The oft-parroted myth about a shortage of good tenors was as far from the truth in New Zealand then as it always has been in England, as I would eventually discover. Few people regarded me as a potential operatic tenor, but that did not worry me; much as I subsequently enjoyed singing in opera, my ambitions and real enjoyment were centred on concert work, oratorio and recitals: all less glamorous, perhaps – certainly to a modern generation obsessed by preposterous media-generated notions of 'stardom'. And in those years there was no shortage of concert work.

The number of my broadcasting engagements increased, and were usually done live from the big Gloucester Street studios with the Christchurch NZBC's superb resident accompanist, Matthew T. Dixon. Matt was a joy to work with, a wonderful sight-reader, utterly unflappable and vastly experienced. I also began to work in university and Eroica Club recitals with Maurice Till, who was making his mark spectacularly as the country's premier resident solo pianist and, especially, as an internationally recognised accompanist through the memorable tours he did with Victoria de los Angeles, Rita Streich and so many others. For the Sunday night ballad broadcasts from 3ZB's Colombo Street studio produced by Grace Green there was either the equally unflappable Maisie McNair, or Jenny Zwartz and her piano trio companions, Frances de Goldi, Teresa Beaven and the soprano Ann Sheehan, sister to both Frances and Mary Mullins. I also did duet recitals with another soprano, Marie Sutherland, whom I'd known since childhood, and who went on to a successful career in Sydney, Britain and Europe (by then known as Marie Landis).

By the time I left the country I had performed more than 50 solo studio broadcasts, which included first New Zealand performances of Benjamin Britten's *Winter Words* song-cycle with Maurice Till, and, with the National Orchestra's oboist Guy Henderson, Vaughan Williams' *Ten Blake Songs* for tenor and oboe. I think I might also have done the first local performances of George Butterworth's *A Shropshire Lad*. I had built up a large song repertoire.

During 1960 the work built up steadily, with *Messiahs* from Dunedin to Greymouth and two memorable visits to Wellington: one for a Bach Mass in B Minor for Stanley Oliver's superb Phoenix Choir, the other for the Royal Christchurch Musical Society's second centenary concert, a Sunday afternoon performance of *St Matthew Passion* to a full Town Hall in July, following a similarly packed-out Beethoven's *Missa Solemnis* with the National Orchestra under John Hopkins the previous evening. John had tried hard to persuade me to help bolster the choir's tenor section in the latter, even offering to lend me a dinner jacket, but I was determined to seize my chance to make an impression in the *Passion* next day, and firmly declined. I got on well with John, in contrast to his predecessor, James Robertson, by now the New Zealand Opera Company's musical director, who could never understand why a potential academic like me preferred singing. Nor did he care for my kind of lightish tenor voice. James was never in the same class as John Hopkins as a conductor, and orchestras sometimes played up during rehearsals, but his witty and off-the-cuff introductions to the orchestra's items were superb and were always a feature of his orchestral concerts.

The *Passion* that Sunday turned out to be the most significant performance of my early New Zealand career and resulted in a great deal of new work.

Most of the major choral societies' oratorio concerts in New Zealand in those days were broadcast nationally on the YC network, but this *St Matthew* was also recorded by Tony Vercoe of Kiwi Records, a division at that time of A. H. & A. W. Reed. After the morning rehearsal he played back various pieces to Bob Field-Dodgson, Winston Sharp and me and we went off happily for lunch. Months later when the recording of excerpts finally came out we were horrified: Tony had forgotten to switch on the soloists' microphones again when he returned for the performance, and didn't realise his error until almost the final series of recitatives. For most of that record we sound as though we are somewhere in the far distance, or singing in an adjacent hall.

Back in Christchurch I at last sang in my cherished but steadily deteriorating Theatre Royal, in a Christchurch Harmonic Society performance of Handel's *Israel in Egypt*. After the Civic Theatre's dry acoustic, the sense of vocal freedom and being able to actually hear what one was doing was exhilarating. Listening to peerless Mary Pratt in sumptuous voice beside me made me realise just how much vocal bloom was lost in the unhelpful Civic. There was also a special sense of occasion to be at last singing in a real opera house. I felt I was vocally growing up.

This was also the year I met Arnold Wall Jnr. At the end of a lunch-hour recital of Shakespeare songs in the Provincial Council Chamber, during which I delivered my own spoken introductions, he loomed over me, darkly gaunt and piratical-looking with his black eye patch, and asked if I'd be interested in doing some radio talks, illustrated with my songs. There would be a double fee for speaking and singing, he added. He was planning an entire day's programme for St George's Day, Shakespeare's birthday, and he wanted me to do an hour on Shakespeare songs.

It was a daunting introduction to radio talks, but I followed it up with several more on such topics as Victorian ballads and Victorian ballad opera. 'Tenors Triumphant' is the one I recall most readily, if for no other reason than I was able to repeat it word for word and note for note for the ABC in Sydney two years later.

Arnold was a delight, and a brilliant producer of radio talks; easily the best I've met subsequently, whether at the ABC, BBC or for Radio NZ. He taught me everything I needed to know about the genre. He also employed Winston Sharp, my frequent baritone colleague of those days, and me to sing Victorian duets and songs for a series he produced on historic Canterbury houses. Later, of course, he became the great editor for A. H. & A. W. Reed.

One of the most enjoyable performances of that year was a one-act opera, *Once Upon a Time*, that Marie Sutherland, Winston and I did with Michael Toovey at the piano. It was a riotous version of a Pushkin story about a boring storyteller and a bored wife by the colourful visiting Welsh composer and academic Professor Ian Parrott, and was part of a Great Hall concert of his music in which John Ritchie, his orchestra and Maurice Till also featured. *Once Upon a Time* was the first – and last – time I was required to attempt a traditional Russian dance. Luckily I was very fit in those days.

I was even busier in 1961, and for the first time performed Handel's splendid *Judas Maccabeus*, which was to remain one of my favourites and, apart from *Messiah*, most frequently performed Handel oratorios. This first performance was done at a couple of days' notice for the NZBC's head of music, Malcolm Rickard, and his Wellington choir. I sang in four or five Wellington concerts for Peter Zwartz, who had taken over Wellington's Harmonic Choir and, in collaboration with Professor Frederick Page and Alex Lindsay, organised a chamber music concert to celebrate Igor Stravinsky's visit. The great man insisted in those days that his chamber music must be conducted, so Alex led a group of the National Orchestra's principals and Pete conducted, after meeting Stravinsky and going through the programme with him. On that incident-packed occasion we gave the first New Zealand performance of Stravinsky's *In Memoriam Dylan Thomas* for tenor and chamber ensemble, which, mercifully, we performed twice. The first was far from perfect, and during the interval, while Fred Page dispensed liberal doses of Scotch whisky (which I reluctantly abjured in the interests of my voice), Alex and Pete furiously accused one another of being responsible for the mistakes and almost came to blows. The second performance later in the second half went much better and that was the one the NZBC broadcast.

There was another memorable occasion in Wellington, on 15 December, when Dunedin's Professor Peter Platt conducted the National Orchestra, Wellington's Harmonic Choir, Rosemary Rogatzy, Honor McKellar, Donald Munro and me in only the second performance anywhere in the world of Britten's new work *Cantata Academica*. This celebrated the formal winding up of the old University of New Zealand and the inauguration of its successors, the universities of Auckland, Victoria in Wellington, Canterbury and Otago, and the Town Hall was crammed with civic and magnificently gowned academic dignitaries. It was a long and quite tedious event of seemingly interminable speeches, though it began dramatically and tragically when, just as I launched into the opening tenor solo, an elderly professor in the far corner collapsed and died. Everything carried on regardless.

I had first met Peter Platt earlier in the year when I went down to Dunedin to sing the *St Matthew* for the Dunedin Choral Society, which he had taken over. Peter and Jean welcomed me warmly into their delightful family and from then on I always stayed with them on my increasingly frequent visits south. Peter was a dynamic organiser and in his time there Dunedin became a major centre of musical activity and innovation as, under his inspired direction, the long-established choral society, his university choir and the revitalised Dunedin Opera Company went from strength to strength. He also gathered around him a marvellously lively and interesting group of friends and disciples, notable among whom and in pride of place as his most outstanding student was the young, brilliant and endlessly amusing William Southgate – destined far into the future to become the first resident New Zealand conductor to receive a knighthood. The young Bill could seemingly play anything and fill in for whatever shortage might afflict the local orchestra. Life was never dull at the Platts' and it was as much a home away from home for me as was the Zwartzes' in Wellington.

During the Easter weekend spent in Dunedin, Peggy came up from Invercargill to tell me that she had finally decided to marry her broadcasting colleague instead of me. It was a hard blow, and John Ritchie prophesied sympathetically that it would probably be some time before I would risk any serious involvement again. I agreed and now resolved not to let any attachment interfere with my career. Mum had always urged me to follow that precept anyway, and during the next year I stuck firmly to my resolution and in the process I fear I came to be quite justifiably regarded as a heel by one or two delightful girls who deserved better. As it was, Peggy's first marriage was no more successful than my own.

Fortuitously, it was not so many weeks after this that McLintock easily convinced me that it was high time I left for pastures new. The occasion was a mild Wellington Friday evening. I arrived for my monthly visit to report on my parliamentarians and found him unusually depressed. He had spent a disagreeable afternoon, he explained, with Keith Holyoake, who had told him that there would be no successor parliamentary historian when he (McLintock) retired and that the universities could take over that sort of thing. Holyoake had also discoursed at length on his belief that history was of no great value anyway, and had struck the table before him and declared that although it had once stood in the old Legislative Council it was nothing more to him than an unattractive and intrinsically useless piece of old wood.

So it was time for me go, McLintock told me, glaring around at the parliamentarians and officials thronging the bar and shouting at one another through the haze of tobacco smoke. There would be no research job for me after his retirement and I was far too young yet to consider a political career. He scornfully indicated the crowd besieging the bar and observed that not one of them was under 50! Nobody under 50 was listened to anyway in this benighted country. I must clear out, sing and write novels, and if all failed I'd always have teaching to fall back on. The main thing, though, was to get out as fast as possible.

That decided me. I would go sooner rather than later, but I

would certainly not creep back to New Zealand as a failure, good for nothing but teaching. I would go for good. The day after I got back to Christchurch I made a preliminary booking on the *Northern Star* for my passage to England in October 1962.

Perhaps the concert I enjoyed most in 1961 was that celebrating Vernon Griffiths' achievements and his retirement, at which I sang a selection of his best songs and later recorded them for the NZBC. Sadly, Griff was already considered passé by the new generation of New Zealand musicians influenced by his former pupils Fred Page and Douglas Lilburn, and along with so much of his vast output of Catholic church music and choral music for adolescent voices, his songs have been forgotten by New Zealand singers unaware of how wonderfully vocal they are. That's a shame. The modern revival of interest in Britain of such notable song composers of Griff's generation as Hubert Parry, Roger Quilter, Peter Warlock and E. J. Moeran has not been mirrored here. Yet Griff's best songs – 'Wrong Not, Sweet Empress' and some Shakespeare settings – can certainly stand comparison with those of his famous English contemporaries.

I also enjoyed singing the marvellous tenor solo 'Onaway! Awake, Beloved' during an Adult Education tour of Samuel Coleridge-Taylor's *Hiawatha's Wedding Feast* around the wider Canterbury region with the English conductor Dr Denis Wright, a power in BBC music administration and a world authority on brass bands. He was an agreeable fellow and throughout my career I revelled in singing 'Onaway! Awake, Beloved' – as do most tenors. I did a similar tour with Denis on his next visit in the following year.

The year 1962 turned out to be not merely another busy one but an even more significant and surprising one. It started splendidly in March when, having again been given time off without pay, I flew with the Royal Christchurch Musical Society on a charter flight to the second Adelaide Festival – first class, a treat I have never subsequently enjoyed. There were abundant in-flight drinks, a very good meal and lots of agreeable female company; and during our stopover in Melbourne we had our first experience of downing ice-cold Australian lager in the manner we habitually downed warm New Zealand beer. It was salutary, but was followed by a less pleasant flight to Adelaide as we flew into an electrical storm and watched lightning playing about the wings.

Our arrival, however, was wonderful: an official event with flowers, fruit and bottles of wine, during which Bob Field-Dodgson gave me news that there was an ABC contract for me to record two radio recitals. Next day I met Dr Perkins, the ABC's head of music in South Australia, and another ABC official from Melbourne who told me about their TV operas and suggested I send a tape to ABC Sydney. With my Dunedin baritone friend Ninian Walden I received open invitations to the ABC's daily cocktail parties, where we met a host of ABC officials and such exotics as Sir Malcolm Sargent, who daily and with extravagant good humour regaled everyone within earshot with Beecham stories about and against himself. There was also the equally colourful Honourable James Smith. Smith was a power in British arts administration and asked after his 'very dear old friend' James Robertson, assuring us that 'they' were keeping a very good job open for dear James when his contracts in New Zealand ended. In London two years later the significance of that conversation became clear to me when James was appointed head of the London Opera Centre, whose founders, the distinguished former singers Joan Cross and Ann Wood, were thereupon declared redundant.

In Adelaide in March 1962, however, the colourfully waist-coated Smith's chortlings and the inner machinations of Britain's curiously turbulent and often Machiavellian music establishment meant nothing to me. I had my ABC recitals to record, my contacts to establish and the Town Hall concert of Kodaly's *Budavári Te Deum* with the RCMS and the South Australian State Orchestra to get over. Not that the Kodaly was very arduous. The solos were brief, I'd sung them before and it went well enough for Lewis Dawe, conductor of Adelaide's Harmony Choir, to ask me back for *Messiah* in December, and for the orchestra's leader to advise me to go to Sydney for regular work.

The remaining days and nights before we flew home were a

prolonged series of parties and dinners. Once back home I rearranged my travel plans completely. I cancelled my berth on the *Northern Star* and, instead, booked an October berth to Sydney. Then I went back to school to see Charlie Gallagher, who announced even before I'd said a word that there was no chance whatsoever of getting more time off that year – even without pay. I replied that I was not asking for time off but I was at last giving in my notice. I was going back to Australia. Charlie was shocked. He seemed to have a far greater opinion of my teaching abilities than I did. He wanted me back before I was 30, and would keep a place on the staff for me until then. Singing was a dicey business, he thought, and anyway didn't I want to be one of the youngest headmasters in New Zealand as he had been, or an administrator or even Director of Education? No, I replied. While grateful and flattered by his offer, I had no ambition to be any of those, and I wouldn't be back.

It was about now that Peter Platt asked me to sing the comic role of the dim-witted Vasek in his Dunedin Opera Company's forthcoming production of Smetana's *Bartered Bride*. I spent most weekends rehearsing in Dunedin from then on and at the first of these met one of Dunedin's rising young sopranos, Beverley Ganderton, another radio announcer and a very ambitious singer who had already sung major roles for the company. This time she was singing the smaller role of Esmeralda the Gypsy, who cajoles Vasek into playing the role of the performing bear for a visiting company of comedians. We rehearsed together a lot and by the time the season began in early July we were spending even more time in each other's company. Playing Vasek was fun, though I didn't think so when, on my first appearance on my first night, I tripped over a doorstep and fell flat on my face. The audience loved it, however, so I left in that bit of accidental improvisation for the other performances.

After the season was over and much to my friends' surprise, I continued to spend weekends in Dunedin when I could, and within a few weeks Beverley and I announced our engagement and plans to marry the following Easter, when I was due back in New Zealand to record radio recitals and do concerts in Wellington and Dunedin. My family and friends were generally astonished – as, in a way, was I. Then Beverley had second thoughts about an Easter wedding, perhaps concerned that I might not return from Australia after all, so everything was rearranged. It was decided that we would get married on 13 October in Dunedin's Catholic Cathedral. The Gandertons – staunch nonconformists and delightful people – were rueful about the Catholic service but accepted it, and Beverley began taking instruction from our friendly priest at St Peter's Beckenham. It was, in retrospect, a rather hectic and even slightly surreal time. (Some years later that priest left the Church, married a former nun and became an Anglican minister.)

My last months in New Zealand were hectic in every other way too. I performed more concerts and a variety of broadcasts, including Brahms' *Liebeslieder Waltzes,* which I have always particularly enjoyed, and Liza Lehmann's superb song-cycle *In a Persian Garden* with my regular concert colleagues, soprano Anita Ritchie, mezzo Edna Boyd-Wilson, baritone Winston Sharp, and accompanists Matt Dixon and Michael Toovey. I also found time to do two amateur productions of Gilbert and Sullivan's *Pirates of Penzance*. The Pirate King for one was the young Rodney McCann, at the very start of what would be an exceptionally distinguished career, and with whom I would continue to work over the next 40 years throughout Britain and New Zealand in oratorio and opera. The other was that unforgettable personality, inveterate controversialist and remarkable painter Alan Pearson.

My last visit to the Zwartzes in Wellington was memorable too, for at one of their parties Denis Glover and his lady companion of those years materialised out of the darkness, tottering unsteadily and creating much noise. Pete introduced me to them as a singer, teacher, historian and writer, at which Glover glowered and growled that it was impossible for one person to be so many things. When I remarked that he had managed to be rather a lot of things too, he shouted that that was altogether different. He then fell back into the darkness and was dragged away bodily by his lady.

I did a final lunch-hour recital in the Great Hall before I left for my Dunedin wedding, and while I was waiting outside in the almost empty quad for my call to go on stage, whom should I see advancing towards me with stately tread but Neville Phillips – smiling. He'd read in the newspapers that I was going to England, he remarked by way of greeting. No, I replied, I'd changed my plans and was going to Australia instead. I'd been offered some good singing work there. 'Australia!' he exclaimed, face contorting with an expression of distaste. 'Australia, Mr Bohan! There are no historians of any standing whatsoever in Australia!' Then he marched away shaking his head. He clearly hadn't grasped the fact that I was going to Australia to sing.

Reactions in Christchurch to my departure and opinions about my prospects varied. C. Foster Browne, the Anglican Cathedral's organist and choirmaster and magisterial music critic for the *Press,* was flatteringly optimistic about my prospects in the last review he wrote before I left – as he had ever been, but not everyone was as sanguine. The mother of another aspiring ex-Boys' High singer and pupil of Clifton Cook declared me to be far too limited to do much: I might be suitable enough for 'light' things like Bach and little Elizabethan songs, but I was no use for opera or real singing. I suspect quite a few others thought the same. However, an abrasive soprano I sang opposite in one of the *Pirates* productions and who consistently made it clear that she was not an admirer, remarked that she had just heard some new G&S recordings with an awful English tenor called Thomas Round, and it made her think that I might possibly do quite well after all.

As it happened, Tom Round was having a splendid run in Britain at that time. He had succeeded the great Savoyard Leonard Osborn as D'Oyly Carte's principal tenor, was currently a principal lyric tenor at Sadler's Wells and, with the Australian June Bronhill (with whom I later sang with the BBC Concert Orchestra), had just had a tremendous success in Franz Lehár's *Merry Widow*. He compensated for a lack of vocal splendour by immense charm and persuasive acting and he had a huge and adoring fan club, some of whom later followed me around the G&S concert circuit. I got to know Tom quite well and we sang together and shared a dressing room amicably in a season of *Die Fledermaus*, but I never dared tell him that particular story about the soprano who so disliked us both.

My final days at Shirley Boys' High were filled with more staff parties and much carousing. The morning after the final one, which had ended very late at Rose Street, saw the staffroom resembling a casualty clearing station. In addition a senior teacher had hit the gatepost as he tried to drive into the staff carpark, and staff wives were reportedly blaming Murtagh and me yet again for leading their husbands astray. Charlie Gallagher and Pat Caird, slightly exasperated, led no more than a handful of staff into assembly that morning and I think they were pleased to finally see me go. Certainly some staff wives were.

Beverley and I were married in Dunedin's St Joseph's Cathedral on 13 October 1962 and the Gandertons spared no expense. That weekend is still remembered by my friends and relations for the succession of spectacular parties that followed the breakfast and our departure for Christchurch, Auckland, then Sydney. Beverley's bridesmaids were her high-spirited friends Catherine Dowling (later the broadcasting personality Catherine Saunders) and Barbara Magna (who married Maurice Shadbolt). Mike Murtagh was my best man and Ray Coats, the Dunedin tenor who had also been in *The Bartered Bride,* was groomsman.

I have to confess, with no pride, that I was suffering a fairly acute hangover because my stag night celebrations had gone on well into the night. I was staying as usual with the Platts and sleeping in Peter's music study, but it was so late by the time Mike and Ian Leggat and I returned there that they decided to sleep over – Mike under the harpsichord and Ian in a double bass case. Peter, slightly surprised when he brought in my early morning coffee but always the unflappable and perfect host, did his best with lots more coffee and amusing advice, but I was still feeling quite remote by the time I found myself at the altar beside the dazzling bride and bridesmaids. That sense of not being part of proceedings lasted into the wedding breakfast itself, along with a feeling of slight resentment that because the photos had taken so long most of the champagne had been appropriated by everyone else. I suspect that only I among all the celebrating throng did not entirely enjoy the afternoon.

By the time Beverley and I were farewelled at the railway station it was clear that everyone was about to have a terrific weekend. To some family surprise, the star of the day with all the young women was Uncle Bill. Father had doubted whether he'd appear, being more likely to choose the races than my wedding, but he came brimming with every ounce of the boisterous charm of which he was capable when it suited him, and enjoyed himself thoroughly. Murtagh, my brother Des and John Mullins were careful, however, to make sure that Father and Bill were safely back in their hotel before the party really heated up: or so I've been told many times since. None of my friends who attended my first wedding have ever forgotten that weekend, and Murtagh is wont to sum it up thus: 'Great wedding but a pity about the marriage.'

FOUR

Australian Interlude and *Arkadia* 1962–63

We found a place to live in central Sydney soon enough: a convenient flat in the comfortable Cahors high-rise block opposite the Alamein Fountain at the heart of King's Cross, where we stayed for six months before moving across the harbour to Neutral Bay. We settled in quickly. Beverley found a singing teacher almost immediately, Leo Demant, at the Conservatorium of Music, and a month or two later I began studying with Godfrey Stirling, a former English tenor who had enjoyed a long and distinguished career in Britain, Australia and South Africa. He was a splendid teacher. But even before I started with him I did my auditions with the ABC's heads of radio and television music and opera, their various conductors and producers.

All had immediate results. Werner Baer, head of music for ABC radio, New South Wales, signed me up for a succession of studio recitals; ABCTV booked me for some Sunday afternoon music recitals; and the head of ABCTV opera offered me the role of Nadir in a production of Bizet's *Pearl Fishers* they were planning. For some time they had been in the habit of using an unphotogenic but very fine tenor for their TV operas in tandem with a more personable actor who mimed on screen. Now they had decided to revise their policy and I, they thought, was suitable to be seen as well as heard.

They also sent me the music for a new opera by the Sydney composer John Gordon. His *Fisher's Ghost*, based on a well-known Australian ghost story of the early 19th-century convict days, was to be the first Australian opera written for television. With the score came instructions about the additional audition I was required to do (to satisfy local union rules) for the central tenor part of John Hurley, and several passages, underlined in blue crayon, that I was to sing.

Accordingly, I presented myself at the TV studios on the appointed afternoon to find just about every other Sydney singer thronging the waiting room. Most were very unhappy. I didn't know any of them (except by sight and reputation) and luckily none of them knew me, so I took a seat beside the door and remained inconspicuous. Soon after my arrival one of the best-known baritones in Australia stood up and made a furious speech. There were rumours, this large and very angry bloke thundered, that some people present had been promised roles already and had even been sent scores! If that was true, why the hell had the rest of them been asked to audition? He was very pissed off. I didn't hear what else he said because I slipped out, clutching my score to my chest, and waited until I was called into the studio to sing my allotted lines. There I found the usual ABC officials, the composer, conductor, producer and repetiteur, who all greeted me cheerfully and confirmed that I had the part anyway. I sang my lines with gusto and left the building as fast as I could.

I went off cheerfully to sing *Messiah* in Adelaide, only to be brought back to earth when I returned to Sydney and was told by apologetic officials that while the head of opera and the producer had promised me Nadir in *Pearl Fishers*, the conductor – who had not yet heard me or been informed about me – had asked another lyric tenor who had recently arrived in Sydney from England (no less than Robert Gard, who was to have a long and very distinguished career with Australian Opera). They were all embarrassed and to solve their problem had decided to offer us both other work but, for Nadir, to revert to using their regular tenor in tandem once more with the actor.

I never did sing Nadir, though in those youthful years I had the right voice for it and for a few years used the famous 'Serenade' as one of my audition arias. Six or seven years later I was offered the role again for the opening of the new Opera House in Cork, but the very day the contract appeared through my London letterbox I also received an anguished call from my agent warning me not to sign it because the season was off. The Cork Festival authorities had omitted to book the new theatre in time and the venue was to open with a pantomime!

From the start of my association with Werner Baer and ABC Radio it was clear that the reason I achieved so many broadcasts in the year we spent in Sydney had to do with the repertoire I offered. Australia seemed to have a never-ending supply of ambitious dramatic and would-be Italian-style operatic tenors, but few of my particular voice type and with my kind of repertoire. So I presented what I had already done for the NZBC, including *Winter Words* and the Vaughan Williams *Blake Songs* for oboe and tenor. And when I met the ABC's head of radio talks I was able to offer him what I had already recorded for Arnold Wall in Christchurch, though I quickly began to present other ideas too.

I was sometimes asked for a new script at little more than a day's notice and would have to work into the night so that I could record them first thing next morning. I even did a long one on New Zealand writing, after one official had asked with typical Australian ignorance of all things New Zealand whether there *was* any writing happening in New Zealand. My talk surprised and satisfied the ABC officials that there was an immense amount of literary activity in New Zealand and they broadcast it nationwide, but it offended the New Zealand-born announcer who sat in the studio while I recorded it. He clearly thought I was not reverential enough to such icons as Frank Sargeson and one or two of our better-known poets and novelists. Had I ever been to New Zealand? he demanded after I'd finished the recording. When I replied that I'd only recently left the place he slammed out of the studio with the curt observation that I should be ashamed of myself.

I enjoyed working with the ABC people (apart from that announcer). They were friendly, very encouraging and far less stuffy and self-important than some of the NZBC men in Wellington. It was also pleasant to find John Hopkins arriving to become Head of Music, though his appointment did ruffle feathers. Conductor Joseph Post had expected the job, and one morning when I arrived at the ABC to discuss future programmes with Werner Baer, what did I find on the steps but a glowering Post, an obviously excited John Hopkins and some uneasy officials. Werner greeted me with unusual warmth, exclaiming that as I lived in King's Cross and obviously knew John, I was just the person to guide him back to his hotel because he didn't know Sydney. We could sort out the next broadcasts and even have lunch later. We'd scarcely reached a bus stop before John had told me his great news. Later in the day Werner admitted that my arrival couldn't have been better timed and had resolved an embarrassing situation. I think it earned me one or two extra recitals.

In addition to the *Fisher's Ghost* contract, ABCTV gave me work on their Sunday Concert afternoon music series hosted by the great Australian baritone Harold Williams, with the unforgettable Henri Penn, for decades Australia's leading accompanist, at the piano. Harold's career in Britain in oratorio especially had been long and very distinguished, and in our school and student days Neil Hartley and I had spent hours playing and replaying his famous recording of Mendelssohn's *Elijah*. Harold was by now one of Australia's most celebrated teachers, and there were few Australian baritones and basses of our generation who did not study with him at some time. Neil did too. Some of the advice Harold gave me was to prove as valuable as any I ever received.

I also auditioned in these first weeks for the Melbourne-based Elizabethan Trust Opera (forerunner to Opera Australia), which was planning a production of Mozart's *Marriage of Figaro*, and initially it looked as though I was going to get the role of Don Basilio, which I was later to play for Kent Opera in England and for Canterbury Opera back in Christchurch 30 years later. Then the old Austrian conductor had a heart attack, the young English director went back to

England and James Robertson arrived in a rush from New Zealand. All changed. New auditions were demanded and when I walked in this time James leapt up, shook my hand warmly and exclaimed how nice it was to see me again, then turned to the panel and explained that I was an absolutely splendid Bach singer but I hadn't done any opera at all and wasn't really suitable. That was the end of that. Three years later in London, James did exactly the same when the Arts Council's Opera For All needed an Ernesto for their *Don Pasquale*. That was even more infuriating because by then I was already singing the role in two separate productions with some success.

My lack of operatic experience was certainly no problem for Douglas Parnell and his enterprising semi-professional New South Wales Repertory Opera. They were preparing a new production of Rossini's *Barber of Seville* and had not yet found a tenor to sing Count Almaviva. It was almost the perfect operatic role for me at this early stage of my career, both vocally and, just as important, temperamentally. I simply preferred comic opera – and I do still. The roles I have enjoyed most (and been most successful in) have been the comic ones. *The Barber* is a sheer delight in every respect. Its libretto is superbly witty and musically it is an uninterrupted stream of outstanding arias and gloriously complex ensembles. It has to be the greatest comic opera, rivalled only by those other Rossini masterpieces such as *L'Italiana in Algeri*, *Cenerentola* (both of which I later performed in Britain) and especially his last, *Conte Ory*, rediscovered in the late 1950s and revealed in all its verve and brilliance by Glyndebourne Opera – to the astonished delight of the operatic world, for by then we were at the start of the great Rossini revival.

In this Sydney production we used a new and slangy American translation – for, strange as it may seem to opera buffs in the 21st century, most opera was still traditionally performed in the language of the country in which the production was taking place. Surtitles would not be invented for another 20 years and the modern insistence on doing most opera (except comic opera and operetta) in the original language was not yet in vogue. Over the next 12 months I sang in all this company's performances around Sydney, with three different Rosinas

– including Beverley – and earned good reviews, especially for my acting. Almaviva would remain one of my most frequently performed roles for over a decade: by the time I gave my last performance in the mid-1970s I had sung four different English translations in seven or eight different productions. The last performance was for Anvil Films as one of an operatic series largely filmed on location at Knebworth Hall, that distinctive and picturesque Gothic country house that had once belonged to the novelist Edward Bulwer-Lytton and is habitually used by TV and film companies.

My brief return visit to New Zealand just before Easter was hectic, with the *St Matthew Passion* in Wellington and Dunedin, and three NZBC recital recordings and a lunch-hour recital in Dunedin with Maurice Till – at which I sang Douglas Lilburn's *Sings Harry* cycle. I had met Lilburn with Pete Zwartz, then his publisher and foremost champion, and Douglas had given me a copy of the work in a tenor key. But generous as that was, I'm afraid I have never warmed to his work, and as British music clubs showed no interest in it I never sang *Sings Harry* again.

Then I was back in Sydney to sing the Evangelist for two performances of Bach's *St John Passion* at St Andrew's Cathedral. And after that back to teaching English and ancient history at Narrabeen Girls' High to bolster the income. Sydney was an expensive place and we needed money if we wanted to move on to London. I also started rehearsals for *Fisher's Ghost*.

Beverley had hardly been idle all this time either. She had joined the National Theatre's production of *Showboat*, which required her to spend a considerable time in Melbourne before their Sydney season, and after that she became ATN TV's Sunday evening continuity announcer. Unfortunately, this separation did nothing for our marriage, which did not really recover its first fine careless rapture: we had begun to realise that we each of us had married the wrong person. For the next few months, though, we did enjoy a bout of being minor television identities and being interviewed by television journalists when we were seen at fashionable restaurants.

Fisher's Ghost was part of ABCTV's current fascination with Australian history. Historical TV dramas such as *The Outcasts*, *The Patriots*, *Stormy Petrel* and *The Hungry Ones* were their staple fare at this time and *Fisher's Ghost* not only fitted that pattern and taste very well indeed, but also fitted into their schedule of presenting made-for-television opera productions (mainly from America) on Sunday evening prime-time television.

It was based on the famous Campbelltown murder in 1826 of Fred Fisher, a ticket-of-leave man who vanished one night and whose body was not found until John Hurley claimed to have seen his ghost and alerted police. I played Hurley, a bit of a drunkard bossed about unmercifully by his wife and sister. Others in the cast included the rising Australian soprano Marilyn Richardson; the veteran Australian character tenor Ereach Riley as Birdlime, narrator and pickpocket; John Brosnan, a Sydney policeman, as murderer George Worrall; and Don McGregor (also a New Zealander) as the tavern keeper.

Not everyone in Sydney's singing world was happy about New Zealanders taking their jobs, though that had been happening for 80 years with a steady stream of ambitious New Zealand singers finding work, especially with J. C. Williamson Ltd's numerous touring shows. At the first rehearsals of the opening scene, set in the old Plough Inn with a male chorus drawn from the NSW Police Choir, that was made painfully clear: not one of this very experienced opera chorus spoke to me. Then a few days later, after I had appeared again on ABCTV's Sunday Concert, one of the chorus tenors tapped me on the shoulder and remarked laconically that they'd all seen me yesterday and had liked what they saw and heard. Then we all went out for drinks. They were a great bunch, though it was a bit of a shock one day in busy Martin Place when a burly cop on duty, pistol protruding menacingly from his holster, held up the peak-hour traffic and ceremoniously ushered us across the road. It was John Brosnan.

We recorded the music with George Humphrey conducting the Sydney Symphony Orchestra, and we were directed by TV producer Robert Allnutt, from whom I learnt a tremendous amount, not least how to act drunk, which was a useful skill I was able to call on often when I later sang Alfred in *Fledermaus* and Nemorino in *L'Elisir d'Amore* – both, incidentally, also among the roles I have most enjoyed. As was the custom, we mimed to our own soundtrack as we filmed.

The finished product was released during September and October throughout Australia, but I don't think it created any great sensation. I have a recollection that one reviewer thought I was perhaps the first person to have uttered the great Australian adjective on primetime telly. The ABC did not keep the telerecording – as they assuredly would now. In those days tape was expensive and the ABC, like the NZBC and the BBC, thriftily recycled their tapes, thereby losing so much of their early TV and radio endeavours.

Even before *Fisher's Ghost* was completed, Bob Allnutt was talking to me about further TV opera productions being planned for 1964. I was certainly very interested, but now our plans were changing. Sir Bernard Heinz, head of Sydney's Conservatorium, had become so impressed by Beverley's vocal potential that he recommended her to London's Opera Centre, at that time the only British institution offering advanced operatic training; Joan Cross accepted her, subject to an audition when she reached London. I would have liked to stay in Sydney for at least another year, but there was no question of my not going to London too, as that had long been my intended destination. So we sold the piano and furniture, regretfully gave away Ptolemy, our little white chinchilla cat, and packed for London.

We spent our last two Sydney days at the Canberra Oriental Hotel in King's Cross where, during breakfast on the morning of 23 November, an aged waitress with thin dyed hair and, in spite of a low-pitched delivery that often dwindled to a mumble, a marked gift for drama, announced the news of John Kennedy's assassination. The effect was startling. I had never admired or liked the man, but the shock of such a uniquely memorable event lingered throughout the next days as we said our farewells to friends, wrapped up our Sydney affairs and embarked on the Greek Line's SS *Arkadia* – a ship once familiar to Dutch migrants as the *Wilhelm Rys* – crewed by an uneasy racial mix of Greeks and Germans. Their relationships were far from harmonious at the best of times, but the dramatic and tragic events of the last week of our voyage plunged them to a new low.

For the next five weeks *Arkadia* was our entire world. We slipped easily into a daily routine of hearty breakfasts, lazing in chairs on the sun deck, long lunches, afternoons reading or listening to records or lounging about in the sun again until the generally excellent dinners. The evening meal would be preceded by cocktails and followed by the nightly game of bingo, then dancing in the Tegean Room to the German orchestra, followed by drinks in the Taverna bar, the Epicure bar and the Orpheus Room. The 'games' organised by a tyrannical Dutch entertainments officer were less interesting, though she and her staff did their best to cheer the more than 200 children on board.

It was a world of gossip and rumour, of quickly made friendships that splintered equally quickly when intimate details of rashly revealed life stories generated new and yet more eagerly disseminated gossip. The majority of the passengers were Greek-, German- or Italian-Australian families returning to their homelands on holiday or on pilgrimage and they kept very much to their own communities. So did our assorted group of English men and women and brash Australians, male and female. We were the only New Zealanders. We shared a dining table with two Australian air hostesses, an incomprehensible Pole, a censorious Australian aunty with her cowed niece, a Scots footballer, a professional English gambler, two rich Aussie girls who were especially ghastly and, our best shipboard friend, Halina, an often spectacularly excitable Jewish girl from Melbourne. Our wider social set included the ship's amusing Irish doctor, a delightful Jamaican couple – a physicist and a language teacher on their way back to teach at the University of Jamaica – and a camp little man and his wide-eyed, silent, sari-clad lady friend. Initial gossip had speculated that he was a Spanish bullfighter and she a dancer. In fact she was simply an archly pretentious art student, and he a would-be avant-garde playwright.

A friendly Greek Cypriot steward attended us solicitously. And ever hovering nearby in the evenings was a cheerful Iranian bag maker and his largely silent family. He was far from silent, though his conversation tended to be limited to reflections about how quickly one's beard grew in hot climates, and an interminable tale of how he'd once lost his grandmother in Rome's railway station.

Conditions were rough all the way around the Great Australian Bight to Freemantle and few of us managed breakfast during that week, but life was far more comfortable as we crossed the swelteringly hot Indian Ocean, and not even the short-lived rumours that Suez was closed because of political trouble disturbed us too much. Eventually, however, boredom set in and grizzling about the ship, the food, the captain and the entertainments officer who tried to satisfy all tastes with a succession of competitions and fancy dress parades became endemic. The larger national groups entertained themselves: the Germans held nightly singsongs and the Greeks danced their traditional dances superbly.

It was a relief to reach the Gulf of Aden, though its dirty green waters contrasted startlingly with the variously deep-blue-black or luminous blues of the Indian Ocean. On a spectacular dawn on 13 December we were anchored out on the roadstead facing the massive orange-brown bare hills lined with the packing-case hovels of the Yemeni refugees rising above flat-roofed stone houses. In late 1963 Aden was entering its last years as a British military and naval base and was under martial law following assassination attempts on its British governor. Arab and Somali boats crowded around the gangway and ferried us ashore and into the market, where an Arab man in a red fez and long white djellaba latched on to us and offered his services as guide and companion. We reached a shop run by two Jewish youths, Simon and Jokai, who, attracted by Halina's Star of David necklace, rescued us and took us sightseeing in their Mercedes, much to our Arab man's fury and the loud astonishment of our passing Australian shipmates, who were determinedly trying to browbeat various Arab silversmiths and perfume sellers and were creating mayhem.

Simon and Jokai were among the last Jewish traders left in Aden, and were themselves winding up their family's businesses and leaving for Israel in a matter of days. Now they shut up their last shop and drove us through the bazaar and around the waterfront eastwards, past the RAF quarters, arid and racially segregated beaches, and a little way into the jagged treeless hills. After lunch they took us westwards towards Crater City, past newer blocks of European flats and up to the observation point at the top of the pass above the Muslim and Jewish cemeteries. From there we had a magnificent view of the crowded bay, before descending into the Crater's maze of crowded stone, plaster and mud-brick houses and tenements and continuing on up to the ancient water storage complex, the Tanks of Tawila, the Queen of Sheba's gardens and a small, one-room museum. An aged, thin and tattered attendant unlocked the museum for us and proudly pointed out clay figurines found in the nearby hillside caves, as well as tombstones, coin collections, maps and archaeological charts.

I could have spent the rest of the afternoon there, but Simon and Jokai, whose contempt for Yemeni Arabs was comprehensive and clearly mixed with some apprehension, were reluctant to linger. They had suffered in violent anti-Jewish riots in the past and there were political agitators now, they thought, haranguing the crowds in the Crater's packed and vibrant bazaars. We had to take their word; certainly the speakers shouting from platforms were getting the crowds excited, but whether it was about politics, religion or commerce was impossible for us to judge. So they drove us at speed out to the airport past the Queen Elizabeth Hospital, the police and British army barracks and the British residential area, and past an open-air cinema advertising *A Touch of Mink*, which seemed rather incongruous. The recording of Jussi Björling singing 'Nessun Dorma' on the car radio seemed weirdly out of place too.

That night the Epicure Bar resounded to everyone's tales of the day, which ranged from a saga of how some of the Australians had defrauded various shopkeepers and hoodwinked the police, to rambling discussions about what benefits – if any – the British had achieved in their 150 years' rule for Aden's Arabs and Somalis. Almost all of us were startled by the squalor and poverty; the exception was one of the English girls. She had spent all day with RAF friends and thought it a simply marvellous place. There were wonderful facilities at the base for swimming and tennis, and, above all, there were endless parties.

Our journey up the Red Sea was a time of torment for all averse to oppressive heat and high humidity, but when we at last reached Suez at midnight spirits revived as the hawkers thronged on board: for the first time we could buy the latest English newspapers, catch up with news of the All Blacks on tour and find out how Dennis Young (a senior player on that tour) was going. For the next day we slowly ploughed through the dirty-green water of the Suez Canal, one of a long convoy of ships, with the low orange-coloured desert to our right and to our left green fields, palms, low mud houses and hundreds of Egyptian soldiers, army barges and pontoon bridges. The region was, as usual, in a time of crisis, but that did not deter a drunken German youth, balancing on the ship's rail, from repeatedly shouting 'Down with Nasser!' and making obscene gestures. Luckily the Egyptian army couldn't hear what he was saying and waved back cheerfully.

We docked at Piraeus early the next day, on a fine, mild morning, farewelled several of our company and, with Chris the Cypriot steward as our guide and translator, headed for Athens, thrilled by our first sight of Europe: Byzantine and Turkish churches and low hills covered with warrens of white-walled, flat-roofed houses with shuttered windows, scrolled iron gates and balconies. After a brief exploration of central Athens around Constitution Square, where the wonderful smell of roasting chestnuts hung heavy in the air, we explored the Acropolis and enjoyed the magnificent views until fading grey light and a chilling wind howling through the ruin-strewn Parthenon forced us back down to the railway station and the train to Piraeus. I could have spent weeks happily pottering around Athens and I could easily have become an addict of Turkish coffee.

Naples, two days later, was cloudy, dull and raining, and the black towering 12th-century Norman castle opposite the wharf looked sinister. Even the black and orange Bourbon royal palace nearby and the closed San Carlo Opera House beyond looked dull and uninviting. The contrasts between the staggeringly expensive arcades and the narrow one-way streets branching off them, the elegant shoppers and the begging friars and more abject begging children glimpsed along the cobbled alleys, were stark and depressing.

The weather did not improve as we set off on a half-day tour to Pompeii through driving rain, past bomb-damaged buildings, unrepaired since the war 20 years before, and terrible slum hovels along the seafront. The Bay of Naples could just be glimpsed through grey haze but things improved slightly once we reached a good highway and the dark-green countryside of villages and villas, orchards and gardens – though Vesuvius remained shrouded by mist. Our driver/guide was amusing, but the afternoon's enjoyment was dampened further by the sheer silliness of some of the Australian girls and a few German pursers who showed their hearty contempt for Italians at every opportunity.

Herculaneum's cameo factory cheered us up and Pompeii, its war damage still being cleared, was rivetting. We were shown all the famous sights before being halted at the entrance to the Vetti house's atrium and garden. Here the men were separated from the furious women and taken inside to see the painting, hidden behind a wooden casement shutter, of a man with vast phallus. Then, guided with nods and winks, we were ushered into a small locked room to see the erotic paintings. The women's resentful mood on our return journey to Naples matched the gloom of the darkening evening.

The general air of depression did not lift the following day as *Arkadia* rolled its way slowly east through heavy weather. Next day, 23 December, we heard the news that our sister ship *Lakonia* (formerly the Dutch immigrant ship *Johann van Oldenbarnevelt*) was burning and sinking 650 kilometres out in the Atlantic. Seven hundred people were believed dead and the news bulletins were declaring it to be the worst peacetime maritime disaster since *Titanic*. Our officers, pursers and stewards were distraught, for most had relatives and friends on *Lakonia* and all the latent antagonisms between Germans and Greeks broke out into open hostility. Later news that there were probably no more than 150 people missing and that 900 had been saved did not lighten the mood.

A day later we were informed that we were going to Madeira to pick up 650 *Lakonia* cruise passengers. This would delay our arrival in London until Sunday, 29 December, but for once no one complained. Instead, there were attempts at invoking some Christmas spirit by having a children's party and Midnight Mass celebrated by the German priest with the small Italian orchestra providing music.

We awoke on Christmas Day in Madeira's harbour, moving on a heavy swell through a flotilla of dinghies from which boys were diving for coins, towards a crowded wharf and concrete breakwater. It was very picturesque, with the old town straggling up steep cloud-topped hillsides and around the bay. In the town centre the castle and the governor's residence had a ceremonial guard clad in Napoleonic uniforms. We were encouraged to go ashore so the ship could be prepared for the *Lakonia* passengers, so we spent the day wandering along the tree-lined seashore promenade and cobbled streets to the white-painted cathedral and uphill, past fine houses with green gardens and orange trees beyond yellow plaster walls and arched gateways. We also took a taxi ride up onto the hills and saw splendid views of town and harbour, though a fiercely cold wind did not encourage us to linger.

Even before we reached the launch to take us back to *Arkadi*a we were hearing highly coloured tales of *Lakonia* passengers' complaints about Greek incompetence and sinking lifeboats. Back on board confusion reigned as traumatised survivors filled the vestibules and lounges, and from now our days and evenings were filled with stories of the disastrous confusion when fire broke out, and of the tragic loss of 128 lives when faulty lifeboats sank. Many stories were contradictory, but all were related with passion and the arguments grew bitter. Although there were heroic stories of how some German and Greek crew had sacrificed themselves in order to guide passengers to safety, the deep-seated antipathies intensified. So, although our menus had been dramatically upgraded to cruise ship standard, it was a huge relief to reach Tilbury at last on 29 December. There we found the *Lakonia* news dominating the newspapers and a massive international incident looming between Britain and Greece. In time the Greek court of enquiry ruled that British maritime authorities ought never to have issued certificates for *Lakonia*'s lifeboats, but Britain never accepted those findings, any more than Greece accepted Britain's findings. The diplomatic impasse, and the ill feeling, lasted for years.

FIVE

ENGLAND 1964

We were met at Tilbury by Ninian Walden and some university and ex-Madrigal Group expatriate friends who guided us about for a few days while we found our feet. We had arranged lodgings at St David's Private Hotel, Westbourne Gardens, where friendly Mrs Benson looked after us solicitously and told us all about the Beatles, of whom we had not yet heard. She soon filled us in exhaustively about them and all their doings; she was an ardent fan and had mementos and programmes arranged all over just about every flat surface in the dining room, sitting rooms and vestibule.

We began flat-hunting immediately, and after viewing numbers of awful and unsuitable places with growing despair, found an elegant basement at 74 Kensington Park Road, Notting Hill. It was owned by a very upper-class lady lawyer and managed by her husband, whose rigid jaw and tightly clenched teeth produced almost a parody of an upper-class accent. It was surprising that he could speak at all. Their smart furnished flat was on the verge of being too expensive, but we took it and stayed there for almost a year, until we split up for the first time.

In order to pay the rent I needed a temporary teaching job at once, and even before Beverley started at the London Opera Centre, I went into the Greater London Council's (GLC) Notting Hill Gate Education Office and was offered a place as head of history at a local comprehensive. I was required to register at County Hall, however, and there, even as I took my degree and teaching certificates from my briefcase and laid them on the desk, I was informed that although they were very short of qualified secondary teachers it would take six months to verify my qualifications with the New South Wales and New Zealand authorities before they could employ me. I left abruptly, raging about GLC rules, but no more than 10 minutes later, through one of those extraordinary coincidences that do happen in places like London, I ran into a woman I'd known at Div. C who told me to go to the Middlesex authorities, and Willesden Borough in particular.

So I dived back into the tube and got to the Willesden Education Office at 2.30, and by 2.35 I had a job and the director was asking if I'd like to start immediately, even though it was late in the school day. I declined and started next morning instead. Supply teaching was a godsend, awful as it usually was and terrible as were most of the schools I went to before I got enough singing work to scrape a living. But when necessary it was a reliable and mercifully temporary source of extra income. And during my supply stints I met some of the unforgettable, fun revolutionaries who delighted in causing chaos in London's education systems as their various Marxist-Leninist and Marxist-Stalinist cells competed fiercely with one another and dreamt of bringing Britain's entire capitalist system crashing into ruins. One or two of them were genuinely amusing colleagues, but they seldom bothered about the wider problems their grand revolutionary ideals and disruptive political tactics were causing their already disadvantaged pupils. Assiduous as most of them were about demonstrating and rallying against the Vietnam War, anything to do with the USA and all things nuclear, and vehemently proclaiming their desire for universal peace, they nonetheless included some of the most inherently violent people I've ever encountered.

I liked London immediately and felt far more at home than I

ever had in Sydney. For a start, people were friendlier. Like so many other newly arrived, liberally minded New Zealand expatriates I became a *Guardian* reader, until its excruciating dullness, its plethora of unintentionally comic misprints (its chief claim to fame in those days) and its relentless left-wing stance and often mindless anti-Americanism drove me to seek better daily fare. The *Daily Telegraph* was too knee-jerk High Tory, though it consistently won the top awards for best British newspaper. Like millions of others at the time, I voted for Harold Wilson – and, like so many, later regretted having been comprehensively conned. *The Times*, however, suited my tastes admirably: its crossword, sports reports, music and book reviews and most of its feature writing were all superior to the *Guardian*'s, and I appreciated its balanced and pragmatic editorial stance, unaffected during my time in Britain by its absorption into the Murdoch empire.

And, of course, the musical life was intense and inspiring. Beverley could get student concessions, so we went to Sadler's Wells opera a lot, and that summer I bought a season ticket to the BBC Prom Concerts. With Beverley fully occupied as a busy student at the Opera Centre and later away on tour with the Sadler's Wells production of Offenbach's *La Vie Parisienne*, I went to most of them on my own or with friends. Hearing all the great and famous was marvellous, and fully as instructive as a whole series of singing lessons. There were significant role models aplenty for young tenors singing in London then, the most influential for me being the great Spanish tenor Alfredo Kraus, the gloriously versatile Nicolai Gedda, Carlo Bergonzi and Richard Lewis. I had first heard Lewis in Christchurch singing Verdi's *Requiem*, and I now heard him at the Proms in magnificent form singing Mozart's Idomeneo, completely overshadowing the all but anonymous young Italian tenor singing his son, Idamante. The young tenor's name was Luciano Pavarotti, and it would be another two or three years before he shot to fame and electrified and inspired all of us lucky enough to hear him singing in Donizetti's *Daughter of the Regiment* at Covent Garden.

At the first school I spent time at as a supply teacher I met the musical director for Unity Theatre, the groundbreaking left-wing company that had already groomed Lionel Bart, Alfie Bass, Bill Owen, Warren Mitchell and so many others. Over the next few months I sang Victorian ballads at Music Hall evenings in their converted chapel theatre in the depths of St Pancras.

Mercifully, it did not take me as long to get singing engagements as some of my far-from-admiring acquaintances back home had foretold, for I lost no time in following the good advice I'd received in Sydney from Godfrey Stirling and Harold Williams. A day or so after landing I wrote to the Ibbs and Tillett Agency, enclosing some of my better press notices and asking for an interview and an audition. Ibbs had been Harold's agent throughout his very illustrious career, and he had assured me that formidable Emmie Tillett, who had succeeded her late husband John as principal, was the most powerful agent in British music and still represented almost all the great and good in the serious music profession: famous pianists, instrumentalists and, especially, the leading oratorio soloists. He had also told me to mention his name and that must have been the magic password, because I received an appointment to see Mrs Tillett almost by return mail.

It was, I later discovered, rare for her to grant interviews to anyone who wasn't already a big name, but she graciously allowed me 10 minutes and made clear throughout that she was granting me a great favour. She was very grand indeed: a relic of Edwardian days in appearance, polite but dauntingly brusque of speech and unashamedly condescending about colonials. She was especially dismissive of my erstwhile conducting nemesis James Robertson, whose career, she assured me, had been finished in England when New Zealand rescued him by giving him its National Orchestra and its fledgling opera. Emmie did not approve of opera. I behaved with suitable deference, but left her presence uncertain how long I might have to wait before I again entered her hallowed Wigmore Street offices. That, as it happened, was to be soon.

Harold Williams had also suggested that I contact Eric Greene, whom he rated the finest English Bach tenor of his generation, its best oratorio coach and a reliable singing teacher. I knew of his reputation already and had long admired his recordings of the *St Matthew Passion* Evangelist.

My letter to him was answered promptly. He summoned me to Wigmore Hall Studios at 11am the following Saturday, and I was to bring with me the oratorio scores I *claimed* (the word underlined firmly) to have sung. I obeyed the summons and was met at the studio door by a dapper little man who informed me as we shook hands that he usually advised singers from my part of the world to go home. The Antipodes, he added, bred voices only; in England they bred *artists*. I remained tactfully silent. His next utterance was a crisp command to produce my scores. We started with *Messiah*, and I sang through its tenor arias and those from *Creation*, *Elijah* and Mass in B Minor to Eric's superb accompaniments but also to his daunting silence. Then he called out recitative numbers from the *Matthew Passion*, and while I hastily scrabbled through the score to find them, he strummed their chord sequences and informed me with disarming immodesty that not only did he know the entire work from memory but he had sung the Evangelist 474 times – more than anyone else – and in his latter days played the harpsichord continuo as well. He had been the greatest English Evangelist ever, he added, and Peter Pears, in comparison, was a fraud who had replaced him for the Bach Choir's annual performances by not charging a fee because his friend Benjamin Britten earned more than £20,000 a year. They were, Eric informed me darkly, 'homosexualists'!

Then we did the highlights, after which he rose and paced the studio with hands behind his back. Yes, I sang those highlights well, but they were, vocally, the easy bits for young fellows like me. We could all sing them well. He, however, had been *great* throughout the entire narration. Anyway, he considered me professional and said he would make sure I did well. I was to attend him fortnightly and his fee was 4 guineas (twice what Godfrey Stirling had charged in Sydney). He would turn me into an artist. Had I been in touch with Ibbs and Tillett?

I had had an interview with Mrs Tillett, I replied.

Eric laughed scornfully. She was of no consequence for singers and she didn't know much about singing anyway, he scoffed. Her business partner, his wife, Kathleen Cheseldine, was the one who dealt with the agency's singers. She would be finishing at the office about now, he added, so perhaps I'd like to come down and have a drink with them at the pub along the street?

I was delighted to have a drink with them.

Kathleen was a small lady of few words but with an impressive ability to put back large gins. Eric was a whisky drinker. And before I went off – immensely relieved, excited and fairly inebriated – I had accepted their invitation to dinner.

That also began with drinks, Eric pouring me the largest whisky with the least amount of water I think I'd ever been offered, and we were well into a third when Kathleen emerged from the kitchen and remarked that Eric said I sang Bach well and that she thought she had a job for me. Would I care to sing something now? How about the first *Matthew Passion* tenor aria?

I was startled, and Eric so amused that he almost fell out of his chair, but we staggered through it and Kathleen confirmed a December date for Bach's *Christmas Oratorio* for the Durham Choral Society. The fee was what she termed 'a good one' – 25 guineas – but she warned me not to expect such a big figure for every concert. The top oratorio fee at that time on the British circuit was 40 guineas and only the famous few got that. Such was my Ibbs and Tillett audition.

Eric also chimed in with his first piece of advice about the English profession: there were two taboo subjects of conversation with concert colleagues, he declared: singing techniques and fees. To discuss these was simply 'not done'. (Nowadays they are young singers' main topics of conversation.) It was also advisable, they both emphasised, to be seen to emerge from a first-class railway carriage, even when one travelled second class. Choral society secretaries had to be impressed and that was one way of doing it. A good overcoat (preferably with a velvet collar), jacket or suit and, of course, a good tie, were other essentials. Appearances were terribly important. It was also essential to sing as well at rehearsals as one did at performances, for it was at rehearsals that the secretaries usually decided whether or not to book one again.

I would find the English class system strange, Eric added, but my being a New Zealander placed me outside it and I would find that people of all classes were likely to speak more freely to me than they might to other Englishmen. I was surprised but, in time, found him to have been absolutely correct.

Eric gave me a great many more items of professional advice during the following years until his death in 1966, and much additional gossipy information about a vast number of famous musicians and singers – most of it libellous. He was, however, a fine oratorio coach and, although not altogether convincing as a teacher of singing technique, adept at providing valuable tips about how to get through performances when suffering from sore throats, debilitating colds, flu and general ill-health. He was additionally a fine accompanist and very good conductor, as I found when I did concerts under his baton for his Twickenham Choral Society and his remarkable Pro Canto Choir of blind singers.

While I did get a steady flow of good oratorio work from Ibbs, I also acted on advice from new colleagues and friends that although Ibbs were still the most powerful single force in British concert music, there were newer and younger agents making inroads in the developing operatic scene, so I wrote to some of them. One, Helen Jennings, immediately found me two minor roles in *Lucia di Lammermoor* and Sir Charles Stanford's *Much Ado About Nothing* at the Wexford International Festival in October, on condition that I also sang in the chorus for Rossini's *Conte Ory* with a contingent from Glyndebourne Opera. She also got me a more immediate job understudying the Germany-based Australian tenor Ken Neate in Hans Werner Henze's *Laudes* for the Leeds Festival, with the London Philharmonic Orchestra under John Pritchard. It is a difficult work that I mercifully was not required to perform.

I had another piece of luck too: one of Beverley's new friends at the Opera Centre was the famous stage director Colin Graham, who suggested I audition for the touring London Opera Players (OP) who were looking for an Alfred for a new production of *Die Fledermaus* to tour the Arts Council circuits around the west of England, the home counties and in Scotland. I lost no time in following that up, and after some hesitation about my lack of height compared with the two sopranos cast to sing Rosalinde, they took me on. So began my friendly and very valuable association with the remarkable Elizabeth Parry, singer, mountaineer and lecturer; and the splendidly eccentric Honourable Phyllis Thorold, pianist daughter of the aristocratic Russell family, lady in waiting to the Princess Royal, and an embroiderer of repute whose costumes featured in many period films and television productions. The OP's costumes were always superb – some of the very best I have worn.

The music director was the conductor and BBC chorus master Peter Gellhorn, a brilliant coach who had learnt his craft at the pre-war Berlin State Opera before he fled to Britain, and from whom I learnt an enormous amount; the stage director (another significant influence on my general stagecraft) was Michael Alfreds. The OP had multiple casts for each opera in their vast repertoire and I shared my roles of Alfred and Prince Orlofsky with another young tenor, Phillip Langridge, who was destined to emerge as one of the most accomplished and celebrated English tenors of our generation. Others in those casts included the Australian tenor Kevin Miller and the French Canadian Emile Belcourt as two of the alternating Eisensteins; both were longstanding Sadler's Wells operetta stars. Emile was perhaps the best operetta actor-singer I ever worked with, and a superb Loge in the English National Opera's *Das Rhinegold*. We sang together a lot in the following few years, not only in *Fledermaus* but also in Monteverdi's *Il Ritorno d'Ulisse* for Basilica Productions, and Purcell's *Dido and Aeneas* at the birth of Kent Opera.

There were other very fine singers I got to know through the OP, but perhaps the most significant for my personal future was the baritone Norman Platt who, like Elizabeth Parry, had been one of Britten's original English Opera Group. He was the OP's resident and splendidly irascible Bartolo in Douglas Craig's production of

Barber of Seville, and we met when I took over Almaviva at two hours' notice. That was a memorable performance never forgotten by the others taking part, because I had merely a nodding acquaintance as yet with Edward Dent's English translation, which all British companies used, and my attempts to combine what I did know of it with the American one I'd sung in Sydney (anathema in Britain) resulted in some bizarre moments.

Touring with the OP – one-night stands and constantly changing casts in performances under every imaginable and even unimaginable condition – was about the best practical training an aspiring young singer could get in those days, long before comprehensively elaborate (and ludicrously expensive) courses in opera were introduced into the music colleges. It was a marvellous way of acquiring repertoire and, because rehearsals were limited, learning one's craft and coping on the job, sometimes at the audience's expense. By the time one had survived a few of those regional arts tours one could cope with anything. And one had learnt to treat costumes with respect, for the Honourable Phyllis sometimes judged one's performance by the way her costumes were treated. Woe betide the soprano who trod on her petticoats or the tenor who maltreated his jackets.

On one famous occasion Philip Langridge accidentally drove his car over some suitcases of *Fledermaus* costumes awaiting loading into the company's van. To make matters worse he had previously that evening caught Alfred's especially beautiful dressing-gown on a nail in the wings, torn a hole in the very fine embroidered fabric on which Phyllis had lavished much care and, apparently, failed to show enough remorse. Phyllis regarded this dressing-gown as one of her finest creations. There in the carpark she became incandescent with rage, I was gleefully informed by everyone in that evening's cast. Poor Philip was not forgiven for many months but I benefited inadvertently by being given several performances for which he had been pencilled in.

Mike Alfreds' *Fledermaus* was a brilliant touring success. As well as performing in it repeatedly during the next four years, until the amount of concert work I was getting forced me to abandon the OP,

I sang half a dozen other roles for the company, including Almaviva and another that became a favourite – the title role in Auber's wonderfully tuneful and hilarious *Fra Diavolo.* It was another very clever production, this time by the unforgettable Dennis Arundell, perhaps one of the most imaginative English operatic directors of his time and undoubtedly one of the most memorable characters I've worked with. We had double casts for all the roles except mine, and as Dennis insisted on rehearsing the two casts separately we had some tense moments when, as was inevitable with touring and clashes of dates, they eventually had to be mixed. By then people had become so used to playing alongside the same cast that some had become rather fixed in their ways and reluctant to adapt. Philip Langridge as the young soldier Lorenzo, and the spectacularly temperamental Australian soprano Madge Stephens as his beloved Zerlina, found it especially difficult to come to terms with one another and their rows were volcanic. Dennis found it all rather fun, but, entertaining though we found it sometimes, it could become rather wearing.

Madge was a very popular broadcaster for BBC Radio 2's light music programmes and was also living with the Head of Light Music, Charles Beardsall, who actually offered me a job as a BBC light music producer. When I turned it down he was astonished that I preferred to be a singer, and he became strangely affronted when I explained that I didn't think I knew enough to take on so responsible a job as telling others what they should be doing. Our paths crossed often later and not always harmoniously, particularly when I became involved from the mid-1970s in music politics and negotiations on behalf of the Incorporated Society of Musicians.

Arundell, Alfreds and Craig were among the very best of all the many operatic directors I've known and each fully deserved the high reputation he enjoyed. So did the very popular composer, musicologist and broadcaster Anthony Hopkins, whose hilarious and very clever children's opera *Doctor Musicus* was specially written for the OP. We premiered it at London's Arts Theatre, and later featured it at the International Festival of Children's Theatre in Leeds, with Tony himself in sparkling form at the piano.

The ladies of Ibbs and Tillett were not interested in this kind of work. The fees were too small, and it was opera and therefore vulgar. It was a different matter with Benjamin Britten's operas and his English Opera Group, however: he was not only the most celebrated and successful composer of his time, he was also hugely socially fashionable and at that time virtually beyond criticism. So they sent me along to be auditioned by the group's conductor and musical director, Meredith Davies, and head of music, Viola Tunnard.

Within a week I had a contract for performances throughout the middle and second half of 1965 as a Pilgrim in Colin Graham's production of the recently premiered church parable *Curlew River*, for 14 singers and seven instrumentalists, and for understudying the role of Clem in a revised version of *Let's Make an Opera* at the Aldeburgh Festival. We were to do *Curlew River* there, record it for Decca, tour it around various English Cathedrals and in France, Belgium and Italy, and record a telecast in Brussels. Oddly enough, Colin had brought the original score with him when he first came to our flat for dinner and I had looked through it and remarked that I was very glad I wasn't in it. It all seemed very complicated: it was extremely stylised and there was to be no conductor, which would naturally throw much responsibility on every single member of the cast and instrumental ensemble.

So, 1965 was to be a year of *Curlew River*. Before that dawned, though, there was the Wexford International Festival of October 1964 to survive.

I flew there with two English colleagues and was met at the airport by the jovial chairman of the festival's committee, who remarked that surely Bohan was a Cork name. I replied that my paternal grandparents had come from villages in west Cork. 'Ah,' he said with a smile, 'y'know we've a saying in this part of Ireland that you can never trust a man from Cork.' We both laughed heartily, but my English colleagues (neither of whom had been in Ireland before) were shocked and muttered darkly about the man's rudeness. I reassured them that such a remark was not rudeness but simply normal Irish humour, the kind I'd been familiar with since birth. They learned a lot in the next few weeks. So did I.

Wexford is one of the most historic towns in a land endlessly fascinating, crowded with ancient places and one for which I have had an affection ever since this first visit. In 1964 the town was still very much an unmodernised and picturesque place of broken walls, narrow streets, grey stone buildings and a charm that remained undimmed for me throughout my stay, in spite of its cold and wet autumn weather. Wexford enjoys a lot of rain, but as I described in a radio talk recorded a few years later at the BBC for the NZBC, not the pouring, bouncing rain of Taranaki or Southland, but soft, drifting, insidiously misty rain that gets into the bronchial tubes and one's shoes. To counteract this, the warmly hospitable people of Wexford had established a great many pubs and bars that were open all hours to provide medicinal drams and strength-giving Gaelic coffee for the festival artists and patrons.

The festival was already well established as a showcase for both British and continental singers, and the local chorus was always bolstered by a sizeable group of young British professionals from Glyndebourne who also played the subsidiary roles backing the big-name stars. So I had become part of the Glyndebourne contingent and had already rehearsed with them. For *Lucia di Lammermoor* I sang Normanno, the forester and betrayer of Lucia and Edgardo.

From the start there were language problems. The director was French and spoke no English or Italian. Direction was minimal and about the only clear instructions I received were to make sure that for the duration of the Act I trio scene with Enrico and Raimondo I stayed between the jovial but ferocious-looking Sicilian baritone Luigi Puglisi, who spoke only Italian, and his boon companion the New York Italian bass Franco Ventriglia. They were notorious for trying to upstage one another and their chief sport was to manoeuvre the other so that he had to sing with either his back to the audience or his face against a slab of scenery. I stoutly did my duty and accordingly learnt more about cunning stage tricks in the next month than in my entire life hitherto. Lucia was played by a Hungarian who also spoke German but no other language, and Edgardo by the splendid Spanish tenor Giacomo Aragall, already being hailed as another

Gigli but who spoke as yet very little English. Arturo was a vast Scot, and Alicia was my very good friend Laura Sarti, the Italian-Slav mezzo. Luckily she was multi-lingual, as was the conductor Antonio Almeida, a wealthy and erudite Portuguese-American fluent in about seven languages.

There were no such language problems with my second opera, Stanford's *Much Ado About Nothing*, in which I played Borachio. It was sung in English by an entirely Britain-based cast, which meant that apart from me, there was a Singaporean Chinese soprano, a Goanese bass, an Australian baritone, two Irishmen, an Anglo-Jewish cantor and two other tenors and a soprano from the home counties.

I shared a dressing room for part of that season with one of the Irishmen: a golden minstrel boy of the moment who had recently returned to his admiring homeland after a wildly successful ballad tour of America. Unfortunately, he had never before set foot on an operatic stage and his knowledge of what he should do was hazy. But he was a good-natured companion and when he asked me if I would tip him a nod when it was nearly his turn to sing I was happy enough to oblige. I was not so happy about being flattened against the wall of our tiny dressing room each time his exuberant fans poured in to get his autograph, take his photograph, get interviews for the Irish press and radio, or simply to clasp his hand with honest pride at his fame and prosperity. Still, even though we all sang bits of his music for him and shepherded him around the stage, he was the hit of Peter Ebert's production as far as the Irish press were concerned – and, as we soon discovered, got far more money than the rest of us.

Stanford's *Much Ado* is a charming opera, we had great fun and I eagerly anticipated more when I saw the young local extra brought in to play the non-singing role of Hero's maid, whom Borachio embraces passionately during his master Don John's wicked scheme to discredit Hero. She was the loveliest-looking Irish beauty one could ever imagine. However, the first time I climbed up to her window to fold her in my arms, what should I find but an elderly and scowling Irish lady in black sitting in the shadows to protect her girl's virtue from the assaults of any wicked British tenor. That was a disappointment for me, and a source of hilarity for the rest of the cast. The lovely girl was never allowed even to speak to us.

Conte Ory was great fun too and has remained one of my favourites because of its wit and wonderful ensembles. Although I never sang the role of Ory itself, for years I used his very high and extremely taxing aria as a vocal exercise. I thoroughly enjoyed this sole experience of singing in an opera chorus but certainly had no intention of ever repeating it. Ory was sung by a marvellous young Italian high tenor, Pietro Bottazo, and I learned much from being on stage with him – as I did from the entire Wexford season. The downside, however, was that I eventually succumbed to flu and the Wexford weather so badly that by the time I arrived back in England laryngitis had struck. A few days later in Dover I perpetrated the worst performance of my career as I struggled through *Judas Maccabeus*.

If that was not enjoyable, neither was the state of my marriage. Beverley and I separated just before Christmas, only to return to one another a few months later when her parents arrived from New Zealand and persuaded us to try to mend our relationship. We moved down to Outwood in Surrey and into the top-floor flat of Copsley Court, a fine country house owned by the delightful and refined lady partner of Beverley's singing teacher, who was the celebrated mezzo Flora Nielsen. We stayed there for the rest of 1965, during which time Beverley was at Glyndebourne most of the time, and I was occupied elsewhere with the English Opera Group.

SIX

DREARY DAYS: ALDEBURGH AND THE ENGLISH OPERA GROUP 1965

On a personal level, 1965 was the unhappiest year of my life, although professionally it was a year of consolidation, of valuable experience gained and ever widening opportunities being offered.

I started rehearsing *Curlew River* at Covent Garden with the English Opera Group soon after Easter. Too soon in some ways because I had had to sing Britten's *St Nicholas* with Eric Greene's Twickenham Choral Society while suffering from a very heavy cold that had lingered too long after another bout of flu that had itself laid me low for a week. I made it through the performance competently enough but at some vocal cost, and I did not fully recover my vocal strength for another month or more. Not that the EOG hierarchy – in particular Viola Tunnard, who was in charge of our musical preparation – seemed to mind. In fact she very much took me under her musical wing and became my champion, allocating me various solo passages and, throughout the next few months, continually labouring to bring me to Britten's attention.

That was a mixed blessing, for within the Britten court and kingdom at Aldeburgh, and inside the small but tightly knit EOG itself, quite brutal factional rivalries were endemic, and Viola, who had given devoted service to Britten as accompanist and assistant musical director, was slowly being sidelined. Not that we knew yet. Two or three years later, when the hitherto almost universal admiration and uncritical hero-worship Britten had enjoyed for so long was starting to show cracks, a bold and perceptive article in one of the quality newspapers likened Aldeburgh to a Byzantine emperor's court, where death came suddenly and unexpectedly from a dagger in the back or poisoned wine cup. Britten himself was notorious for declaring anyone of his circle whom he no longer wanted to be 'dead'. The bodies, metaphorically speaking, piled up remorselessly.

Curlew River, the first of the church parables and with a libretto by William Plomer, was based on a mediaeval Japanese *noh* play, transposed to mediaeval England, in which a group of monks on pilgrimage to the scene of a miracle re-enact the story of a madwoman's quest for her lost (and murdered) son. Colin Graham's production, conceived in close consultation with Britten, Plomer and Pears, was a stylised ritual, with every movement, gesture and facial expression rigidly prescribed.

The company was a very small one: Peter Pears and Robert Tear were alternating as the Madwoman, though Peter did not join us at first; John Shirley-Quirk, then the British musical establishment's leading oratorio bass-baritone, was the Ferryman; my marvellously good-natured fellow New Zealander Bryan Drake from Dunedin was the Traveller; and rotund Scots bass Harold Blackburn, who had for so long been a Sadler's Wells Opera Company stalwart, was the Abbot. Two boy trebles alternated as the Voice of the Spirit; and eight of us – all solo singers – were the remaining Pilgrims. Once we reached Aldeburgh the 'Players' – virtuosi from the English Chamber Orchestra – joined us. Viola conducted our rehearsals and Britten himself conducted the recording we did for Decca at Orford during June. In performance what direction was required came from Philip Ledger, who presided over the small portable organ, but for the present acted as an impatient rehearsal pianist, openly scornful of thick-headed opera singers who were by no means near faultless sight-readers like the choral scholars with whom he had hitherto mixed at Cambridge.

It was, to put it mildly, a high-spirited company, and no one was more high-spirited than Bob Tear, the most amusing of companions, though his relentless clowning and irreverent but very funny and uncannily life-like impersonations of Pears meant that he was always skating on thin ice. Indeed, within another couple of years Britten turned on him, very publicly and just before a performance. That was the end of their association. Bob never forgave Britten and certainly didn't forget his humiliation; rather he spoke of it frequently in public and wrote of it bluntly in his memoirs. Admired by the 'establishment', if not by rival tenors, his career flourished and his ultimate knighthood was (as with John Shirley-Quirk's and Philip Ledger's) inevitable. He was, I think, at his best in the character roles he filled so vividly for the Royal Opera at Covent Garden. I liked him and we got on well.

Harry Blackburn was, apart from Pears, the eldest and operatically by far the most experienced in the company, but almost from our first rehearsal he was openly scornful of the mannered and stylised production, and what he regarded as the excessive precocity of the company's vocal style. He refused to attend Claude Chagrin's daily mime and movement classes, which were obligatory for the rest of us. Socially he was our self-appointed father figure and the most formidable of drinking companions, along with the baritone Edgar Boniface, with whom I shared rooms on tour, and Peter Leeming, a bass with whom I had sung often in oratorio. I fear we drank rather a lot that year. Far too much. Drinking was an occupational hazard for British singers and musicians generally in those days – just as it had been in New Zealand.

Bryan Drake was by far my closest companion throughout these months. We shared so many mutual friends, a distinctly New Zealand sense of humour and independence of mind, and a curiosity for all the places we visited on tour. Known generally as the Mad Kiwis, we were known for our insatiable sightseeing and fascination with picturesque churches, art galleries, ruinous city walls and castles.

Britten admired Bryan's distinctive voice and forthright delivery and wrote a succession of roles for him; Bryan was cannier and more tactful than Bob Tear, Harry Blackburn or me, and he held his place among Britten's singers far longer than most. Bryan and I happened to be the understudies for the festival's revival of *Let's Make an Opera*. Britten and his librettist Eric Crozier had completely reworked its appalling, dated and by now risible Introduction and it was not an arduous assignment. We had sung our roles previously and were seldom called on to fill in at rehearsals; instead we spent most of them helping Meredith Davies with the *Times* crossword. Meredith was now believed to be the latest under Britten's sentence of 'death'. Not that it seemed to worry this urbane and witty man in the slightest.

Life at Aldeburgh, where I shared a pleasant cottage with three colleagues, was agreeable enough in the weeks of early summer, but I never liked Aldeburgh itself or felt at ease there. The Fenlands of East Anglia are my least favourite parts of England, with their sluggish and dark, winding streams, brooding and slightly sinister flatness, and the relentlessly chill winds from the North Sea, even in the height of summer. I found Aldeburgh's stone-covered and, in those days before they were cleaned up, oil-stained beaches vaguely oppressive too. They were a far cry from Invercargill's Oreti Beach and Christchurch's New Brighton and Sumner sands. What did make the place bearable was the social life and the music as preparations for the festival intensified.

With the performances and the recording looming we rehearsed intensively on our specially designed set in nearby Orford Church, and our music daily in the library of Britten's and Pears' Red House. They were hospitable hosts and Britten, though demanding, was more understanding of and patient with singer's foibles and shortcomings than other and lesser composers with whom I've worked. Perhaps that was because of his lifelong companionship with Pears who, with apologetic and rueful honesty, would freely admit to his musical shortcomings: in particular his less than perfect sense of pitch and his very fallible memory. The rest of us found that somewhat consoling, though Bob Tear also found it a wonderful inspiration for his impersonations. Britten's forlorn cry of, 'Peter, we really must get that passage right!' and Peter's equally despairing reply, 'I'm so sorry, Ben. Yes, I will look at that!' became regular features of all our sessions, and later during almost every rehearsal for every performance Peter sang in for the rest of the year.

I sat next to Pears during all the sessions at Red House and learned much from him. Perhaps no other tenor had so great an influence on my generation of young British tenors, though not all of it was beneficial. Sure he could be excessively mannered and, when afflicted by a memory lapse, bland to a quite remarkable degree as he dispensed with consonants and simply sang a seamless legato of vowels; yet at his best he could be unforgettably incisive and moving. For all that many dismissed him as a mere light-voiced, white-toned English tenor of the type widely disliked in Europe and America, by the time I knew him his voice had developed formidable power and depth. His was, in truth, the loudest tenor sound I have ever sat beside. He spoke freely about that, maintaining that his discovery of a new teacher (Lucy Mannen) when he was about 50 (he was 55 when I knew him), had so completely transformed his voice and attitude to singing that if he had met her when younger he might have matured into a Wagnerian. Above all, Pears was a superb artist. He was also a man of charm and intelligence, and I found him much easier to get along with than I ever did Britten, to whom I never warmed, though I continued to admire much of his music. His writing for the tenor voice was, naturally, always very good, and Peter's fallible musical ear means that entry clues in musically difficult passages are always there if one knows where to find them.

I sang a great deal of Britten, especially the *Serenade for Tenor, Horn and Strings*, the *Spring Symphony* (easily my favourite), the song-cycles *Winter Words* and *The Holy Sonnets of John Donne*, the folksong arrangements and the *War Requiem*. Stravinsky had famously and with characteristic acidity once declared that the *Requiem* was the only work ever proclaimed to be a masterpiece before anyone had heard a note of it. Certainly it has generally remained popular, but as a performer I developed reservations, for the more I worked on it and rehearsed it the less I liked it. This is unusual in my experience. With most other works my fondness for them has intensified the more I have sung them and got to know them. In performance, though, the *Requiem* never failed and one was inexorably caught up in its drama and the atmosphere it generated.

I found the Aldeburgh Festival itself completely absorbing and during it the little town became alive and vibrant; it was not unusual to come face to face with the great and famous browsing companionably in the small bookshop. I first saw the aged Zoltán Kodály there, accompanied as always at that time of his life with his assistants and acolytes, who included Cecilia Vajda, conductor and champion of his music, under whose direction I sang four years later in concerts at London's Purcell Room and at other venues.

Membership of the English Opera Group did have its perks: free entry to Covent Garden stage rehearsals had been one of them; now it was free attendance at all the Jubilee Hall concerts, provided we sat motionless and silent in the wings behind the stage. From there we heard some memorable events (all recorded by the BBC): what became an historic concert of Schubert piano duets played by Britten and Sviatoslav Richter, and song recitals by Pears and Dietrich Fischer-Dieskau, who with Britten gave the first performance of the *Songs and Proverbs of William Blake*. There was also a splendid Monteverdi concert, memorable subsequently for Bob Tear losing his temper (the only occasion in all the time I knew him) when a tactless baritone remarked on how similar he and Pears sounded in their duets.

There were other concerts in the local and nearby parish churches: Imogen Holst's Purcell Consort and Purcell Singers and the English Chamber Orchestra conducted by Britten; a concert of Zoltán Kodály's music by the Kodály Choir of Budapest; and, unforgettably, Fischer-Dieskau and Richter performing Brahms' *Magelone Lieder*. The parish church was packed for that and the concert was relayed by loudspeaker into the churchyard, where Peter Leeming, Edgar Boniface and I sat on tombstones and enjoyed every note and every minute. At the end Pears and a stony-faced Britten emerged and Peter asked how we'd enjoyed it. I waxed enthusiastic. I liked Brahms' symphonies and chamber music and I especially liked his songs. Britten was withering. I had not realised hitherto the depths of his almost obsessive hatred of Brahms. The music was meretricious, he declared; it had all been great artistry utterly wasted on rubbish. I had clearly fallen into great error – sinned, even – and I don't think our relationship recovered. Pears shook his head sadly, and the great men went on their way. The rest of us went to the pub, where everyone gathered every evening, and I fell into another argument about Brahms and Britten: this time with Edward Greenfield, one of the *Guardian*'s music critics and at the time one of Britten's most ardent, not to say fawning, admirers, with whom I enjoyed several heated arguments about music and related topics during that fortnight. Debate in the pub at Aldeburgh was always robust.

We began touring a week or two after the festival ended and the first excursion was across to France and down to the delightful city of Tours on the Loire for Richter's Festival of Touraine, another splendid feast of great music from not only Richter himself but the Borodin Quartet and Virtuosi di Roma. We performed *Curlew River* in the vast and extraordinary mediaeval Grange de Meslay on our special set that went with us always. Grange de Meslay had once been a mammoth storage barn of an abbey and had no modern facilities such as we had grown up with. Pails of water were brought in for us by attendant French farming ladies, and I shall never forget Pears sitting looking anxious, abstracted and slightly lost as he applied his Madwoman makeup in the makeshift dressing room, rigged from barely adequate screens set up on bare earth. The barn's acoustic, however, was superb and the atmosphere almost magical. Our first performance there was probably our best anywhere, from the moment Pears appeared on the high platform with small bats circling his head attracted by the single beam of white light that was the only illumination in the cavernous darkness. His performance that evening was one of the three most remarkable I've ever been on stage with. The others were the English soprano Jennifer Vyvyan's singing of the *Matthew Passion* in a Good Friday performance at the Royal Festival Hall in 1972 (not long before her death), and Sir Donald McIntyre's Hans Sachs in the last act of *Die Meistersinger* in Wellington during the 1990 International Festival.

Later in the year we toured in Belgium and performed at Courtrai, Louvain and Brussels, where we filmed the work for Belgian television, winning, I believe, a major European award. I missed seeing the telecast when it was shown in Britain later and lost no sleep about that – by then I was more than disenchanted by both the work and the company, increasingly riven by personality conflicts and the inevitable internal politicking that seemed to permeate Britten's realm.

In September we went to a festival in Perugia, where soon after our arrival (with many of us suffering hangovers after too much rough local red wine the previous evening) we were suddenly and unexpectedly summoned to put on a special morning performance for the Italian musical press who, with unusual artistic honesty, would not review anything they had not previously seen or heard.

There was one other memorable incident from that visit, though of significance only for New Zealanders who, as a nation, glory in being universally popular. One morning as our entire company sat around two vast breakfast tables, a waiter who spoke excellent English and had been assiduous in his attendance on us, asked why there were so many different English accents among our company. Amid lots of good-humoured banter, the flautist Richard Adeney replied that we were drawn from many different parts of Britain and the Commonwealth: there were Englishmen from various regions, Welshmen, Scots, Irish, an Australian and even, he ended, pointing to Bryan Drake and me, New Zealanders. The mood changed immediately. The waiter turned away abruptly and angrily, put down his tray on an adjacent table and walked out of the dining room with a parting glare and a muttered ejaculation that 'It was the war!' The head waiter was profusely apologetic and murmured that in some parts of Italy there were bad memories. We didn't see our favourite waiter again. He refused to wait on New Zealanders or, indeed, anyone else in our company.

The Covent Garden management who administered English Opera Group and arranged its tours had originally promised us much work. It was not, I fear, a very efficient management but neither, in my experience, are many other operatic managements. Or maybe I've just been unfortunate with those I've dealt with. Several dates now fell through and I returned to remote Outwood, nestling in Wealden Surrey and our flat in Copsley Court for weeks on end, faced there with a steadily disintegrating marriage and having little profitable to do, though I was at least able to get down to Glyndebourne occasionally.

I welcomed the end of summer and the start of the autumn and winter concert season with immense relief, though I did not enjoy our final bout of *Curlew River*. By the time we went off during October for visits to Chester, Newcastle, Edinburgh and Durham, the weather was cold and most of us were heartily sick of our church parable, whose charm had definitely worn thin. The last performance in Durham Cathedral bore many of the characteristics of an end-of-term celebration. Bob Tear was especially frenetic that night, and when Bryan Drake and I chased him around the cloisters before we began we really did intend to throw him into the nearby pond. Luckily, we were summoned into our ranks to process into the hushed, expectant and full cathedral. There, for the last time, Tear did his full impersonation of Pears while one of the baritones, who over the months had been steadily perfecting what he called his Rigoletto faces, achieved such extraordinary feats that at the work's climax, when the company turned away from the audience to the high altar as the pure voice of the murdered Boy pealed out, just about every bowed monkish shoulder shook with silent laughter and our Abbot's voice quavered.

The audience had mercifully not noticed anything untoward and the work delivered its message unerringly. The applause was ecstatic, and among the crowd that clustered into our changing space was a quite overcome Malcolm Rickard and some other NZBC officials eager to congratulate their fellow New Zealanders, Bryan and me, for helping to deliver such a moving experience. As we hastily changed and raced for the London train we deeply regretted our very unprofessional behaviour and vowed to be better people for ever after.

SEVEN

Dublin – and After

I FIRST MET THE agent Norman McCann in Bournemouth during September 1965, just before the last *Curlew River* tour. Beverley was playing Kate Pinkerton in McCann's British National Opera Company's *Madame Butterfly* and I was unexpectedly summoned to Norman's presence during the interval. He was already a controversial figure in London's music scene, a Cockney of direct and aggressive manner whose shoulders were scarred and weighed down by chips of massive size. He had been an aspiring tenor who had discovered he could make more money hiring singers out than singing himself. He was even shorter than me and sported a beard and distinctive hairstyle modelled on Caesar Augustus, whose bust he had recently gazed on in the British Museum and decided that there was such a distinct likeness that it must be emphasised for all to recognise. Unsurprisingly, the ladies of Ibbs and Tillett looked down on him as being hopelessly common, vulgar and unacceptably pushy. They warned me to have nothing to do with him. Unlike them, however, he was passionate about opera and was getting more and more singers more and more work.

He did not waste words. We had not met before, he began, and he'd never heard me sing. Up to now he had never hired anyone he hadn't heard, but those whose opinions he valued had recommended me. Anyway, I wouldn't get anywhere sticking to Ibbs. They were old hat – and snobs. His was the agency of the future. Would I sing Don Ottavio in Mozart's *Don Giovanni* in December for the Dublin Grand Opera season?

He continued to be frank. He was asking me only because his first choice, a brilliant Welsh tenor he was nurturing for international stardom (who did attain such eminence soon after and enjoyed a stellar career), couldn't learn the role in such a short time.

I expressed surprise. The season was at least two months away, Ottavio was not a long role, and didn't every tenor know his two famous arias anyway? Two months was surely long enough for anyone.

Norman told me not to be a smart-arse. That was none of my business. Would I do it or not? The Dublin season would be a starry one because he was gathering singers from America, Germany and Covent Garden, etc. He repeated that he was taking a risk hiring me.

I hastily assured him that he needn't worry and we settled the details there and then.

I got on well with Norman. He had an acute, if sometimes mischievous sense of humour, and, for all his driving ambition to become a millionaire, a sense of proportion. Above all, he treated me well and got me a lot of good work during the next two or three years, until his Welsh tenor star and protégé abandoned him for a more fashionable agent. In disillusionment and disgust, Norman sold the artist management side of his agency to his secretaries, concentrated on being an impresario and eventually made the fortune he had dreamed of. In December 1965, when we experienced Dublin, all that was in the future.

The Dublin season was a truly grand and traditional event, with four performances each of *La Bohème* (with the superb Charles Craig, perhaps the finest British operatic tenor of his generation), *Faust* (starring that excellent Canadian soprano Sylvia Stahlman), *Carmen* and *Don Giovanni* at the marvellous old Gaiety Theatre, as Norman had boasted there would be, with London-based conductors and casts from Britain, Europe and North America.

There were other expatriate New Zealanders too: Warwick Braithwaite from Dunedin, who had long been one of Britain's most senior and experienced opera conductors, conducted *Carmen*; and John Matheson (also from Dunedin), incorrigibly bouncy and abrasive, had come from his abruptly truncated tour of Australia with the Sutherland-Bonynge Opera Company to conduct *Faust*. Richard Bonynge had been so anxious to banish him from Australia that he continued to pay him for not being there. Four or five of us used to accompany John to the Dublin Post Office to collect his weekly remittances from Australia and help him celebrate at the pub just across the lane from the Gaiety's stage door. The *Faust* cast also included Auckland's John Hauxvelle, for years one of the best high baritones in Britain, as Valentine, and Beverley as Siebel.

Our *Don Giovanni* cast was typical of the mixes one met during the Irish seasons in those years: the Don was the Lancastrian Forbes Robinson, vast of voice, personality and bulk, who had already been one of Covent Garden's principal basses for nearly 20 years. Leporello was the distinguished French Canadian Robert Savoie. Donna Anna was the Australian soprano Elizabeth Rust, and Donna Elvira was Ireland's current pride and later the country's most distinguished voice teacher, Veronica Dunne. Commendatore was the elderly American bass-baritone James Pease, in the twilight of a notable international career in which he had achieved much, from being the first Don Giovanni televised from New York's Metropolitan Opera to creating Balstrode in early performances and recordings of Britten's *Peter Grimes*. Masetto and Zerlina were performed by Dublin singers of some local reputation. Glyndebourne's chorus master Myer Fredman conducted, and the veteran Welsh opera producer Harry Powell Lloyd directed.

Our major problem, however, was lack of rehearsal time. Opening night was 10 December but the complete cast did not assemble until about two days beforehand.

Norman had booked Liz Rust and me to leave London for a

Belfast *Messiah* on 4 December – that was an interesting experience for two lapsed Catholics. The large combined choir we encountered was entirely made up of grim-faced Ulster Protestants whose management greeted us unsmilingly in a green room stacked with sheaves of the most virulently anti-Catholic tracts and assorted propaganda I had ever encountered.

Our rail journey south across the border early next day was eventful too. It was the custom in those days to take one's costumes to the Irish opera seasons and mine included a rapier that for all its elegance, embroidered scabbard and sparkling hilt was still a weapon, and it was illegal to take weapons of any kind into the Republic. Irish Customs at the border became alarmed and we feared an 'incident', maybe even arrest, until we explained we were singers on our way to the Dublin Opera season. That made everything different. That was fine. Laughs and jokes all round. But had I heard of John McCormack? the Garda asked. Count John was a Dublin feller and a great Ottavio. He'd sung that role at the Gaiety too! How could I ever match the great man? I asked. No one argued. I was allowed to bring my rapier into the Republic and the train was allowed to proceed.

We made our first scheduled rehearsal session that afternoon, 5 December, with five more days till opening night, and now learned that Forbes was still tied up at Covent Garden and Bob Savoie was still in Italy. Pease was already in Dublin, having been booked to sing in *Bohème* too, though he was supposed to be in Germany rehearsing Baron Ochs in a new production of *Der Rosenkavalier*. Dublin was being bombarded with telegrams demanding to know where he was. Finding that out was a continuing problem, because he would drift out of the upstairs crush bar where we rehearsed and disappear for hours on end, and invariably when we needed him, before returning with some curious prop or ancient helmet from the wardrobe that had taken his fancy. By then we would usually be doing a scene for which he was not needed. So he would wander off again 'until you need me'. Sometimes he wouldn't return at all.

The season had already been packed with drama. Faust, a tall Canadian with a mighty voice and a distracted manner, couldn't remember much of his role – either music or words – and was wandering around the stage at rehearsals muttering the few phrases he could recall whether or not they bore any relevance to the scene presently being rehearsed. He was fired at the final rehearsal and replaced by an English tenor of my age, currently being hailed by London's press as the new Heddle Nash and potentially one of England's greats. He never fulfilled his promise. Within a few years vocal problems forced him to leave the profession and return to the building trade, where he became a very rich man indeed. Years later when we were both members of London's Savage Club he occasionally drove me in his beautiful Mercedes to catch a late train.

That final *Faust* rehearsal was a particularly dramatic one, during which the Radio Telefis Eirrean Orchestra (led by Janos Fürst, their brilliant leader and later a notable conductor) walked out after John Matheson had shouted at them once too often. Myer Fredman, with typical conductor's charity, was delighted.

The Dublin flu then struck *Faust*'s cast: Beverley (Siebel) collapsed dramatically on opening night, appropriately at the very moment that Valentine (himself all too obviously ill and losing his voice) cursed Marguerite in front of the horrified company. Equally horrified, I rushed backstage and took Siebel (still in costume) off to Dublin hospital and, eventually, back to our hotel. By the time the second performance came round she was able to stand so she went on, as did Hauxvelle, struggling heroically and still able to produce that distinctive quality that made his such a beautiful high baritone voice.

The story went that Britten had Hauxvelle's voice in mind when he wrote the role of Billy Budd, but that Hauxvelle had scornfully rejected the idea of singing it. Knowing him, I'm inclined to believe it was probably so, but true or not, it's sad, I think, that New Zealand forgot – or never heard – John as he was in his prime, just as it has forgotten so many other very fine and successful expatriate singers. For years he was the first choice for most London performances of *Carmina Burana*, the ultimate test for any high baritone, and he was widely popular for his many BBC appearances, especially the enduring *Friday Night is Music Night* that always attracted the biggest listening audiences of any BBC music programme.

The flu, however, wasn't the only hazard afflicting *Faust.* One night Forbes Robinson and I, having dined and wined far too well, found our way into the gallery in time for the moment in the last act when Faust discovers Marguerite lying on straw in her prison cell and resolves to rescue her. The stage was divided diagonally by wooden bars and a door with a large lock, but Faust now discovered that there was no key (as there should have been) in that lock. It was still in the pocket of a stagehand who had left the theatre for quick refreshment in the pub across the lane. Faust was in a quandary because Marguerite was waiting patiently in her straw, and the producer had been adamant that he had to be inside that cell and on his knees beside her in time for the great final trio. He stared about wildly and shook the door ineffectually. Then he drew his sword – the one I had brought from London. He had left his own at home so I, foolishly generous but in the time-honoured yet all too often unappreciated tradition of tenor solidarity, had lent him my elegant dress rapier. Now he thrust that into the keyhole and shook it violently. It stuck. He struggled unsuccessfully to withdraw it amid mounting audience frenzy. His music cue was almost on him. He lost his head, abandoned my sword to quiver in its lock, thrust his hands between wooden bars and smashed them apart. The audience cheered and beside me Forbes, sobbing uncontrollably, fell off his seat and became wedged between the rows of gallery seats.

The theatre rocked with gargantuan Dublin laughter, for wasn't this wonderful night turning into the kind of glorious and memorable operatic disaster Dublin audiences loved?

Appalled at what was happening to my sword, I tried to free Forbes and drag him out. It was difficult because he was about twice my size and helpless with laughter, so we kept tripping over and adding to the general chaos in the cheering gallery. But on stage Faust had achieved what the director had demanded: he was on his knees in the straw and the Scots bass William McCue (for a variety of bizarre reasons the third Mephistofile in four performances) was calling him to take horse for Hell while the heavenly choir backstage lustily summoned Marguerite to Heaven. It was all very affecting and the audience was almost out of control.

My sword, however, would never be the same. Its fine buttoned point was bent and it would not fit back in its sheath. Faust kept apologising, promised to buy me as many drinks as I wanted, and the props people assured me everything would be right for the next *Don Giovanni.* They'd see to it for sure. They didn't. When I drew it to threaten disguised Leporello in Act 2 the following night it stuck fast until, as I heaved it free, it flew out of my hand and hit Donna Anna. She, stately and imperturbable, ignored me as I scrabbled to retrieve the weapon and sheath it. I had great difficulty doing so.

I was required to sing my second aria, 'Il mio tesoro', to Elvira, Masetto and Zerlina, who were downstage with their backs to the audience. This night, though, they made faces and strange gnomic signs. I was mystified. I knew my flies were not gaping open because there were no flies in my 17th-century breeches, so I ignored them. Apart from the Garda at the border, kindly Dubliners who had actually heard the great McCormack in this same theatre had been regularly reminding me of his wonderful singing of that aria, so I was not inclined to fool about merely because others in the cast were having a giddy evening. There had, in fact, been some horseplay during each performance, but right now I concentrated hard, ended with a flourish and spun on my heels, as instructed, to make my grand exit. What my colleagues had been vainly trying to warn me about, however, was that my scabbard and belt had been steadily unravelling and slipping down my side. I caught my heels in its wreckage and went out head first into the wings.

Our most memorable disaster, and one that has gone into operatic history, had happened on opening night: a grand occasion because President Éamonn de Valera and the entire Irish government were present. Surprisingly, given our minimal rehearsal time, the performance started well and went on uneventfully until at the opening of the cemetery scene the curtain went up too soon. No one had told Commendatore it was about to start and now he was revealed with feet encased in his statue's concrete boots and pacing nervously in circles. The audience were delighted but quickly simmered down and there were no more alarms until the last act, when Elvira failed to appear on cue. She was, it transpired, engaged in amusing conversation with Colonel William O'Kelly, a famous veteran Irish Republican soldier and genial chairman of the Dublin Grand Opera. On stage, mystified and alarmed, Don Giovanni and Leporello sang on desperately, asking questions of thin air, while in the pit Myer tried to understand what was happening and hoped he was dreaming. When Elvira finally did arrive, shoulder to shoulder with Commendatore, she could do little but give her agonised shriek (as marked in the score) and exit immediately.

The event for management followed the final curtain, when we were escorted upstairs and into a small, dimly lit room to be formally presented to the tall, saturnine and blind de Valera and lesser ministerial mortals such as the Taoiseach Seán Lemass. A flustered Colonel O'Kelly, overcome by the moment, introduced us in turn, and managed to get almost everyone's name wrong except the Irish singers. We shook the great man's hand and were then allowed to escape to celebratory drinks.

As we walked back to our hotel much, much later, I remarked to Forbes Robinson that my father would consider my meeting Dev a wonderful event. Forbes shook his head sadly. It had been, for an Englishman conditioned throughout his life to distrust the Irish, an ordeal. He believed de Valera to be the very personification of evil; an evil, he declared in oracular tones that reverberated in the cold Dublin air, overwhelming and palpable in that small reception room.

I certainly had never shared Father's opinion of old Dev but I'd not detected any dark suffocating shadows of evil lurking about us, so we agreed to differ amicably. And I was right about Father; for the rest of his life he considered my brief meeting with Dev to have been the high point of my career. Not even my meeting the Queen Mother a few years later after a Royal Festival Hall performance could come anywhere near to matching it. That was hardly surprising. Our family had never been ardent royalists.

The Dublin season was a leisurely sort of event, and with several days between performances I was able to fly across to Bristol to sing *Messiah* for Ibbs at Bath Abbey. It was, both Ibbs ladies had assured me, very important because they were sure Clifford Harker, organist at Bristol Cathedral and conductor of three of the biggest choirs in the southwest, would like my voice. He did. For the next 22 years I was his tenor soloist for at least one of those choirs (and often for all three) every year: the Bath Choral Society, the Bristol Choral and the Bristol Cathedral Special Choir. The Bristol Choral was one of the biggest in the land in those days, with a mighty and predominantly Welsh tenor section with whom I regularly drank after concerts. In that time, apart from the annual *Messiah*s, I sang a wide range of standard works and enjoyed all of these concerts: especially those traditionally majestic *Messiah*s in the soft light and wonderful atmosphere of an always packed Bath Abbey, and also the last one of the year a few days before Christmas at Bristol's Coulston Hall. Harker was, I think, the best *conductor* of all the many church and cathedral organists I ever worked with.

The Dublin season itself had important results too. It was nice to be praised by the Irish music critics but it was of far greater importance to impress conductors and an agent like Norman McCann. My ignorance of British operatic matters, however, led me into making one of my most serious career mistakes. During an after-performance meal one night, Myer Fredman remarked that there would certainly be a place for me at Glyndebourne the following season. At that stage I was still weighing up the possibility of another year with the English Opera Group, whose company manager had assured me just before I left for Dublin that there was definitely a place for me again if I wanted it. They were doing Britten's new work, *The Burning Fiery Furnace*, there were principal roles available and Pears was considering retirement. If he did retire I could be sure of one of them. So I asked Myer what roles might be on offer at Glyndebourne. None as such, he replied, but there would be understudies, and naturally I'd have to be in the chorus, which, he added proudly, was the best in the world because it was filled with the best rising young singers. I was unimpressed. Tactless as ever, I replied that I hadn't come 12,000 miles to sing in a chorus – even if it was the best in the world.

That was a mistake – compounded three years later when Myer and Jani Strasser, Glyndebourne's head of music, offered me the understudy of Ferrando in *Cosi fan Tutti.* I turned it down too because the basic fee was merely a lump sum of 25 guineas, for which I was to be available for six weeks' rehearsal and all the performances. If I had to go on, of course, I would get a good fee per performance, but I also knew the Welsh tenor who was singing Ferrando and knew for sure that he would go on even if he were at death's door. By that time I was getting a lot of work, doing over 100 performances a year and I was also about to become a father. I simply couldn't afford to give up even one Sunday evening Gilbert and Sullivan concert at Eastbourne or Brighton for Glyndebourne's derisory fee. I don't think I was forgiven. Some 10 years later when an agent recommended me for a major role that had just become available, Glyndebourne told her that while I would certainly be suitable I had turned them down twice, so was not one of 'theirs'.

The Dublin season also, in effect, marked the end of my first marriage. It was amicably done and Beverley and I even spent time deciding what name she should use professionally from now on. Henceforth she was Beverley Bergen, and went on to have a successful career in Germany, back in New Zealand and especially in Australia.

The news of my marriage break-up did not surprise any of my family. Father had recently married again: a pleasant Northern Irish lady, May Docherty, who looked after him devotedly. His letter in reply to mine was characteristically forthright: he had always known my marriage would fail, but he hadn't tried to dissuade me because he knew I wouldn't take any notice.

I left Wealden Surrey and moved back to London, where I found a convenient and comfortable enough bedsit in Clarendon Drive, Putney, over the road from my Christchurch friends Nelson and Janet Kenny. They let me practise in their music room and often fed me as well. I had known them since university days when, as art students, they had been part of that extraordinary group who were by now revolutionising New Zealand painting. Nelson was still painting, though by day he was the New Zealand Press Association's agent in London, and Janet was studying singing and starting to get work as a mezzo-soprano.

But 1966 did not start particularly well. No sooner had I moved to Putney than the English Opera Group's manager rang and, with profuse apologies, broke the news that there wouldn't be a role after all in Ben's new church parable: Peter had decided not to retire. I was not altogether heart-broken, but this did leave me with an uncomfortable gap mid-year in between the oratorio seasons.

True to his promises made in Dublin that he would push me, Norman McCann rode to the rescue. Within weeks he had booked me for a Hans Werner Henze one-act opera, *The End of a World*, with Basilica Opera at the St Pancras Festival; *Hiawatha* in Aberdeen; concerts with the Band of the Life Guards; and he was negotiating a contract with Cambridge University's Clare College for me to sing the lead in a scholarly revival of Edward Loder's long-forgotten 1840 Romantic opera *Raymond and Agnes*. Basilica Productions had also wanted me for their London production of Monteverdi's *Il Ritorno d'Ulisse* (the first production since the 17th century, it was proclaimed) but I was already booked for oratorio concerts on the relevant dates.

Basilica Opera was a new and ambitious company founded by a memorable triumvirate: the aristocratic but startlingly ineffectual director, Roland Holt Wilson, who had a titled, wealthy and indulgent mother; Frederick Marshall, an entertainingly raffish and endearingly alcoholic Ulster conductor; and Raymond Gubbay, a very young and ambitious administrator from Golders Green, devotee of Gilbert and Sullivan, popular Italian opera and Viennese operetta, but a musical rebel against his mother's passion for chamber music and his father's idolisation of Mozart.

Their Henze triple bill for the St Pancras Festival (renamed the Camden Festival a year later) had the superb English Chamber

Orchestra in the pit (many of whom had been colleagues on the *Curlew River* tours the previous year), and it was in many ways the most significant of my early British engagements in its consequences and the direction into which my subsequent singing career was channelled. I had a marvellous role to start with: Herr Fallersleben, the narrator and central figure whom Henze wanted to be modelled on the Charlie Chaplin of *City Lights*. I was surrounded, too, by a starry cast in smaller roles, including, among others, Monica Sinclair, Geoffrey Chard, John Kentish and that remarkable international specialist in contemporary music, the soprano Dorothy Dorrow. Each of their characters lampooned notables of the English musical and critical establishment and the whole thing was an outrageous satire on artistic pretension. My role was a gift and I grabbed it with hands, feet and everything else.

Apart from some good reviews in the influential papers, I immediately got a veritable avalanche of work. Ray Gubbay asked if I sang Gilbert and Sullivan. Of course I did! I wanted as much work as I could get! He intended to start his own concert-promoting business, he informed me, but in the meantime he was putting together a series of G&S concerts for Basilica headed by the well-known Australian baritone John Cameron. The soprano and mezzo were to be Savoyards from D'Oyly Carte, and he and Cameron wanted me as their tenor. Their first tour would be in the north: 11 concerts (with piano) in a fortnight.

Ray also booked me for a season of *Fledermaus* and *Ulisse* in Sunderland's wonderfully impressive Empire Theatre, one of the finest acoustics I have encountered, and for seasons of *Don Pasquale* in Harrogate's fine Georgian theatre and in London. So I became a regular with Basilica along with Cameron, Thomas Round, Marion Studholme (with whom I later sang more often, I believe, than with any other soprano and who became a lifelong friend), Emile Belcourt, Laura Sarti and Roger Norrington (as ambitious a tenor then as he was an aspiring conductor), before the company's money ran out and their cheques bounced. None of that was Ray Gubbay's fault. By the time the terminal decline set in he had already set out on his own to create his empire as impresario, concert promoter and, intermittently, artists' agent. His first office was just off Oxford Street, near Tottenham Court Road, and was no bigger than a large cupboard.

He succeeded spectacularly and 10 years later took me out to a splendid lunch in one of London's best restaurants to mark my 500th concert for his ever-expanding organisation. By then I was appearing in London in his G&S or Viennese galas at the Albert Hall, Festival Hall or the Queen Elizabeth Hall on average about once a month. Thirty years later, while Gillian and I were on holiday in England, he gave me an even better lunch at his Country Club and admitted to being a multi-millionaire.

In spite of the success of *End of a World*, I was relieved to finish with Henze, as the *Birmingham Post*'s music critic noted with some amusement when I sang a Mozart Mass there under Sir Anthony Lewis three days later; and it was an even greater contrast to start rehearsals for the Cambridge University season of *Raymond and Agnes*.

Nicholas Temperley, the eminent musicologist, music lecturer and Fellow of Clare College (and later Yale University), had rediscovered this Gothic Romantic opera, all but forgotten since the 1850s, and had produced a performing edition. He was also a friend of Peter Platt, himself a Cambridge man, and Peter, on sabbatical in Cambridge at this time, had recommended me for the tenor hero, Raymond. So had Norman McCann, who naturally took the credit for landing me the work.

It was a good role and I had some lovely ballads, and even better duets and ensembles (especially a quintet in Act II) that were musical gems. The baritone villain, the Baron of Lindenberg, had a magnificent mad scene that, sung by Ronald Lewis – at the time one of Convent Garden's longest-serving stalwarts – remains vividly in my memory. It really was an opera that, but for its execrable libretto, could have taken its place in a stronger operatic culture than England provided, alongside Weber's *Der Freischütz* and even early Verdi. The

Mum – Elsie Maclean (1896–1959) – about the time of her marriage.

Father – Edward Bernard Bohan (1897–1985) – also about the time of his marriage.

Left: Aged 2. I disliked that jacket and, I'm told, had a tantrum until a bribe of a penny reconciled me to sitting for this photo.

Below: 3L 1948. The future writers: Derek Round, back row fourth from left; me, back row fifth from left; Niel Wright, back row third from right; Joseph Musaphia, front row third from right; John Broomfield, far right front row.

Standish & Preece

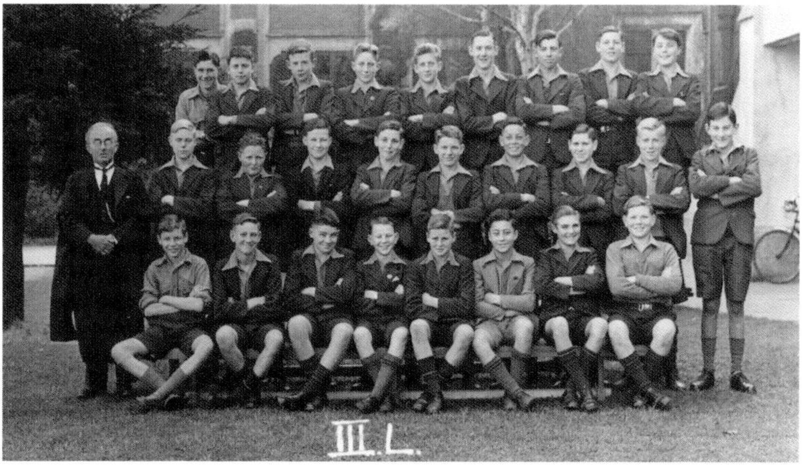

Father's retirement evening, 1957. *Left to right*: Bernadette, me, Father, Erle, Trish, Mum, Des, Margaret.

Fisher's Ghost, ABCTV, 1963 – as the inebriated John Hurley, the first of my stage drunks.

John Pearson Photography Pty, Sydney

En route to England: Beverley and friends in Naples, December 1963.

December 1966 in Folkestone: My new friend Gillian with Sebastian, who hated my fur hat.

L'Incoronazione di Poppea, San Carlos Opera House, Lisbon, just before the wig flew. *Left to right*: Ann Pashley (Nero), Janet Hughes (Valetto), me (Lucano).

San Carlos Opera, Lisbon

London Concert Artists outside Ivor Novello's former home, 1975. *Left to right*: Jennifer Partridge, Robert Bateman, Margaret Eales, Jean Temperley, Julia Meadows, Bruce Lochtie, Gillian, Michael Wakeham, me.

The happiest reunion of all the happy reunions of 1985: Gillian, Sarah and I with Bernadette.

Die Meistersinger von Nürnburg, Wellington 1990. *Left to right (ignoring the two actors standing top right)*: Conal Coad, Sir Donald McIntyre, Georg Voelker, Richard Weston, Roger Wilson and me (front right).

Woolf, 326 Lambton Quay, Wellington

Above: As Monsieur Triquet in *Eugene Onegin*, Wellington City Opera, 1997.

Wellington City Opera

Ulli the cat checking the Stafford manuscript.

Tales of Hoffmann, Canterbury Opera 2001: Spalanzani under threat from Paul Whelan's Coppelius.

Canterbury Opera

The Canterbury University History Department's centennial celebrations dinner, 2009. *Left to right*: Emeritus Professor David McIntyre, me, Jim Gardner, Marie Peters.

Geoffrey Rice

The British Ambassador to China and family outside their Beijing residence. *Back*: Isobel, Sebastian, Henrietta. *Front*: William, Nok, Florence.

Sarah and John Ashton.

Frederick and Grandpa.

On Sumner sands a week before the earthquake of 22 February 2011: Sarah, Vanessa, Sebastian, Gillian, George and me.

full original libretto, by the infamous Edward Fitzball, had mercifully been lost, so our producer, resourceful Max Miradin, had written new dialogue and done his best to improve what remained extant. Fitzball was one of Victorian England's most prolific playwrights and had also provided Loder's contemporaries, including the more famous and successful Michael Balfe and Vincent Wallace, with libretti that, sadly, have done much to plunge their musically effective and once universally popular operas into undeserved obscurity.

I enjoyed the rehearsals, and Cambridge in early May was charming. So was the company. Clare College welcomed us warmly and our social life was lively, with the exuberant young John Rutter's playing of his Beatles arrangements (soon to be nearly as well known and popular as his splendid choral music) especially memorable. So was a lunch at Christ's College as guest of two Americans from our chorus who were doing postgraduate study there, and through whom I met the eminent Cambridge historian Sir John Harold Plumb who, when he discovered I was a Canterbury University history graduate, recalled that Neville Phillips was an 18th-century man too, albeit a Namierite. Over a decade later I told Neville about that meeting and he glowed with pride. All went so splendidly, in fact, that I even began to revise my attitudes towards Oxbridge in general. Then came the opening night at the Arts Theatre.

It should have been a triumph. Instead it was all but disastrous. It started well enough as Agnes and I sang an aria each and our very good duet. Then the sinister Baron, black-clad Ron Lewis, swept onstage and the booing began. There was uproar. It was the most terrifying experience of my career because it was so utterly unexpected. I stood half hidden behind a picturesque ruined wall at the back of the set and my stomach froze. It was even worse for Lewis. Booing does not happen in opera anywhere unless a volatile audience hates the set or decides that a particular singer has been too awful to tolerate any longer, and that usually only happens in Italy. Lewis hadn't even sung a note before the booing and catcalls started. He struggled manfully through his opening aria and we somehow managed to plough on to the trio that ought to have been one of the evening's highlights. Instead, we just managed to get through it before the curtain fell, not a bar too soon.

Backstage, pandemonium ensued and Lewis was incandescent with rage and affronted operatic dignity. He and I were ready to leave the shambles and return to London immediately, until a shocked McCann and distraught Temperley arrived with the explanation.

It seemed that the conductor and musicologist Raymond Leppard with his cohort of King's College men, none especially well disposed to Clare College's operatic venture, had decided, as they put it, to enter into the spirit of Victorian melodrama, so surely it was okay to boo the villain, wasn't it? They were told in no uncertain terms that it was not. The interval was rather protracted.

We limped through the rest of the opera and the reception afterwards was by far the briefest and most sombre I've attended. I found it a particular irony that one of the King's College men was a tenor who had originally been cast as my understudy but had withdrawn because he found the role too demanding. So I had been lumbered with all seven scheduled performances, including those originally planned for the understudies, all promising Cambridge students. He went on to have a considerable career; we even sang together once in Bach's *St John Passion*, but we did not have much to say to one another.

The reviews of that first performance were predictably far from flattering, but luckily half of London's critics' circle had stayed in the capital that night to review a visiting German company and they didn't get to us until our second performance. By then we had recovered and the reviews this time were good, but Cambridge no longer felt the same as it had and I have never been able to feel kindly disposed to what, inside the British singing profession, is known, not altogether jocularly, as the Cambridge Mafia. I was glad not to sing there again. It was some consolation to discover that our experience was by no means unique. A year or so later Bob Tear (himself an ex-King's man) told me of suffering a similar jeering audience when he did Britten's *The Turn of the Screw* at the Arts Theatre in Cambridge.

I was 30 by now, often an awkward age for tenors as the voice matures and changes and youthful natural ability needs to be supplemented by sound vocal technique. The role of Raymond was by far the most demanding I had yet sung and it did reveal some potential problems, so after taking advice from other singers whose judgement I trusted, I started lessons with the elderly and remarkable Viennese Gustave Sacher, perhaps the best 'voice doctor' in London and a man who for many years managed to salvage voices all but ruined by some of the more celebrated, fashionable and expensive London singing teachers. He and his charming wife were two of the gentlest and nicest people I have ever known. Our first lesson was a revelation, and I left his studio with my problems solved – theoretically anyway. It just required time and practice. Best of all, people began to notice the improvements almost immediately, especially when I sang the central role of Popritchkin in the first stage performance of Humphrey Searle's one-act *Diary of a Madman* (adapted from the Gogol story) at the Jeanetta Cochrane Theatre. I had regular weekly lessons with Gus for the next few years, and after we discontinued those regular sessions I consulted him whenever I had new and vocally difficult roles to cope with. He continued to give sound practical advice to huge numbers of singers until well into his nineties.

I had certainly not forgotten my dream of becoming a writer, and from my arrival in England, and while I did the rounds of singing auditions between days of supply teaching and a steadily increasing number of concerts and rehearsals, I ploughed on with efforts to have published what I churned out on my almost antique typewriter. In Sydney I had drafted a few stories retelling Aborigine and Maori myths and legends. I experimentally sent these to what I imagined was still one of the most prestigious children's book publishers, Constable, and received a rather curious reply from the editor. They liked the Aboriginal tales and were interested in them, she wrote, but they were not at all keen on the Maori ones – least of all *Kahukura and the Fairies* (one of Maui's escapades), which, she declared primly, was morally suspect because Maui had not, after all, acted very 'nicely towards the poor fairies'. I didn't persevere, though perhaps, in retrospect, I should have. *Kahukura and the Fairies* was published a few years later in *Child Education*, for which by then I was also writing the occasional article and a number of book reviews.

Instead, I tried a short comic novel (*Turn Down an Empty Glass*) based on our voyage on the SS *Arkadia*. When it was turned down as being 'too Australian' and too flippant I abandoned that too, and wrote *The Silent One*, a rattling yarn for boys set against the background of a Chinese revolt against Rajah Brooke of Sarawak. I finished it sometime during the summer of 1966, I think, and with fingers crossed sent it off to a publisher and tried to forget about it while I went on singing.

That summer turned out to be a better one than I had earlier feared it might be, enlivened by a *Barber of Seville* season for the grandly titled and long-established Imperial Opera Company at the open-air Court Theatre in Holland Park and using yet another new (for me anyway) translation – my third in four years. Imperial Opera was more or less an offshoot of the famous but by now defunct Carl Rosa Opera Company, and in its productions of *Butterfly* and *Faust* it boasted some of Britain's most famous – if ageing – opera stars, including the veteran tenor Walter Midgley, whom I had admired since my youth, and the dramatic soprano Victoria Elliott, a woman of immense vocal power and extravagant 'diva' personality who was, in her time, considered a near peerless Butterfly and Tosca. I did several concerts with her and they were unforgettable. Vicky had powerful arms and in duets she used them to try to manoeuvre her tenor into singing with his back to the audience. I always fought back, so our duets often seemed to degenerate into arm wrestling contests, which always gave Ray Gubbay, watching gleefully from the wings, immense delight.

I had no such problems in the Holland Park *Barber* with my two Rosinas, one of whom was the very successful Christchurch-born coloratura soprano Edna Graham. Edna was my University Madrigal Group soprano colleague Diane Parsons' sister, and had enjoyed a very good career, having been one of Sir Thomas Beecham's favourite singers for some years, while for Carl Rosa she had shared the coloratura roles with the popular English soprano Gwen Catley. She had also sung major roles at Covent Garden and Glyndebourne. She was, alas, yet another of the expatriates New Zealand had largely forgotten about. Others prominent in British musical life at this time – apart from Drake and Hauxvelle – included the veteran baritone Denis Dowling, a fixture in just about every Sadler's Wells production for decades; the tenor Andrew Gold (who became the BBC's Head of Light Music); and the soprano Estelle Valery. By now, too, Jon Andrew, Heather Begg, Noel Mangin and Donald McIntyre were consolidating their places in the operatic world. One New Zealander who was not forgotten back home was Inia Te Wiata. And others of my generation who were doing well included three more sopranos: my Christchurch friend Marie Landis, who had also just achieved a triumph in Donizetti's *Maria Stuarda* at the recent St Pancras Festival; Suzanne Green; and of course Beverley. The younger Kiri Te Kanawa, Malvina Major, Patricia Payne, Rodney McCann and Anson Austin (among many others) were just starting to arrive in London.

Unlike the Australians, however, who always maintained strong supporting links, we were each more or less on our own, though clarinettist Murray Khourie and diplomat Jeremy Commons did their best to create interest in what New Zealand musicians were doing in London. After Jeremy left London, New Zealand House seemed to lose interest – unlike the Australian Federal and State High Commissions, who assiduously encouraged and supported the many young Australian singers trying to make their way in Britain's very competitive world. I did not find it a very welcoming place and I soon stopped calling in there, even to read the New Zealand newspapers.

EIGHT

GILLIAN – AND THE FIRST BOOKS

DURING A SOUTH-WEST Arts Council tour of *Barber of Seville* early in 1966, baritone Norman Platt mentioned that he was planning a new operatic venture and that I'd be hearing from him soon. And so I did: an offer to sing the Sailor and the Spirit in a short season of Purcell's *Dido and Aeneas* at the Swan Theatre, Worcester. It was to be a showcase for the Arts Council and other interested parties potentially inclined to finance the new company he and Roger Norrington were forming, provisionally called Regional Opera.

This was very much a group of friends: Norman himself was the producer, Roger was conducting, Laura Sarti was Dido, Claire Walmesley was Belinda, and Emile Belcourt was Aeneas. When I eventually made it to my first rehearsal, later than scheduled because of two longish Arts Council tours of *Fledermaus* and *Fra Diavolo*, I met soprano and actress Gillian Neason, playing Second Lady, a witch and a shadow dancer for good measure. She was a friend of Laura and Claire, who had met her during the year's run of Minos Volanakis' famous production of *Lysistrata* in London's West End. She was an actress who also sang in those days and they had encouraged her to take lessons from their singing teacher – the gloriously colourful and often riotously behaved mezzo Bruna McLean – and take her singing seriously. Eventually she became Laura's first pupil at the start of what was to be Laura's spectacularly successful and very distinguished teaching career. So Gillian gradually turned her professional attention towards singing, and had understudied good roles at Glyndebourne. She also had sung opposite Roger Norrington in the premiere of Nicolas Maw's first opera, *One Man Show*, at the Jeanetta Cochrane Theatre, directed by William Chapple and conducted by Norman del Mar and Myer Fredman. I had auditioned for this celebrated production, but found that all the tenor roles had already been cast.

Our first meeting was not entirely successful. She kept calling me Mark (the French dress designer Marc Bohan was much in the news) and she thought I was Australian. When Norman sent us off together to buy the fledgling company's makeup supplies she began to harbour doubts about my too-careful analysis of different kinds of body makeup. I'd just discovered that my costume as the Sailor was to consist of nothing but a Grecian version of a mini-skirt, and the truth was I hadn't a clue about makeup, whereas she knew a great deal. I thought she was extremely attractive.

The *Dido* season at the Swan was successful and a lot of fun, although, as was becoming my habit, I had problems with my costume. At one performance it disintegrated, just after I'd sung my sailor's song and swept up the little principal dancer to bear her off into the wings where the rest of the cast were watching with vast and ribald amusement. Luckily I was wearing black briefs, lent to me by the little dancer, as Gillian has occasionally reminded me in subsequent years.

At the end of the season I was careful to get Gillian's phone number. Regional Opera got its Arts Council approval and, not long afterwards, sponsorship from Kent County Council, thus becoming Kent Opera.

My next meeting with Gillian was sooner than either of us might have imagined. A day after I got back to London I was in a Putney laundrette waiting for my washing to spin and gazing into the dull, cold afternoon drizzle when I saw her passing, shrouded in overcoat and fur hat and literally being dragged along by a black and white spaniel and two very lively small boys. I rushed out, discovered that she lived around the corner in Balmuir Gardens, just off Richmond Road, and arranged to have drinks together at the Arab Boy pub that evening. I also met Sebastian, one of the small boys, though he took no notice of me. He and his friend Mark and Patch the dog were having some chasing game of their own and were as preoccupied as only five-year-olds and frenetic dogs can be.

Sebastian did take more notice of me when I arrived to collect Gillian that evening. He was sitting on the stairs and peering through the banisters. He did not reply when I greeted him, but next day asked his mother who that man in the fur hat had been (everyone was wearing Russian-style hats that cold winter), and when she replied that he was a singing friend, Sebastian announced that he did not like that man. He hated the hat. Maybe he also had a premonition that he was going to have to see a great deal more of me in the future. He did, of course, and almost from the start I treated this very intelligent and lively little boy as though he were my son.

Gillian's estranged husband was the undoubtedly brilliant but difficult John Wood, very much a rising theatrical and television star. I had seen and admired his performance as Sydney Carton when the BBC's *Tale of Two Cities* was shown on ABCTV in Sydney. Gillian and John had met while members of the Old Vic Company, which she joined after her two years at RADA, for their celebrated *Midsummer Night's Dream* at the Edinburgh Festival and on a long American tour. This was a notable production featuring most of Mendelssohn's incidental music (conducted by Hugo Rignold) and starring Robert Helpmann, Moira Shearer and Stanley Holloway. As well as understudying Hermia, Gillian sang first soprano in the female trios. John, who had already achieved critical success in an Oxford University production of *Richard III*, had come into the company later for the London season of *Othello, Macbeth, Romeo and Juliet, Troilus and Cressida* and *The Winter's Tale* – another famous season headed by such stars as Richard Burton, John Neville, Wendy

Hiller and Claire Bloom, whom Gillian understudied. And not long after that, setting aside much advice from colleagues, she married John.

Sebastian was born three years later, but John, a proudly and relentlessly serial Don Juan, left home one night on the pretext of going to buy cigarettes and, to Gillian's understandable astonishment and fury, went instead to live with Sylvia, a TV floor manager of whom Gillian had not previously heard. By the time I appeared on the scene, John and Sylvia had produced a half-sister for Sebastian, and Gillian, assisted to a greater, or sometimes lesser, extent by a succession of German and Swiss au pairs, was holding the fort in the Putney matrimonial home.

My first meeting with John (who was visiting Sebastian and also doing some floor sanding while I was doing my daily singing practice at Gillian's piano) was very civilised and during it he explained, more or less apologetically, that he hadn't *really* meant to leave Gillian, and had intended to return to her some day. I replied as tactfully as I could that all that was rather a pity but it had been four years ago and I had no intention of disappearing. We got on quite well, really, and for a few years while Sebastian was small and when John wasn't filming abroad or acting in New York he would drop in at weekends, ostensibly to see Sebastian, but often to agonise about his career and get our advice. He even took that advice once or twice. He also, on one occasion, added horrendously to our telephone bill by ringing Trevor Nunn and talking for an hour. He hadn't told us that Nunn was currently in Edinburgh.

It did not take either Gillian or me very long to decide that we should settle down together, and after spending most of the 1967 summer in Chichester – where Norman McCann had sent me to be a singing wedding guest in the Chichester Festival Theatre's production of *The Italian Straw Hat* – I moved into Balmuir Gardens permanently. Chichester was fun. Peter Coe's dazzling production in that big arena theatre and Eleanor Fazan's choreography were hilarious, and it was a wonderful experience to work with them and actors such as the great Bill Fraser (the absolute master of comic timing) and Michael Aldridge, Anton Rogers, John Standing, Peter Egan, Sarah Badel and Fenella Fielding.

Gillian was busy too, singing Papagena in Sadler's Wells' *Magic Flute* in a new production by Frank Hauser, with whom she had previously worked as an actress at the Oxford Playhouse, and conducted by either Charles Mackerras or Bryan Balkwell. She remained part of that production for the next three years.

There were inevitably some complications before we were able to get married: our divorces, and also, for me, untangling myself from one relationship in particular that had already become very difficult. This was not easily accomplished and culminated in the lady in question visiting Gillian and rather forcefully, I believe, discussing the situation. I was glad I wasn't there. I was doing *Don Pasquale* in Harrogate. But Beverley had, with commendable solicitude, warned us of the angry lady's intended visit and I think Gillian must have dealt with it effectively. We did not hear from her again.

The divorces took longer, mainly because John was constitutionally averse to answering letters and signing papers and was in New York, playing *Sherlock Holmes* on Broadway. A lawyer's assistant finally secured his signature by visiting him backstage to congratulate him on his performance and serve the necessary papers at the same time.

So Gillian and I were married at last in 1968 at Wandsworth Registry Office, attended only by our witnesses. In agreeable contrast to my first wedding the ceremony was very short. We left Balmuir Gardens just as a baritone colleague was beginning a BBC morning recital; we got back before he had finished. Sebastian, in bed with tonsillitis and solicitously tended by the au pair, was not even aware that we had gone out.

Settling down with Gillian finally sealed my decision not to move to Germany, which several people had for years been advising me to do. At this time a lot of British singers were getting contracts there, but invariably most of them were not getting much work in Britain. By 1969 I was, so it seemed pointless to abandon all that for a country and an operatic system based on rigid specialisation that I profoundly disliked. I'm very glad I didn't go. A few years later an agent sent me to audition at Frankfurt for what I was assured was a lyric tenor vacancy but which turned out to be one for a spinto (a heavier voice than mine), although Frankfurt Opera's intendant, Cristoph von Dohnanyi, told me that if there had been a lyric vacancy they would have offered me a contract. I don't think I would have accepted it.

In December 1968 our daughter Sarah was born, although I was not present at the birth.

It was not my fault. December was a very busy month and as an anxiously expectant first-time father I was acutely conscious of having to earn as many good fees as possible. Between October and Christmas I did 38 concerts, and in December itself, apart from *Messiah*s in Harlow, Morecombe, Kendal, Bath and Bristol, there were two *Creation*s in Ulster, Rossini's *Petite Messe Solonelle* at Harrow and Bach's *Christmas Oratorio* in Newcastle. The Bach was the problem. It was on the 18th and I had three free days before it. Sarah was due on one of them but she kept everyone waiting. I spent almost all day on the 17th at the hospital with Gillian, but by 11 at night she was falling asleep in mid-sentence and the nurses sent me home, assuring me that probably nothing would happen for another couple of days. They were wrong. I was woken about two in the morning with a call to say that Sarah had been safely delivered, that mother and daughter were both very well and that the nursing staff was sorry they had forgotten to let me know earlier. Elated, I woke Sebastian and rang my father-in-law in Folkestone. Then John Wood rang from New York to know if Sarah had arrived and to give me the news that he and Sylvia were expecting another child – and that he had a suspected cancerous growth. He was amazingly cheerful about that. It was a false alarm and he lived to be 81, by which time he was rightfully acknowledged to be one of the country's greatest stage actors. But by the time our conversation ended back in December 1968, it was almost time for me to get up and head for Euston and the early train to Newcastle. I caught the sleeper back to London after the concert but did not see Sarah until she was more than a day old – for which dereliction of paternal duty I have not yet been fully forgiven.

The other notable event of 1968 was the acceptance by Hutchinson Junior Books of my ripping yarn *The Silent One*. Two other publishers had rejected it, so Hutchinson's brief letter of acceptance was one of the most exciting and cheering letters I've ever received. I rushed to meet Dorothy Tomlinson, director of their vast children's division, and her chief editor, Paul Langridge.

Our meeting went well, especially after they had satisfied themselves that my historical research had been sound. It was vital, they warned, that historical novels for any age had to be based on soundly researched history. Paul emphasised that if the background facts and historical settings weren't accurate they would be inundated by waspish letters from bright young Etonians, and that would be embarrassing for everyone. So I explained my academic background and they offered me an advance of £100, which I hastily and gratefully accepted. There was only one snag: *The Silent One* was 70,000 words long and currently children and young adults' books were required to be no longer than 35,000. I would have to reduce it.

I waved my hand airily, declared that task to be no problem, and rushed back home to start the chore immediately. But it was neither easy nor successful. Luckily, I had already finished a second, and much better, historical tale – *The Writ of Green Wax* – about Jack Cade's Rebellion of 1450, set largely in Wealden Kent and Surrey, that intriguing countryside I had come to love. *The Writ of Green Wax* was accepted in place of *The Silent One,* which, in both long and short version, was consigned to a bottom drawer and never subsequently disinterred. Just as well. It would have dated very badly – and quickly.

This book was, I suppose, in the long-established tradition of Rosemary Sutcliff, Henry Treece and Geoffrey Trease, though by now I was becoming familiar with the hugely popular (with middle-class parents anyway) Leon Garfield, who was steering the genre in new and sometimes controversial directions. I liked most of his work and reviewed *The Drummer Boy* most enthusiastically for *Child Education* when it came out in 1970. He certainly influenced me and, I suspect, every other contemporary writer of historical fiction for young people, by widening our horizons and elaborating on what could henceforth be permissible in young adult fiction. *The Drummer Boy* is really a very dark tale indeed of destructive obsession. I did tire somewhat of Garfield's mannered prose style and I did not care much for his later books. Overall, I think, his most successful work was his completion of Dickens' hitherto unfinished *Mystery of Edwin Drood.*

The Writ was, incidentally, the first of my manuscripts to be subjected to Gillian's careful reading and ferocious but constructive criticisms. It came out in 1970, adorned with Val Biro's splendid dust jacket and striking woodcuts, for which I remain grateful. Hungarian-born Balint Stephen Biro was undoubtedly the foremost book jacket designer and illustrator of the time and had enhanced the appearance of just about every English author from Evelyn Waugh and Joyce Cary to C. S. Forrester, Neville Shute, Rafael Sabatini and a host of children's authors. It has been estimated that between the late 1940s and the 1970s he produced at least 3000 dust-jackets alone, as well as providing the *Radio Times* with at least one drawing almost every week and producing an enormous number of his own children's books.

For all Biro's fine work, however, *The Writ* made no great splash and caused few discernable ripples, though the *Scotsman* welcomed it as 'a more than promising debut'. Its publication date coincided with Hutchinson's lavish and heavily publicised launch of a book of less than distinguished poems by the charming and long-suffering Mary Wilson, wife of Prime Minister Harold Wilson. And for Hutchinson *The Writ* was just another addition to their huge list of almost every kind of book. Dorothy Tomlinson and Paul Langridge did apologise for the lack of publicity but I can't say I cared very much. Being published was enough. I was more excited by the *The Writ*'s publication, I think, than I have been by any of the 30 or more books I've written or contributed to during the 40 or so years since its appearance.

I was already at work on my next, *The Buckler*, a wild romantic tale involving family feuds amid the clash of Gaelic and English cultures, set in the Scottish Borders in the immediate aftermath of the Battle of Flodden, 1513. By now I had become even more fascinated by those extraordinary borderlands with their darkly forbidding peaks and distinctive evening skies than I had been by Wealden Kent and Surrey; during a few free days in a prolonged concert tour for the Scottish Arts Council I had explored Flodden Field and the remote valleys of the Cheviots, with their grim surviving stone pele towers and little churches. The story's genesis, though, was a display of 'curses' – ancient votive offerings dedicated for the destruction of enemies – that I had seen in Bath's museum.

Unfortunately, there were no Val Biro illustrations this time, and when I received the final proofs I was appalled to discover that the artist had not only confused Flodden with Culloden (1745), but had conspicuously ignored my careful descriptions of some characters. So the ragged Highlanders of 1513 were portrayed in 18th-century garb, and an emaciated and half mad-Border laird was portrayed as a stout and bluff grandee in buff-coat and wig. I complained furiously. Paul Langridge was shocked, apologetic and mortified, and the artist had to hastily make good his errors. I hope he lost sleep or had a ruined weekend and I didn't much care for his revised efforts, but by now printing and publishing deadlines for October 1972 were too close for any further revisions.

The illustrator's inadequacy did not hinder *The Buckler's* success. Reviews were good – especially in the *Times Educational Supplement*, the *Scotsman* and the *Times Literary Supplement* (although the revered *TLS* complained about some of the illustrations and the publisher's careless placing of them). I was stricken with flu that December and had to cancel some concerts – almost the only time I was forced to do so throughout my British career – so when Paul enclosed photocopies of the reviews he added his hope that they would gladden my heart and cure my sore throat. And, he added, a touch ironically I think, 'I am sorry that the TLS felt we had maltreated you!'

They didn't soothe my throat but they certainly did gladden my heart. So did Elaine Moss's choice of *The Buckler* as one of the best children's books of the year and its inclusion in the Children's Book Society's list of recommended titles. It sold steadily enough to provide modest but always welcome annual royalties for several years.

I now started on another book called *The Mound of the King* (the 'mound' in question being an ancient Irish burial site) set in 16th-century Ireland, but by the time it was finished everything had changed. Hutchinson had been reorganised, taken over and left with no more than a skeleton staff after most – including Dorothy Tomlinson and even its chairman, the almost legendary Sir Robert Lusty – had been made redundant. And there was a change in the literary climate. Naomi Lewis, a powerful influence in British children's and young adults' literature, had announced that historical novels were passé; fantasy and gritty contemporary realism must henceforth rule supreme. The violence of the IRA onslaught against mainland Britain was no help either, and several publishers, while flatteringly complimentary about the story, suggested I concentrate on purely English (or even Welsh) settings. I persevered doggedly, but a letter from Oxford University Press summed the situation up: 'This is a powerful story and you are right not to be repentant about writing Irish fiction nowadays,' the editor wrote, but the problem was that 'historical fiction seems to be in the doldrums', especially that for 'older children'. It was, he concluded, 'a shame, for the love story you tell is ageless'.

I had also sent a copy to the family firm Dennis Dobson, specialists in children's and young adult books (Dobson's son was at Emanuel School with Sebastian), but they lost it during their move from London to Brancepeth Castle near Durham. After that, more or less as a joke, I would send an ironical reminder postcard on the anniversary of its despatch until, 10 years later, I unexpectedly received an apologetic letter informing me that they had at last found it hidden behind padding in a packing case. They liked the book very much and wished they could publish it. The economic recession had proven so devastating, however, that they were no longer publishing any new work and were sustained only by their backlist. Even that soon failed. Not long after this depressing letter, Dennis Dobson ceased to exist.

The Mound of the King joined the mangled *Silent One* in a bottom drawer, and although there was intermittent interest from several publishers in an Arthurian children's fantasy, I gave up trying to write for young adults. Also, I was finding less and less spare time to concentrate on my ideas for novels. By the late 1970s my time was almost entirely taken up by our family, my singing career, the often bruising politics (so integral a part of British musical life) on behalf of the Solo Performers' Section of the Incorporated Society of Musicians (ISM) with whom I was increasingly heavily involved, and a business venture started in partnership with Raymond Gubbay. The badly dislocated British economy, sliding inexorably into serious depression, made worse by the disastrous shambles of James Callaghan's disintegrating Labour government, was playing havoc with publishing and many firms were collapsing.

By now we were living in Wimbledon, having been able to buy our first house there, at 124 Faraday Road, largely because of the very good money Gillian earned playing the leading role of the Prioress for over a year in Martin Starkie's long-running *Canterbury Tales* at the Phoenix Theatre in the West End. A few years later, as the specialist stamp dealing business Ray Gubbay and I had established began to generate a satisfactory extra income, we moved around the corner into the elegant and much larger 124 Queen's Road.

NINE

General Practitioner of Singing

Henry Wendon, a fine English tenor of an older generation, used to describe himself and the majority of male British singers with wives and families as 'general practitioners' of singing, required by simple economic necessity to accept all kinds of engagements rather than to specialise. Without a doubt the need to specialise, especially in opera but also in the burgeoning fields of early and baroque music, was strongly advocated by the London Opera Centre's principals – Joan Cross, and James Robertson who displaced her – and by the various cliques who dominated early and baroque performance. Rightly or wrongly I preferred 'general practice', confident enough in my vocal versatility and ability to cope adequately with whatever style I was required to conform to, but also acutely aware of what I could *not* do. I did not enjoy the avant-garde and 'contemporary' opera, and though I had had success with Henze, and Searle's *Diary of a Madman*, I certainly did not want to be regarded as a 'specialist' in that genre. Searle, with whom I got on well, had wanted me to sing some of his other works, and I discovered that the BBC had me on their list as a 'contemporary specialist'. I asked them to remove me from it and, although surprised (singers did not usually rule themselves out of possible BBC work), they obliged.

Based on both my own experiences and the often disastrous ones of so many colleagues, I was unwilling to rely exclusively on notoriously unreliable and often treacherous opera managements. Opera was still very much a minority interest in musical Britain. Many splendid singers enjoying fine – if often short – bursts of London fame at Covent Garden or Sadler's Wells remained utterly unknown to the wider musical public outside London, as many of my friends discovered when their contracts were not renewed (often for reasons far removed from their abilities as singers) and their careers foundered. So I battled on as a freelance, and year after year managed over 100 performances annually, ranging from Gilbert and Sullivan and Viennese operetta to Bach and Monteverdi, accumulating a repertoire of over 170 choral, orchestral and operatic works in addition to several hundred songs with piano. I also enjoyed the sheer variety of my work, and I took some pride in the fact that, for example, at Easter 1972 I sang the tenor arias in the London Choral Society's *St Matthew Passion* at the Royal Festival Hall on Good Friday, and two days later on Easter Sunday sang in the first of what would become regular G&S galas at the Royal Albert Hall.

I had first sung for the ageing and idiosyncratic John Tobin and his splendid London Choral Society at the Festival Hall on Good Friday 1969, with Bob Tear as Evangelist, John Carol Case, Jennifer Vyvyan, Maureen Lehane and John Barrow, and with New Zealand's Alan Loveday leading one of the orchestras and Peter Gellhorn and Adrian Skeaping heading the continuo group. Tobin was a man of strong opinions and he believed that 'Mr Bach' and 'Mr Handel', as he termed them, spoke to him directly. He did not hold with Sir David Willocks and the Bach Choir's polite but more pallid and, he argued, less 'committed' style. His instructions to me brooked no argument: even in the opening 'Oh grief!' and 'I would beside my Lord' I was to be forthright and sing with my full tone while, he added, the choir would sing beneath me 'in terrified whispers!' That suited me. He usually chose a different tenor aria soloist each year. I was one of the few he employed more than once.

The *St Matthew* continued to be of significance during these years, though as my voice matured I was becoming a less obvious choice for Evangelist because many British choral societies preferred much lighter-toned tenors than I now was. There was one performance, however, that produced dramatic results. This was for the Harrow Philharmonic at Southwark Cathedral in March 1970. Roger Norrington had originally been booked for it, but a day before, Helen Jennings rang to say that Roger had laryngitis, so was I free? As it happened a Bach Mass in B Minor somewhere in the north had had to be cancelled and I was feeling disgruntled; to be without a concert – and the fee – on as busy a concert date as the Saturday before Good Friday was dreadful! So I accepted with alacrity and some amusement. Roger's conducting engagements were increasing by now and his singing was becoming less important for him, so he had been in the habit of asking me to substitute for him, sometimes at short notice. Oddly, the work was usually *Judas Maccabeus*, and a day or so before the date he would ring the particular society, put on a strangulated voice and explain that he had laryngitis but was sending a capable deputy. This time, however, just as Gillian and I were laughing at what was probably another of Roger's mock ailments, Roger himself rang. For once he really did have a bad throat, and he croaked that he had needed the fee. I commiserated but assured him that I did too.

The performance at Southwark Cathedral turned into a disaster. Though no one knew it yet, the conductor, a pleasant man and a good musician for whom I had already done a number of concerts, was terminally ill (he died a few days later) and lost control of the two chamber orchestras and the double choirs. Alone in the pulpit and aloof from the chaos, I was quite glad that Roger's name and not mine was on the programme; I concentrated on my narration and tried to shut out what was happening in the rest of the cathedral.

Early next morning Helen Jennings rang to offer congratulations. She had been there with Harold Holt, the international agent, and I had impressed him so much that he was booking me to sing Britten's *War Requiem* in Rio de Janiero in October. The fee, by British standards, was large. Some months later, during rehearsals for Kent Opera's *Marriage of Figaro*, while Roger and I, to the amusement of the rest of the company, were having one of our quite frequent arguments, he remarked that he was sorry to have dropped me into what he'd heard was a somewhat fraught *Matthew* at Southwark. I told him not to apologise, because as a result I was going to Rio to do the *War Requiem*. Roger, slightly shaken, later that day in the pub told me he was finally going to give up singing and concentrate on conducting.

The first South American performance of Britten's *War Requiem* was a fascinating experience. The *Sinfônica Brasileira* under the dynamic young Isaac Karabtchevsky, and the big combined choirs drawn from Rio de Janiero's numerous choral societies, were wonderful mixtures of colours and nationalities. The performance was fully as intense as performances of that work invariably are, though it was daunting to arrive at the splendid and historic Teatro Municipal to find it ringed by dozens of machine-gun-wielding soldiers. There had been threats made to the British ambassador and Brazil was in the midst of one of its political crises, though the unrest did not diminish the warm reception my colleagues – English soprano Elizabeth Simon and baritone John Gibbs – and I received. We were lodged in a luxurious hotel facing Copacabana Beach and the hospitality from orchestral management, British Council, members of the British Embassy and several of the participating choral societies was all but overwhelming, especially after the concert, when we were invited to a succession of suppers (the German Society's was the best) and parties. At an extremely late hour we were taken up to the figure of Christ watching over Rio to see the sunrise, which was unforgettably spectacular. The car ride, however, through the (mercifully) all-but-deserted centre of Rio and up the steep, winding hill road to the top was one of the two most terrifying rides I've known because our driver, a diplomat at the British Embassy, was very drunk. The other terror ride was the one back down to the centre of Rio.

I always enjoyed singing into the Albert Hall's vast spaces and to its large audiences, though for our first G&S gala there in April 1972 we had no idea how large – or small – that audience would be. Ian Wallace and I arrived early and simultaneously at the artists' entrance, and I wondered aloud if we'd get any kind of audience at all, because this was very much an experiment for both Gubbay and his former employer, Victor Hochhauser, in those days London's major impresario. Ian laughed with delight. There was already a queue extending as far as the Albert Memorial. There'd be an audience all right. Walking out onto that stage and seeing thousands crowding the hall is a remarkable experience.

Quite early in his career as impresario, Ray Gubbay had established an orchestra, with the very experienced Marcus Dods – one of the very best 'singers' conductors' I ever worked with – as its principal conductor. To start with, the concerts were outside London, but from 1969 large audiences in Wembley Town Hall and at the Fairfield Halls, Croydon, helped persuade the management at London's Royal Festival Hall complex to risk a G&S night. On 26 December 1971 Marion Studholme, Jean Temperley, John Heddle Nash and I performed a G&S centennial concert (it was 100 years since Gilbert and Sullivan's lost *Thespis*) with Marcus conducting the New Promenade Orchestra at the Queen Elizabeth Hall. It was sold out within two days and Victor Hochhauser immediately booked it for the Albert Hall, with the addition of a chorus and a second baritone for the comic songs. That, to everyone's delight, was Ian Wallace, one of the most popular singers in Britain and a radio and TV celebrity; from then on Gubbay concerts started to dominate London's concert schedules.

The reason was simple: they were almost always sold out, in stark contrast to most other kinds of orchestral and choral concerts. Indeed, if a particular kind of programme failed to attract at least a 90–95 per cent capacity, Ray would not bother repeating it. Throughout the next decade the G&S or Viennese Evenings, Johann Strauss Galas with dancers, and operatic concerts never failed. Ray became the most successful concert promoter in Britain and his New Promenade

Orchestra, initially made up mainly of players from the English National Opera's orchestra, became either the London Concert Orchestra (for a while led by the brilliant John Georgiadis), or, for the Strauss galas, the Johann Strauss Orchestra, led by the superb Polish violinist Jack Rothstein.

I also appeared in similar concerts for other managements besides Ray's, such as the Royal Philharmonic Orchestra at the Albert Hall and Fairfield Halls, at the Norwich Triennial and Swansea Festivals, for the Ulster Orchestra and Belfast Philharmonic Choir, the Northern Sinfonia in Newcastle, and for Victor Hochauser (again at the Albert Hall). Hochauser had a dry wit. Once as we approached a door together he stood aside, gestured for me to go first and remarked laconically, 'Art before exploitation, my boy.' And that, after all, summed up so much about the music profession.

I worked with many interesting people under Ray Gubbay's management, but one of the most entertaining was the composer, pianist and revue celebrity Donald Swann, as entertaining off stage and off camera as he was in his famous double act with Michael Flanders. There was, however, a very serious side to Donald: he was anxious to be regarded as a genuine composer. Before he dedicated himself to composing his rather remote and strange mix of spiritual and science fiction operas, we did several recitals of his songs that always included his deservedly popular John Betjeman settings and his Tolkein song-cycles. The *Set by Swann* evenings were popular, and later Donald regretted having abandoned them. The last time I saw him, at the Savage Club a few days before I left England in 1987, he gave me copies of the songs I'd sung in those concerts and asked me to continue to sing them whenever possible. It is a real regret now that I didn't.

During 1975 Ray Gubbay also came to an arrangement with the large recording company Polydor to record a disc of G&S favourites. On 18 July 1975 Marion Studholme, Jean Allister, Ian Wallace and I, accompanied by Marcus Dods, the London Concert Orchestra led by John Georgiadas and the English Chorale, recorded a *Gilbert & Sullivan Spectacular*. I wish I had been on a royalty arrangement instead of my concert fee, although at that time, before the years of dramatic inflation that soon followed, it seemed a good one. This recording sold well and steadily under a series of labels on disk, tapes and CDs, and it stayed in the catalogues for more than 25 years.

By far the weirdest recording I ever made was of a Nigerian Opera by a high-powered Nigerian official. Each of us sang several roles; none of them really suited our voices, and they were sung in Ibo, for which we were coached carefully by the composer. We were very well paid and we recorded this strange work at Abbey Road in the same studio the Beatles had used. I've never heard this recording and I don't particularly want to. It was strictly for Nigeria, but I'd be amazed if it has ever become a treasured cultural icon there.

There were downsides to being versatile, and these were pointed out to me often enough by those who imagined that anyone singing light music could not possibly do 'serious' things. This attitude was, of course, pure musical snobbery but it did affect me. Some time in the late 1970s, I think, at a time when I was doing many Verdi *Requiem*s and other large-scale works such as *Psalmus Hungaricus*, Beethoven's Ninth Symphony, Janacek's *Glagolitic Mass*, Britten's *Spring Symphony* and Delius's *Mass of Life* outside London, Ibbs and Tillett's new director, Wilfred Stiff, deplored the fact that I did so many G&S and Viennese galas in London and, horror, was singing frequently on BBC Radio 2. I should be doing the big Verdi and Elgar works in London instead, he announced, and should certainly not be appearing in the BBC's *Friday Night is Music Night* with the BBC Concert Orchestra – despite its many good conductors. I replied that I always sang at least one operatic aria in that programme, and at least four million people listened. That surprised him, but he wouldn't dream of listening to it or anything else on Radio 2. Nor, although he liked my singing, would he go anywhere near a G&S gala at the Albert Hall. He considered that I had sung far too much G&S, and that had affected my reputation among serious musicians. We agreed to differ. I continued to do around 100 performances a year, and within another three or four years Ibbs and Tillett went out of business, having got into trouble for not passing on fees due to their performer clients.

Wilfred Stiff was not the only one to be surprised by my wide repertoire and musical tastes. Some of my specialist colleagues were too, especially English baroque practitioners who preferred a more bland and bloodless type of tenor voice. Nevertheless, throughout my career I sang much early and baroque music: a very great amount of Bach, Handel and Haydn, and Heinrich Schütz for Roger Norrington.

I sang the role of the amorous young courtier Eurimacho in *Ulisse* at Basilica's season in Sunderland's Empire Theatre, and after arriving back in London received a call from Tom Hammond, head of Sadler's Wells music staff. They were changing the two major principals of their successful production of Offenbach's *La Belle Helene* and he thought I had the right legs for the role of Paris. And, he hastily added, he had also liked my singing. I did a special stage audition singing 'The Judgement of Paris' (already one of my regular concert items) and, with the staff accompanist Richard Nunn reading other roles, a longish dialogue sequence. It seemed to go well, the company's directors and conductor checked my availability for 20 performances and I went home with them pencilled in my diary. Then Hammond rang next day, apologising profusely. One of the directors had decided I was too short. Admittedly, he added, Nunn was well over six feet, but their new Helene also happened to be just on six feet tall. I was unlucky, he added, because I would have been the ideal height for their previous Helene.

My lack of height was to continue to haunt me, for the newer generation of English sopranos now starting to appear were, almost without exception, quite tall girls.

Coronation of Poppea was Kent Opera's first production under its new name in 1969 and over the next eight years height was not a problem as I sang the roles of Lucano, Nero's drunken poet friend, and the very grumpy 1st Soldier. We sang it in English initially and used Raymond Leppard's easily available but far from satisfactory realisation, though Roger completely re-barred the work and Norman Platt improved some of the unsatisfactory translation. Those first performances at Canterbury and Tunbridge Wells had Laura Sarti as Poppea, Adrian de Peyer as Nero, Benjamin Luxon as Ottone and

Sarah Walker as Empress Octavia. It was Sarah's operatic debut and set her remarkable career off to a spectacular start. In subsequent years we sang it in Italian in an entirely new musical realisation by Roger and the American scholar Alan Curtis, with the soprano Anne Pashley as Nero, the young John Tomlinson as Seneca, Laura Sarti, the Welsh tenor Kenneth Bowen as Ottone and at different times Sarah Walker or Sandra Browne as Poppea. We were always accompanied by an array of Britain's finest lutenists, including Nigel North, Anthony Rooley and Robert Spencer, the brilliant Nicholas Kraemer as harpsichord continuo and a splendid baroque orchestra led by John Holloway.

We performed this version at Portugal's San Carlos Opera House in Lisbon and in Oporto, at the City of London Festival and a number of provincial theatres, including Oxford's Sheldonian Theatre and Bath's beautiful Georgian Theatre Royal, before reverting to another English translation – Norman's this time – as demanded by the BBC for their 1975 Promenade Concert Season at the Albert Hall. The Norrington/Curtis version was about as close to Monteverdi's original as even the purists could hope, and as I recall it did not differ too markedly from Nicholas Harnoncourt's celebrated edition that saw the light in Europe about the same time.

During opening night in Lisbon I once more distinguished myself by losing my curled blond wig during the duet with Nero as I spun on my high cork heels and launched into a series of roulades in praise of singing, love and glory. I turned it into a brief comic moment by sweeping up the wig from the floor and replacing it with a flourish as though it was deliberate, while the two sopranos singing Damigella and Valetto had hysterics behind a pillar. Norman Platt told me next day that one of the Lisbon papers was describing me as 'a comedian extraordinaire' and asked if I'd keep it in. I didn't.

I parted company with Kent Opera eventually because I was unhappy about being cast specifically as a character tenor. I had already (rashly perhaps) spurned the English National Opera's suggestion that I might sing Monostatos in their *Magic Flute*, but even more important was the fact that I could no longer afford to be tied to the long rehearsal periods opera companies demanded. At this stage the BBC were apt to ring at short notice to offer broadcasts and recording dates for which Norman, in particular, would not release me – though he did not pay me for rehearsals – and my concert commitments were more demanding than ever. And being so consistently busy meant that I often had to turn down offers of high-profile work – most painfully, a BBCTV opera. So I ruled myself out of opera for a few years, before returning in the early 1980s for various festival performances, many of them with the London Chamber Opera. And throughout my British career I did many concert performances of operas such as Verdi's *Nabucco* and *Aida*, and Bizet's *Carmen*, all favourites with the larger choral societies. Then there was Master of the Queen's Music Sir Arthur Bliss's only opera, the interesting but flawed *The Olympians*, revived at the Royal Festival Hall to celebrate his eightieth birthday. The sight of Bliss and his librettist J. B. Priestley running on stage hand in hand to milk the applause at the end was one never to be forgotten. The baritone Raimund Herincx, a larger-than-life personality and himself a genius at milking applause, declared the manner in which these two little old men did it to be as sublime a lesson in the art as any he had seen, and one the rest of us must emulate.

The other memorable incident of that evening involved Prime Minister Edward Heath, as arrogant in his musical opinions as he was about everything else. At the reception afterwards, as the male principals waited in a group while the Queen Mother chatted long to the sopranos, Heath, not a man for small-talk, broke the awkward silence by observing jocularly that during the interval he had remarked to Bliss that much of his music reminded him of Richard Strauss's *Ariadne auf Naxos*. 'And do you know,' he guffawed with shoulders heaving in that manner so often imitated by political satirists, 'Sir Arthur said he'd never heard *Ariadne auf Naxos*!'

None of us offered comment. We knew (because Sir Arthur had told us several times) that he disliked Strauss greatly. As Forbes Robinson later observed in his rumbling murmur that could resonate throughout any reception room, it was surely the height of tactlessness – and rudeness – to inform an old man on his birthday that his favourite composition was like that of another composer whom he loathed.

Herincx was a man of tremendous energy and a huge, not to say overwhelming personality around whom legends grew. Many of the legends were true; I know because I was with him so very often when the events on which they were based occurred. When he was on form he was unforgettable and fully what he always claimed to be: Britain's best bass-baritone. Certainly few singers of any voice sang a wider range of music or had a larger repertoire, and in every respect he was a singer of wide international reputation and experience. He was also the perfect and generous host for those of us invited to do the Sunday concerts he put on in the concert room of his beautiful Elizabethan country house.

I was lucky enough to work with a very large number of memorable baritones and basses and some, especially Ian Wallace, became lifelong friends. No other British operatic and concert singer was so widely recognised by the general public. Wherever he went people would approach him in the streets to shake his hand, request his autograph or to simply tell him how much they enjoyed *My Music*, his recordings of Flanders and Swann songs or his latest TV appearance. He was always affable and grateful for their attention. Ill-health shortened his career and he retired from singing in his late fifties, though he continued his radio, TV and light-hearted one-man show evenings until well into his eighties. Our friendship with him and his delightful wife, Pat, continued after we moved to New Zealand through letters and, after his Parkinson's made writing difficult, by very long phone calls during which he would sing and recount his newest comic experiences. He was a superb raconteur. His last call, a mere few weeks before his death at the age of 91, was just as hilarious, and his voice was as youthful and clear as ever.

Even Ian could not quite compete, as far as vocal longevity went, with the extraordinary baritone George Baker, whose recording career began in 1909 and who, under a variety of names, made thousands of recordings, the last for Glyndebourne Opera's groundbreaking Gilbert and Sullivan series under Sargent in the early 1960s. In 1966, when he was 81, I sang two performances of *Trial by Jury* with him, and he was as lively and sounding as vocally fresh as he had in the famous recordings of that work he had made in the 1920s.

Not all my colleagues became abiding friends, of course; least of all the baritone John Heddle Nash. He was, more than anyone I've ever known, a cautionary story of why one should never follow in the professional footsteps of a famous parent. His father was the great English tenor Heddle Nash, who had not simply a supremely beautiful voice but a truly charismatic personality that won him a vast following. Perhaps few English singers of any era have been so adored by the British musical public and remembered with affection so long after his death. His son John had too much to live up to, yet make no mistake, he too had a beautiful voice – an easy, lightish high baritone – and on stage a charm, personality and artistry that made him popular with audiences; and, like so many tall and overweight men, he moved on stage with elegance. He did have a good career, but he was not his father and people often reminded him of the fact: like the mayor of a large Lancashire town who at an after-concert reception spoke at length to the large attendant throng about his late father, old Heddle: 'Your father could sing everything, and he was great in everything, John!' the mayor declared. 'You're good in the lighter things, John boy, but you'll never match your Dad.' Nash flushed dark scarlet with rage, though he continued to smile. Our pianist, my soprano colleague and I put down our drinks and fled for our hotel.

No one else I've known could find insults in even the most innocent remark so effortlessly or hoard their memories so long. Our relationship started badly. When John and I first met I told him how much I had admired his father and he thanked me and gave me a beaming smile. I thought we were getting on really well. Then he took Ray Gubbay aside and complained that I was getting at him. And so it went on for years until we both mellowed: Nash complaining about me, and me complaining about his paranoia. Ray coped with us with good-humoured tact and tolerance, for the fact was that on stage we worked together well and audiences enjoyed our duet singing. It did not take me long to discover that Nash was as suspicious of every other singer, conductor and accompanist in the profession as he was of me. It was a sad fact that he had no professional friends, and late in our association he confessed to having hated his father too. Twenty years or so after we started singing together, and after he had suffered a minor stroke that slowed him down a little, he came into my dressing room before an Edinburgh concert and, haltingly, apologised for having misunderstood me for so many years; he added that he had taken too long to grow up. I've never felt so sad for anyone. John Heddle Nash was in every sense a tragic figure. He died not long after we left Britain, and the only mourners at his funeral were his wife and Ray Gubbay.

Naturally I worked with other vivid personalities who were not singers. Quite a number were conductors, and of these few could compare as 'characters' with the old Welshman Rae Jenkins. Having started as one of Sir Henry Wood's violinists, he was for many years a BBC conductor with over 6000 broadcasts to his credit, and he had conducted all the British and most of the European orchestras. He had a wonderfully abrasive and mischievous sense of humour and I always enjoyed working with him with both the Royal Philharmonic Orchestra and his Wembley Philharmonic Society. The first concert we did together was with the RPO. I was away when he rang to arrange rehearsals, so he asked Gillian if I was any good, and when she said I was he discoursed at length about the shortcomings of all the famous tenors he'd conducted during the previous 50 years. When I did meet him he repeated all that to me. He could be gloriously rude to orchestral players – often advising the strings to put chalk marks on their instruments if they couldn't hear that they were out of tune – but they liked him; he had given most of them their first jobs. The orchestras he assembled for his Good Friday *Matthew Passion*s at Wembley included an array of London's best players from whom he drew splendid performances. I have never heard any violinist match John Georgiadis playing for him the great violin solo for the bass aria 'Give me, O give me back my lord'. John was leader of the London Symphony Orchestra at the time and liked to claim that he never practised. Before the *Matthew*, however, he spurned tea between rehearsal and performance, and shut himself in the loo to practise that sublime solo.

Another unforgettable character was Carl Dolmetsch, virtuoso recorder player, son of old Arnold Dolmetsch who had been one of the first to fly the flag for early music and who founded a dynasty of instrument makers and performers who battled on through the long years before early music became fashionable. Unlike Rae Jenkins, Carl was an intensely serious little man of almost painful thinness, who seldom if ever, during the two years I sang with his ensemble at his Haslemere Festival, gave any sign that he had a sense of humour. He was always friendly but, being a militant vegetarian, discouraged meat eating in his presence. Meals at the Dolmetsch house were uncomfortably spartan, and could consist of little more than sliver-thin slices of homemade bread with almost invisible traces of margarine. Excuses had to be made so that we could flee into the town to find enough sustenance to get through the concerts.

Inevitably visits to Ireland always brought wonderful encounters with big personalities – like the chairman of the Limerick Festival Opera who met the English baritone Geoffrey Nielson Taylor and me at Limerick airport and whisked us off to what he described as the festival's committee room. This was the snug bar of an inner-city pub where, for several hours, glasses of Guinness were pressed on us and we were royally entertained with an avalanche of funny stories about just about every topic under the sun. Sometime after midnight our chairman rose, announced that as Geoff and I were required to be at rehearsals for *The Barber of Seville* at nine in the morning it was time we were taken to our hotel. Then the lights were put out, everyone lined up in the pitch-black hallway and an acolyte was sent into the street to check that there were no Garda about: 'For wouldn't it be a terrible thing if we were all up before me in the morning!' the chairman called out. He was the local magistrate.

Geoff Taylor was a very fine baritone and was also renowned

inside the profession for having paid his way through training at the Royal Academy by playing first division professional football for Fulham (his brother played cricket for Yorkshire and England). The first time he came to dinner at our place, an awed nine-year-old Sebastian (already a fanatical Manchester United supporter) interviewed him solemnly in the approved TV sports correspondent style on his sporting career. Geoff's singing career was shortened by severe arthritis, but he became an influential singing teacher at the Royal Scottish Academy.

Visits to Northern Ireland were not always as light-hearted and packed with fun as those to the Republic as the 'Troubles' broke out and worsened. During 1968 and 1969 I sang a series of *Creation*s (always one of my favourite oratorios) in Londonderry, Coleraine and Strabane (the town almost straddling the Donegal border) for the University of Ulster and the Strabane Choral Society, which boasted a wholly Catholic tenor section, a wholly Protestant bass section and happily mixed soprano and contralto sections, with both denominations willing to remain on stage for the singing of 'God save the Queen' *and* the Irish Republic's national anthem. I used to stay in Strabane with the hospitable Smyths, Anglo-Irish and Protestant Ascendancy establishment mill-owners since the early 18th century, and delightful people who had worked hard to foster toleration and inter-denominational harmony. The revival of the IRA and the renewal of communal violence destroyed that – and Strabane itself.

Music making continued to be attempted further east, and Gillian sang Frasquita in a comparatively uneventful season of *Carmen* for the Belfast Festival in 1971, but after 30 January 1972, Bloody Sunday, things got progressively worse. By the time I sang in Ballymena a few months later, civil war was being waged, lovely peaceful-looking Antrim was a war zone, and parts of Belfast were fast becoming a maze of shattered buildings, sand-bagged police guard-posts, boarded-up shops and closed hotels. By then assassinations were almost daily occurrences. That concert was incident free and went well. I flew back to London next morning, to learn when we turned on the news that the Grand Central Hotel, where I had enjoyed a good lunch the previous day, had just been blown up, with more than a dozen injuries. Foggy London suddenly seemed like paradise, and quiet Putney the only place I wanted to be in.

But I went back to Belfast in subsequent years: most memorably in early 1978 for concerts with the Belfast Philharmonic Choir and the Ulster Orchestra in the Ulster Hall, where distant bomb explosions could be heard from time to time during the concerts. No one in the packed hall turned a hair, but the Ulster Orchestra management took no chances with Marcus Dods and me. We were ferried from our hotel door to the Ulster Hall's artists' entrance in bulletproof limousines, and from there to the BBC Club a mere block away. At one of the receptions during that visit I met a leader of Ulster's Protestant Defence Force, a vast and charming fellow who explained, in the nicest possible way and with appropriate regret, that if I had lived in Belfast, with my Irish name and blue eyes, I would have probably been shot by his 'people'. He assumed I was a Catholic.

Sometime in the mid-1970s when the old Ibbs and Tillett-dominated agency establishment was undergoing great strain and radical changes, and famous groups such as the Amadeus Quartet were taking over their own administration, Ray Gubbay decided to discontinue promoting vocal concerts with piano. There was still a huge demand for these from music clubs, miscellaneous arts organisations and local authorities throughout Britain, so a group of us decided to take on the task of promoting ourselves as an independent co-operative. London Concert Artists now came into being. Pianist and accompanist was Jennifer Partridge; Margaret Eales and Gillian were the sopranos; Jean Temperley and Julia Meadows the mezzos; Robert Bateman and Michael Wakeham baritones; and Bruce Lochtie and I the tenors. Jenny Partridge and I shared secretarial duties. When necessary we could call on other singers to join us if particular members were unavailable.

We offered recital programmes for three or four singers with piano in as wide a range of music as possible, and we succeeded far beyond our expectations. Over the 10 years Gillian and I were associated with LCA the group did just on 800 concerts, had a return booking rate of over 90 per cent and a repertoire of 46 different programmes, some of which included all eight singers: opera, Gilbert and Sullivan, Viennese operetta, French operetta, songs from the shows, Novello and Coward evenings, Victorian evenings, lieder and song recitals. We toured from the Channel Islands to the Orkneys, for all the regional arts councils and for scores of music clubs. Sometimes we would be presenting two different programmes on the same nights at opposite ends of Britain, and when this happened pianist Peter Pettinger would become an additional member, as he did when we needed a second pianist for Brahms' *Liebeslieder Waltzes*. We also made four commercial recordings: the first (*When Song is Sweet*) on our own LCA label specifically for sale at our concerts, then *Sweet and Low* for the new ASV label in 1981 (reissued as *Salut d'Amour* in 1991) and later for RCA Victor and Bandleader labels with the Band of the Welsh Guards. We usually sold enough records at each concert to earn ourselves an extra fee.

The reasons for our success were simple: the programmes fitted the current tastes of Britain's concert-going public, our style was relaxed and informal, and our various combinations of voices and personalities worked well together. Audiences liked us. To begin with, Ray Gubbay and other agents forecast doom: performers could never manage themselves, they declared, and we would probably fall out disastrously and scratch each other's eyes out. We proved them wrong. We did argue sometimes about programme details and items, and great care was taken to ensure that no one of the same voice performed fewer concerts than his or her fellow. For the most part, and for the next decade, we remained the close friends we had been in 1975.

Sometime in the early 1970s, after a concert for the Broadstairs Festival, Ray Gubbay received a letter from Jan Dyer, indefatigable mover and shaker of the London Symphony Orchestra Supporters' Club, the BBC Promenaders and an honoured life patron of the

Northern Sinfonia, requesting a list of all my forthcoming concert dates. Vastly amused at what he termed 'the prof's fan club', he sent it on to me, I duly replied and, for the rest of my British career, Jan, her mother and her friends – loyally and with unfailing cheerfulness – came to as many of my concerts as they could manage; not simply in London, where at the Elizabeth Hall they would regularly fill the front two or three rows, but as far north as Newcastle and York Minster and as far south as the Isle of Wight. She bought the records and books and also recorded every BBC broadcast I did and sent us copies of the tapes – which in more recent years she also did with Jared Holt, Gillian's prize pupil, when he was making his way in the British music world.

More than all that, Jan adopted our family – taking Sarah to see the Royal Ballet, getting us all into the Last Night of the Proms (in the face of some hostility from promenader colleagues) and never forgetting a single birthday, Easter or Christmas. After almost every concert she would appear at my dressing-room door with a shopping bag crammed with chocolates, homemade jam and other gifts. Nor has she forgotten us yet, in spite of her own uncertain health and the vast distance between us, which she bridges with long phone calls and letters crammed with shrewd critical analyses of LSO concerts and the annual Prom seasons. When the 2010/11 earthquakes struck she was among the first of our anxious British friends to ring and reassure herself that we had survived. Whenever I've wondered whether singing for a living was worthwhile after all, I've been reassured by remembering Jan, her friends and so many others like her for whom going to concerts and listening to music means so much.

TEN

Musical Politics – and Folkestone

The suggestion that I get involved in the Solo Performers Section (SPS) of the Incorporated Society of Musicians (ISM) came on a cold and miserable afternoon in April 1976. Ian Wallace was slowly driving Marcus Dods and me around Sunderland in search of somewhere to eat before a Gilbert and Sullivan gala at the Empire Theatre. Almost all our conversation since we left London that morning had been about musical politics. Ian was the warden and chairman elect of the SPS, due to take over from Dame Evelyn Barbirolli; Marcus was a committee member (and would eventually become warden too); and both were worried about new policies being promulgated by the BBC and the Arts Council that were going to have profound impacts on our profession. They were anxious that the Society must modernise and shake off its reputation for stuffiness and suggested proposing me for an upcoming committee vacancy.

I wasn't sure. I didn't know if I had the time. They reminded me that they were busy men too. Then Ian issued an ultimatum. He wouldn't stop the car at any likely restaurant until I agreed, in spite of the fact that none of us had eaten since breakfast. Hunger won. Within the week they had proposed me for the vacancy and later in the year I took my place. For the next decade ISM matters loomed very large in my life, for almost immediately I was drafted onto the specialist sub-committees in continuous negotiations with the BBC, the heads of the music colleges, the Arts Council, the agents' committees, the Musicians' Union (MU) and Equity, the Actors' Union. If that were not enough, I also became one of the small editorial group helping Douglas Craig and Susan Alcock to produce the society's house *Journal* three times a year, and in 1983 I succeeded the superb English violinist Ralph Holmes as SPS warden and chairman. I also served on the society's executive council for four years.

The ISM had been founded in 1882 as a professional association to promote music and represent the interests of Britain's musicians. With a membership of about 5000, it was organised geographically into 54 centres throughout Britain, and generically in three specialist sections: solo performers for conductors, solo instrumentalists, chamber musicians, composers, pianists and solo singers; private teachers; and Music in Education for teachers in schools, universities and colleges. Its list of presidents was a who's who of Britain's great musical names of the past century, and in recent times had included Sir Thomas Beecham, Sir Malcolm Sargent, Gerald Moore, Sir Peter Pears, Richard Lewis, Sir Charles Groves and Sir Yehudi Menuhin. The list of SPS wardens was likewise impressive and included John Coates, Eric Greene, Isobel Baillie, Pears, Groves, Alan Civil, Evelyn Barbirolli, Denis Matthews and Reginald Jacques.

In short, the ISM was the 'Establishment' and, dangerously in our developing musical environment, traditionally antagonistic to the MU and Equity, though there was change in the air, with a young and dynamic group of administrators headed by the immensely able general secretary Susan Alcock, the celebrated contralto Pamela Bowden as administrator and Elizabeth Poulsen (another New Zealander) taking over at headquarters at Stratford Place (just off Oxford Street). By law in those times of compulsory unionism all orchestral players had to belong to the MU, and all operatic principal singers as well as choristers had to be members of Equity. Both unions (affiliated to the Labour Party) resented the ISM for the influence on government it had exerted since Beecham's dynamic time, on the issuing of work permits for foreign musicians, and on its right to set minimum solo broadcasting rates with the BBC. From now on we worked hard to break down that resentment.

Several major topics preoccupied us throughout the 10 years I was involved: the policies and decisions made by the Arts Council and its offshoot the National Federation of Music Societies, which funded choral and orchestral societies and music clubs; BBC matters; relations with the concert and opera agents; Young Musicians Awards and concerts – perhaps the ISM's most useful endeavour; and relations with the two unions and the heads of the music colleges.

Dealing with the BBC radio heads and their officials was always an exasperating experience. With economic conditions worsening almost monthly, the BBC was not only striving to reduce spending in general, but in particular spending on Radio 3 (its serious music network) and its orchestras. When they proposed in 1980 to disestablish most of the orchestras and replace them with players hired on an ad hoc basis, the MU called a strike. To the BBC's astonishment and the horror of some of our older members, we supported them.

The meeting at which we committed ourselves was tense and dramatic. All that long afternoon our delegation sat on one side of a long table in the directors' luxurious suite on the top floor of Broadcasting House, facing an angry group of heads of radio sitting opposite, shocked that we should criticise their proposed cuts and, especially, that we were at one with the unions. They agreed that regional musicians in the north, in Scotland, Wales and Ulster would 'howl', as one of them put it, but they would simply have to put up with what the BBC decided. That was a simple and immutable fact of musical life. And yes, they agreed that there would be some 'tiresome' public discussion (the major newspapers were already fulminating against their plans) but it would all be forgotten soon enough. 'These things always were.'

During the refreshment breaks, while we were served fine malt whisky and delectable savouries, I came under particular pressure from Charles Beardsall, Head of Light Music. I was by now broadcasting a lot on Radio 2 and Charles assiduously filled my glass, took me by the arm aside from the others and murmured that if I changed my vote there might be even more broadcasting coming my way. I wondered aloud if he was not, by any chance, trying to bribe me. His disavowals were unconvincing. So were the BBC arguments; so much so that before the afternoon was over the head of Radio 3 left the room white-faced with anger. He later told us he was ashamed to be sitting alongside his fellow officials and trying to defend their indefensible policies.

The ISM now joined the MU's campaign against the BBC policy. Susan Alcock joined MU general secretary John Morton in a delegation to lobby MPs, we wrote to the newspapers and some of our most distinguished and titled members, including Dame Evelyn Barbirolli, Sir Charles Groves, Sir Lennox Berkeley and Sir Geraint Evans, joined the picket lines outside Broadcasting House and achieved nationwide publicity. Ultimately the BBC backed down, but neither graciously nor with any intention of abandoning its cost-cutting and redistribution of spending. The Reithian ideals of public-service broadcasting were on long notice, and nothing in the charter (least of all serious music) was sacrosanct.

The spat with the BBC had some positive results for our relationship with the MU in particular; and the BBC executives' annual all-day festive jaunt on the Thames for the regular negotiating teams from MU, Equity and ISM also drew us personally closer together, because several of those involved were friends. John Morton's right-hand man and successor, Dennis Scard, was principal horn in Ray Gubbay's London Concert Orchestra; Equity's singer rep on their council was John Noble, a baritone colleague and friend with whom I did a lot of work; and the respective officials got on excellently. In October 1980 a formal ISM/MU agreement was signed by Dame Evelyn and Ian Wallace, giving us some additional negotiating right with ITV companies and clarifying the status of chamber music players, so laying to rest some very ancient and bitter grievances.

It had been easier to deal with the MU leading up to the agreement than with some of our older members. The special SPS meeting at which the officials and I explained the reasons for and the details of the agreement was rowdy and ill-tempered. We carried the day but I doubt if some elderly Establishment figures ever forgave either our general secretary or me.

Reaching understanding with the unions during this period of steadily worsening economic recession was, in retrospect, easier than dealing with the new ambitions of either the agents or the heads of music colleges. The days when the ladies of Ibbs and Tillett had been all powerful in British music were long gone. There were now over 70 competing agents, and some of this new and younger generation were determined to brush aside the old limits on foreign performers and, especially, to bring even more American singers into Britain's opera companies: their fees were bigger and there were possibly reciprocal benefits for a very small number of British singers and instrumentalists in America. A few were also dismissive of British artists and the British music scene in general. It was, they considered, not lucrative enough for them. For our part, we wanted a code of practice that would give artists protection against some blatantly manipulative and unethical agents.

The British Association of Concert Agents (BACA) represented only 27 of the country's agents but included some of the most important. Our meetings with their committee were extremely lively and the usual chairmen – either Sir Charles Groves or BACA's president, my old friend Norman McCann – had their work cut out. I still got on very well with Norman, but less well with others, such as the influential Jasper Parrott, who succeeded him as president and who challenged the ISM's very right to exist as a negotiator with BBC and Department of Employment. He and I clashed repeatedly and, on our respective organisations' behalf, wrote letters to *The Times* attacking one another's opinions. The tone of our exchanges during my year as warden was summed up in the minutes of one of our 1984 meetings: 'The discussion [on foreign artists] which had already become heated, became more so ... with very strong feelings being expressed by Jasper Parrott and by the SPS warden.' I think it was later that afternoon that Jasper, in exasperation, rang Gubbay to ask why his friend Bohan, a New Zealander after all, was acting as the champion of British singers.

I don't know what the situation is now, nearly 30 years after these tense but always entertaining events, but when my term on the executive ended in mid-1987 and I left Britain for good in October that year the ISM's negotiating powers remained undiminished. Although besieged, we had held out successfully.

In stark contrast to the disputes with the agents, our disagreements with the heads of music colleges had a certain flavour of a family dispute, for they were all ISM members. Some, notably the Royal Northern College and the Royal Scottish Academy, were now expanding their activities in such a way that they were affecting future employment inside the wider profession. Some were, in effect, becoming agents for their senior students, offering oratorio soloists and chamber musicians to the choral societies and music clubs at heavily discounted rates, and even free orchestral concerts to local authority entertainment officers. By the 1980s, for example, several of the major northern choirs had written apologetically to me and many of my colleagues that they would no longer be booking us for their annual *Messiah,* Verdi *Requiem* or other major works, because they could employ four senior students from Manchester for a total fee that was less than our individual concert fees. As we tried to explain to the college principals, all that was fine for their senior students but potentially disastrous to the wider profession, and for those same students when they left the colleges and were succeeded by the next wave of senior students.

Our arguments fell on several very deaf ears. Meredith Davies from Guildhall and John McCabe from the London College of Music were, as active performers, sympathetic; others, including my erstwhile English Opera Group colleague Philip Ledger, were downright hostile and implacable. We lost that war and the results have been exactly as we warned they would be. The British music profession, always difficult and always by its nature financially precarious and intensely competitive, changed forever within the decade.

On the whole I enjoyed my years immersed in musical politics, and during them I worked with congenial and first-rate colleagues. In addition, through my connection with Ian Wallace and Susan Alcock I became the ISM's historian. Sometime in late 1980, Ian, newly installed as president in succession to Sir David Willcocks, rang me, sounding suspiciously and ominously conspiratorial. As I already knew, he explained with many characteristically amusing but artful digressions, the society's centenary was looming and was to be lavishly celebrated in October 1982. Apart from concerts and so forth there was to be a centennial history. Sir David had commissioned a friend who had duly produced a manuscript, but the executive was not happy about it so wondered whether I might help them 'knock it into shape'. Of course there would be a fee. Yes, I'd be interested I replied cautiously, but there wouldn't be too much work involved, would there? Good heavens no, laughed Ian. Would I be at home for the next hour or two? I would be. Wonderful! He'd bring the manuscript over to Wimbledon immediately (he lived in Highgate). He laughed again and rang off abruptly – which was not his habit. His phone calls invariably lasted at least an hour.

Gillian was immediately suspicious. She hoped the task would not be arduous but feared it was likely to be. How on earth would I find the time? I brushed her fears aside. Ian had mentioned a fee, after all. Then he arrived, carrying a vast mass of manuscript. Uncharacteristically, he did not linger for more chat or even a sherry, gin or Scotch. For the first and only time in all our long friendship he left his beloved Jaguar's engine running at our gate, and, having thrust the bulging folders into my arms, actually ran back down our front path. He was clearly overjoyed to have got rid of the thing (and later cheerfully admitted it).

The first cursory glance at the manuscript confirmed my growing concern and Gillian's worst fears. It was a mess. I would have to start the entire project from scratch – both research and actual writing.

It was a massive task and I had a strict deadline – less than six months, I think – but the fee *was* a good one. I found the time (amazing how one invariably does), I enjoyed the challenge and I was marvellously well supported and helped by Susan and the society's head office staff. *The ISM: The first hundred years* came out on time.

Now I cast about, but in a necessarily desultory kind of way, for some new and purely historical project in which to involve myself, but came up with little that seemed viable. I was surprised and pleased when I discovered that the new *Oxford History of New Zealand*, edited by Bill Oliver, not only listed my Master's thesis, *The 1879 General Election in Canterbury*, in the bibliography, but even quoted from it. The old research bug was biting again and a renewed interest in New Zealand history was stirring, but my time was taken up with earning a living in hard economic times. The specialist stamp-dealing business Ray Gubbay and I had operated for a few years had done well, but had eventually become just another of the hundreds of British businesses that fell victim to the recession. From late 1982 Gillian and I were hard at work (between my continuing concerts) in a new venture – establishing a singing teaching practice in Folkestone on the Kent coast near Dover, in Victorian and Edwardian times a fashionable watering place for the aristocracy and such literary lions as Dickens, Thackeray and H. G. Wells.

We moved there (we had been considering it for years anyway) not only to keep a sharp and constant eye on her father who was all too obviously failing fast, but to take advantage of the inflationary surge in London house prices and shed ourselves of our mortgage. We had spent lavishly on the Queen's Road house but we did very well from its sale; and our newly acquired Folkestone house, on the corner of Bournemouth Road overlooking Radnor Park, was a handsome delight and, thanks to Gillian's astute negotiation with its previous owners and estate agents, a bargain.

Gillian was a Folkestone girl, though born in Coventry, for her father, Harold Alfred Neason, had become Folkestone's Borough Treasurer a year or so before World War Two and remained so until the late 1960s. During the war Folkestone was designated a front-line area. It was regularly bombed, just as in World War One, and shelled every afternoon by the German long-range guns dug in along the French coast 30 kilometres away. Harold administered its affairs under the Home Office's overall command. In the hope that they would escape bombing and shelling, he sent Gillian, her mother and Gillian's older sister Pam successively to Ashfield (from where they watched overhead dogfights during the Battle of Britain), the New Forest (just before Southampton was flattened) and finally to Stratford on Avon (in time for the devastating raid on nearby Coventry). Back in Folkestone, Harold's office was bombed and one of his best stories was how he arrived there after the raid to find men digging for his body.

Harold was an amusing and highly accomplished man who wrote music criticisms for the local newspaper, was a nationally recognised authority on the arcane art of managing municipal finances, on which he had written a textbook, and had instigated and encouraged (with ratepayers' funds) the London Philharmonic Orchestra's regular concerts in Folkestone's Leas Cliff Hall. He had survived quite severe wounding in World War One (about which he told very entertaining stories), and was the most generous of hosts, an indulgent grandfather, and fond of an argument. Every summer we (and our cat Paws) would move down to spend the long school holidays with him in his large comfortable house and sunny sheltered garden at 124 Cheriton Road, from which Gillian and I would emerge to do our summer concert rounds.

They were great summers: Folkestone's cricket ground was a mere couple of blocks away and there was a festival cricket week every August when Kent hosted two county games and a Sunday limited-overs match. Harold would sit in state in the mayor's tent – though like most local government officials of his autocratic generation he was jocularly contemptuous of mayors and elected councillors – and Sebastian and I (Sarah, too, eventually) would seek better vantage points, though Sebastian was always invited into the mayor's tent for afternoon tea and to meet the players. We played cricket for hours on Harold's front lawn, putting his windows and the neighbour's fences at risk.

We were also able to enjoy long rambles in the countryside and up to Caesar's Camp, along the edge of the Downs to the Martello Tower on the headland, where a Roman naval commander's villa had once stood above the ancient port, and down into The Warren, a wild tumble of chalk and bracken where one had to keep an eye out in hot weather for vipers. Harold never ventured inland, could never understand our enthusiasm for doing so, and could be tetchy if we didn't return in time to make him afternoon tea. His long and vigorous daily walks were always along the sea front. In fact he was agoraphobic, the result of having been caught by German machine-guns on a long open slope and trapped there for a day. There were scarred furrows across his back and he often had nightmares, when he would rear up with a shout and raise his hands as though to ward off the bullets.

It was always difficult to arrange family holidays further afield because, for 14 years, I didn't have a gap longer than 10 days between concerts, though we did manage to organise a very happy interlude at Ventnor on the Isle of Wight to coincide with our regular summer concerts there; and later, though Sebastian was by now at Oxford, Gillian, Sarah and I had a wonderful time based at Oban, exploring the spectacular surrounding countryside with its remarkable mountain vistas and sea- and skyscapes, and crossing to Mull to visit Duart Castle on its commanding promontory, the spiritual home of Clan McLean.

ELEVEN

Connections with New Zealand and the Expatriate's Return

Apart from regular correspondence with the family, I had only spasmodic contact with New Zealand during my first decade in Britain, but, largely through lobbying by Vernon Griffiths, I believe, I was asked to sing at the opening of the new Christchurch Town Hall in 1972. Unfortunately, I was already heavily booked up, and the concert was to be in September – a time of the year when I could not afford to be so far from Britain. Instead, I returned to Christchurch in July/August 1973, when I sang Honneger's *King David* with the NZBC Symphony Orchestra and the Royal Christchurch Musical Society, and recorded two radio recitals with Maurice Till.

My major reason for this visit was to see the family again and, especially, to help celebrate the 76th birthday of Father and his twin, Aunt Margaret Younger. It was marvellous to have so many enjoyable reunions with so many friends, but New Zealand itself had not changed enough to attract me to return, even if I had been able to: my family life and my entire career were based in London.

At the end of the *King David* performance Vanco Cavdarski, then conducting the Christchurch Civic Orchestra, and others involved with the old New Zealand Opera Company, came to my dressing room and asked me to stay on to sing Rodolfo in a season of *La Bohème*, with which they were hoping to revive the company. I had successfully sung eight performances of Rodolfo in a festival season not long before and I would certainly have accepted under different circumstances, but apart from being anxious to return home I was heavily booked until Christmas: 40 concerts in all, including the Norwich Triennial Festival with the RPO and 13 concerts at the Queen Elizabeth Hall. Being in New Zealand, even in the English summer, had already cost me a series of 20 Sunday concerts at Bournemouth. I explained all this but they seemed slightly offended that I wasn't enough of a Kiwi patriot to stay on immediately and help them. I assured them that I would happily return for operatic engagements provided that they gave me plenty of notice, and I gave them my agent's address. Neither she nor I ever heard from the New Zealand Opera Company or its successors again.

One especially hot afternoon sometime in the early 1970s, during a break from Kent Opera's rehearsals near Westminster, I went into New Zealand House, mainly to get out of the sun. I ran straight into Len Hewland, whom I had not seen for 10 years, but he didn't even greet me; instead he reeled off a list of deaths and disasters: my Div. C girlfriend Judy Passmore and her husband had died in a car crash in Scotland, he began without preamble, and Tubby Moore had had a sudden fatal heart attack when he was 27. On and on he went until I managed to mutter that I had to get back to rehearsals and fled into London's burning noonday sun again, comprehensively shocked and rather depressed.

Nor did a chance meeting with Alan Pearson in Wimbledon High Street a few years later cheer me up as he recounted his experiences during the 'punch a Pom a day' time in New Zealand and fulminated – as only Alan could – at very great length.

And my hitherto cordial relations with the Welsh and Wales, where I sang several times every year, suffered a temporary but annoying setback after the All Blacks–Wales game of 1978 when Andy Haden suffered his brainstorm and leapt through the lineout, after which Brian McKechnie kicked the winning penalty. It was for another infringement but that didn't matter to the Welsh. Andy Haden in particular and New Zealanders in general became objects of Welsh loathing.

I had watched the game in my Bristol hotel room, and when I got to the Colston Hall for the evening's concert with the Bristol Choral Society I was confronted by my distraught Welsh chorus friends who demanded to know what I had thought of the game. I replied cheerfully that I had enjoyed it immensely. They howled with rage and one actually had tears in his eyes as he turned his back on me. He didn't speak to me again for three years. Even when I went to Bridgend for *Judas Maccabeus* a few months later, my reception from the conductor, his committee and the chairman of the Welsh Arts Council was frosty in the extreme: all because of Andy Haden.

My only previous dispute with the Welsh (and a very brief one) had been back in the 1960s when some Welsh colleagues informed me that there was a move being made by Geraint Evans and others to get the Welsh Labour MPs to sponsor a bill to prevent Australian, Canadian, South African and New Zealand singers working in Britain and taking Welsh singers' jobs. I pointed out that such a bill would contravene the new immigration laws. My colleagues were thunderstruck. They had thought those laws applied only to Indians, Pakistanis, West Indians and Africans. They gave up their campaign.

Mercifully, other New Zealand sportsmen did not generate such fury as had Andy Haden, and one of the greatest pleasures of every cricket season was to follow the fortunes of Glen Turner at Worcester as he not only tamed every other county attack, but often destroyed them as he marched on towards his century of centuries. To me he wasn't simply our greatest batsman since Bert Sutcliffe, but the ultimate professional, and I can't offer higher praise than that for anyone, whether singer or sportsman. Richard Hadlee's remarkable deeds at Notts added greatly to my enjoyment of English summers too.

Brick Lynch's arrival in London as our deputy high commissioner was another cheerful lift to the spirits, and from now on we were invited to the regular receptions at New Zealand House, where I met up again with a large number of friends, including Don Walker and Derek Round. I also gradually began to catch up on much that had been happening back home that I had not heard about from the family's letters.

It was always a tremendous pleasure to be visited by New Zealand friends on their OE excursions. These included at various times the Murtaghs, Leggats and Mullins, and Clifton Cook too. He emerged from a taxi at our gate clutching a colossal bunch of flowers and a bottle of wine, much to the delight of Sarah and Sebastian watching from a window, with seven-year-old Sarah exclaiming that he looked 'a dear little man'. But he was a very unhappy little man. He had been terrified during his flight in case the plane fell down, he was desperately homesick for his Fendalton home and furniture, and he was cutting short his holiday and returning to their comforts as soon as possible; though he still hoped to see his other former pupils, Anson Austin at Glyndebourne, Richard Greager at Scottish Opera and Christopher Doig, who was studying in Vienna. He was profusely apologetic that he wouldn't be remaining long enough to see me at the BBC Proms in the Albert Hall.

One of the best New Zealand House receptions was for the first New Zealand Youth Choir. Bryan Drake and I were slightly surprised to hear this fine choir singing the national anthem in Maori, and perhaps for the first time started to appreciate what monumental changes were happening back home. But the greatest surprise and delight was to find such friends as John Ritchie and Bill Hawkey accompanying the youth choir, and bound for the 1982 International Society of Music in Education conference in Bristol, where by a pleasant coincidence I was already booked to sing the tenor solos in Kodály's *Psalmus Hungaricus* with a combined international youth choir (including the New Zealanders) and one of the best county youth orchestras.

That concert turned into a great reunion occasion, during which John, Bill, Peter Godfrey and several others suggested that maybe it was time I sang back home again and that I should resume contact with the New Zealand Symphony Orchestra.

So I did, and though its chief executive, Peter Nisbet, wrote gloomily that New Zealand opera was 'in a murky state', having suffered financial disaster with seasons of Kurt Weill and Britten (hardly surprising given both composers' indifferent box-office appeal at the time), he offered me the choice of two concert tours during 1985: a series with Sir David Willcocks for the Bach–Handel Tercentenary in July/August, or a shorter tour with the American Robert Shaw in October. There was really only one option for me, much as I would have liked and preferred to work with the celebrated Robert Shaw: from September to Christmas and from March to May were still, as in the past, my peak earning periods and I could not afford to be out of Britain then. So, although Sir David and I had not had a harmonious relationship over ISM matters, I accepted the mid-year tour of seven performances of the Bach Mass in B Minor and Dvorak's *Requiem*.

John Ritchie also wrote encouragingly, though with a warning that New Zealand's music had its problems: 'a lack of vitality, and certainly a great lack of financial support for music in particular, and the arts in general. The outlook is depressing.' He at least had the cheering news that Maurice Till was back at Canterbury University with the violinist Carl Pini and the German cellist Walter Godde. Maurice himself wrote enthusiastically to arrange a recital for us at the James Hay Theatre of Schubert's song-cycle *Die Schöne Müllerin* and, joined by Walter Goode, Schubert's 'Auf dem Strom'; and David Childs booked me for his Harmonic Society's *Judas Maccabeus* – also to be conducted by Willcocks.

The major attraction of the tour was the prospect of seeing Father and the family again, and introducing them in person and at long last to Gillian and Sarah, who were accompanying me. Des had died of cancer in 1982, and although badly affected by his death, Father had been battling along quite well, even after May, my stepmother, suffered a massive stroke and had to go into Nazareth House. Then, a fortnight before we flew out for New Zealand, he died on 14 June, two months short of his 89th birthday. So our family reunions in

Auckland and Christchurch were bittersweet, but heart-warming.

The reunions with friends were heart-warming too – especially the old Shirley Boys' High staff welcome home party at Tony and Margaret Cooper's two days after we arrived, for which Mike Murtagh came down from Wellington (where he was now a power in the Qualifications Authority).

The harsh reality, however, was that despite jet-lag and an ominously persistent and worsening sinus infection that necessitated a course of antibiotics, I had to knuckle down to work with Maurice for the two radio recitals, which we recorded for the Concert Programme on 5 July, and for our James Hay recital on 3 July, and to rehearse with Willcocks for the Harmonic concert on 6 July. The schedule was far too tight and that was my own fault for having tried to pack in too much. It was a relief to find Willcocks genuinely friendly and we got on remarkably well for the entire tour, though he did gently remind me that over the last few years my policies and what he termed my 'radical opinions' had not won me friends among the British musical establishment. I was already aware of that. It was of greater immediate significance that we got on so well musically and personally.

We needed to: we rehearsed Dvorak's *Requiem* and Bach's Mass in B Minor solidly for five days at Symphony House and the Michael Fowler Centre in Wellington, and performed the Dvorak on the 13th, the Bach in Hamilton on the 17th, Rotorua on the 18th, Tauranga on the 19th, in Auckland's St Patrick's Cathedral on the 21st, then back south for Lower Hutt on the 26th, Palmerston North the next evening (in a wild storm), and finally at the Michael Fowler Centre in Wellington again on the 28th. It was rather a relief to fly out of Auckland on 2 August bound for Singapore and a brief reunion with Sebastian, who was in Bangkok on his first posting for the British Foreign Office.

While I had been travelling and singing almost continuously and feeling under the weather throughout the month, Gillian and Sarah had enjoyed themselves greatly. In Christchurch the family and Maurice and Leila Till had showered them with hospitality. In

Wellington the Zwartzes had welcomed us, and so had longstanding family friends Margaret Austin (then a rising Labour MP) and her daughter Faith (a viola player with the NZSO), and we had stayed with the Lynches, who hosted a delightful reunion evening with the Murtaghs and Hensleys. In Auckland Trish and Don and their family had again looked after Gillian and Sarah solicitously while I completed the last stages of the tour.

It had been marvellous to meet so many friends again and I found New Zealand changed out of recognition in so many ways – and entirely for the better. The *Rainbow Warrior* disaster, tragic though it was, did not, perhaps, shock us nearly so much as it did New Zealanders in general. We had, after all, endured the continuing IRA threats and disruptions to London's life for years, and Gillian and I had come face to face with their consequences in Ulster itself. In comparison, New Zealand was still an unthreatening haven of tranquillity.

I had reservations about my own performances, however. I certainly have never sung as well in New Zealand as I had in my vocal prime during the 1970s in Britain: at no time on this tour was I in my best vocal form. I became aware of resentment from some local singers that I was there at all, and one was particularly blunt. He told me several times that he couldn't understand why I and baritone Barry Mora, a splendid singer, the most amiable of colleagues, currently resident in Frankfurt and with whom I toured in the Bach, had been booked when there were good resident baritones and tenors who had sung our roles. One day when Barry and I were discussing how nerve-wracking it was to be singing in one's home town after so many years away, he remarked that there was really no need for us to be nervous because no one here had heard of us anyway.

I was also disappointed with some of the choral singing. It did not seem that choral standards generally had risen markedly since 1962, nor the standards of what passed for music criticism. But there was no such equivocation about the New Zealand Symphony Orchestra. It was superb. Not long before I had left for this tour Sir Charles Groves had assured me the symphony was world class, but as we were sharing a few drinks at the Savage Club in London at the time I didn't know how much of what he said was down to the whisky or his sympathetic knowledge that I was a New Zealander. Now I knew how right he had been. I was not entirely sure about its management, however.

Our New Zealand trip had caused us to reconsider our future. Life in Folkestone was as pleasant as ever, and our joint singing teaching practice was flourishing with pupils coming to us from all over Kent. Having retired from performing, Gillian was also developing an additionally busy schedule as a teacher of drama.

Pamela Bowden had often remarked on how much enjoyment I seemed to get from singing; but one day, she warned, I would wake up with a dark cloud hovering somewhere in my mind and wish that I didn't have to get up and sing again. I had always laughed at the idea, but now it happened for the first time – and went on happening far too often. And I was restless to get down to some writing again. In short, as I celebrated my 50th birthday I was, Gillian decided with some amusement, entering the male menopause.

I had also grown tired, at last, of the incessant travel, so much of it on British Rail, an organisation that more than ever seemed intent on discouraging its patrons from using its increasingly unreliable services. At least my years spent travelling on its frequently delayed and interrupted trains had enabled me to get through an immense amount of reading: on any and every subject that took my fancy. This was often to the amusement of colleagues, who assumed that tenors weren't capable of managing more than lavishly illustrated girlie magazines. Adelina Patti's ancient jibe that tenors were congenitally stupid because the ringing of their high notes in their heads gave them brain damage was still a given for many other musicians. It was a slander, though an amusing one, and I have raised a lot of laughs over the years by repeating it. It's an interesting fact, though, that most of the academically qualified and intellectually inclined singers I've known have been tenors.

Gillian and Sarah now suggested that we might well make a

complete break and move to New Zealand. They had liked what they saw of the country and they had very much liked our wider family and all my friends. Also, prices for large Folkestone houses were rising steadily to near London levels, and they had taken note of the comparatively low housing prices in New Zealand. If we sold we would have, as Gillian put it, lots of 'spare change', and without my hectic round of British obligations I would have time to concentrate more on writing, and maybe pick up whatever singing work came up – if I still wanted to do it. We could also set up another singing teaching practice. Sarah would be finishing at Folkestone Girls' Grammar in mid-1987, and Sebastian was well set on his Foreign Office career. Making a move towards the end of 1987 would allow me to work out all the engagements I had already booked.

She convinced me, so I ended my own involvement with London Concert Artists and rang the agents to instruct them not to book me for anything after 1987. Ray Gubbay assured me that I wouldn't ever leave, and I don't think the others believed me either until I started turning down work for 1988, including the usual *Messiah*s and a proposed European tour of a new opera. I also informed my New Zealand contacts, some of whom were becoming very despondent about New Zealand affairs in general and music in particular. Ever the optimist, I took little notice of their gloom. And among the many letters I now sent off was one to the Ray Richards Literary Agency in Auckland, outlining some ideas for future novels. Ray's answers were encouraging. This was the beginning of another friendship and a very productive one, though he had grave doubts about one of my proposals – a novel about expatriate New Zealanders in Britain. He did not think New Zealand readers would be interested in expatriates.

Our last few months in Britain passed in a whirl of activity as, variously helped and hindered by estate agents, we steered our way through the tortuous process that accompanies all British property transactions and we wound up our affairs. I sang my last oratorio in England (Bach's Mass in B Minor for the Upminster Bach Choir), gave my last recital (in Folkestone) and, fittingly perhaps, the last engagement of my British career was in Bath, my favourite English town, where I sang the elderly villain Massimo in a festival production of Handel's *Ezio*.

Typically, completion of our house sale (exchange of contracts) was scheduled for the very day we were to depart. There were dramas, too, the day before that when our removal firm decided that moving the Egyptian embassy's London home took precedence over our furniture packing and despatching, though they eventually agreed to send a B team – very much a B or even a D team as it turned out. It wasn't their fault that they got fog-bound, but losing their way for an hour or two on the motorway was. So was bringing a container that was too small and leaving behind various household effects and some furniture, and allowing some of our best pieces of furniture to get wet in a rainstorm, though we didn't realise the damage that caused until everything was unpacked months later in Wellington.

Our last night in Folkestone was one of increasingly torrential rain and wild wind, though when we set off for Gatwick Airport next morning the weather seemed pleasant enough. In high spirits we boarded our flight to Los Angeles, where we spent a pleasant day or two at the art galleries, unaware as yet of the chaos we were leaving behind and the turmoil into which we were headed.

Our ever-cheerful Folkestone solicitor had assured us that exchange of contracts would go ahead as planned and it did, I discovered when I eventually rang him. That was a relief, but otherwise his news was grim: we had left Folkestone not a day too soon. The next day southeast England was torn apart by the worst series of storms to strike in living memory, and his conversation was mainly about the loss of his own roof and the widespread devastation of properties and fallen trees. He promised to forward the money from the house sale as speedily as he and the bank could manage, but we knew that at the rate he and that particular bank operated we could not expect it soon.

We were in Auckland now, staying with Trish and Don before going down to Wellington where we planned to settle – and then New Zealand was plunged into its own series of storms: economic ones. The sharemarket had crashed and so had the New Zealand dollar. While Don watched his large and numerous shareholdings plummet in value, we watched (with some satisfaction, I confess shamefacedly) the value of our sterling funds climb. By the time our solicitor and one of Britain's most notoriously laggardly banks did finally remit all our money we had made a handsome profit. With the high interest rates being offered by banks and building societies we now could enjoy a comfortable income, for the present anyway. For the first time we had no need to search for work.

That was just as well. The movers and shakers of New Zealand music did not welcome me back with open arms and offers of work. They were, in fact, cool, apart from Bill Southgate, Jeremy Commons and David Childs of the Christchurch Harmonic Society. The management of Radio New Zealand's Concert Programme was coy; I would be required to audition if I wanted radio recitals. That, after all the broadcasting I had done during the past 30 years in Britain, Australia and back home here was not something I was prepared to do. Nor were they interested in the ideas I offered for radio talks. My great friend Pete Zwartz, in spite of his abilities, had been effectively cold-shouldered by now too except by the brass band world. I was even warned that it would not do me any good to be seen to be associated with him. I reacted angrily to that, and the Zwartz household remained another home away from home just as it always had been.

Pete had high musical standards, and his major problem for Wellington's musical elite was his devastating honesty and his complete inability to disguise his true feelings and opinions about the quality of performances. He bruised far too many sensitive egos.

Initially, the new Canterbury Opera and the secretary of Dunedin Opera did seem likely to offer work, especially when Bill Southgate, grown older as we all had but not a jot less amusing and friendly, assured me that I'd be ideal to sing Eisenstein in the *Fledermaus* he was to conduct with Canterbury and Dunedin. It would have been the perfect role for my return, but neither company thought so. Bill was snubbed and the letter I received from Dunedin was little short of insulting; yet Canterbury Opera's rejection hurt far more. If I had returned purely to continue my singing career I would have gone back to England almost immediately and never set foot in New Zealand again. Although when I did eventually see the Canterbury production from my old bench seat in my beloved Theatre Royal's gallery I was relieved that I wasn't in it.

History and the historians came to the rescue. A day or two after we moved into our rented Karori house, I read a newspaper article about Bill Oliver and his projected *Dictionary of New Zealand Biography*. I sent him a note. First thing next morning he rang and suggested I come in for coffee. I did, and we got roughly up to date with our respective doings in the previous 25 years and reminisced about old Canterbury days, Neville (inevitably) and other old acquaintances. I met Claudia Orange and the rest of the dictionary's staff too, and Bill suggested that if I didn't have anything better to do I might care to produce an essay on Edward Stafford for his first volume, due out in 1990. There wouldn't be any fee and the deadline (May) was daunting, he admitted, but no one had wanted to write it. I was astonished. Didn't Keith Sinclair want to write about the most interesting and important man in New Zealand's early politics? No, Keith thought Stafford was too boring. Since I had left the country few younger historians had been interested in 19th-century political history; they were preoccupied with far more modish things such as social history, feminist and Maori perspectives. I jumped at the idea, and had no sooner done so than Keith himself appeared and the reminiscences began all over again.

I started work that same afternoon and for the next four months worked night and day, reading everything on New Zealand's 19th century that had been published since my departure in 1962, going through the Stafford papers and various other colonial collections in the Turnbull Library, and becoming dismayed at the lack of interest in the period's politics and politicians. How could one fully understand modern New Zealand if one was almost totally ignorant about the actual events, personalities and social realities of our colonial years, and make assumptions about them purely on old myths? It was difficult enough to understand modern New Zealand and its topsy-turvy politics.

The reception my Stafford essay received from Bill, Claudia and Keith – who uncharacteristically and freely admitted now that he had 'got Stafford wrong' – decided me to embark on the first full-length biography of that remarkable man, who had been at the centre of New Zealand affairs from his youthful arrival in Nelson in 1843 to his departure for London society and its business world in 1878. My resolve was strengthened when, coincidentally on the same day, Bill, Claudia and Keith each separately suggested that the full biography was the next logical step. So I drafted a book proposal for Ray Richards; he set out to find a publisher while I settled back into my research.

The Stafford project occupied me for the next seven years and was greatly assisted by the Ministry of Internal Affairs awarding me a handsome sum from Michael Bassett's newly established History Awards scheme in 1990. My historian friends and of course my initially bemused family, gave me every encouragement too, though I repeatedly had to explain who Stafford was to everyone who asked me what I was working on. No one had heard of him, and that made me even more determined to bring him back to life and into his rightful historical place. He had, in effect, been written out of New Zealand's history and that was intolerable. How could we – and least of all our historians – continue to ignore the most influential and visionary politician before Richard Seddon's emergence in the 1890s, the fourth longest-serving premier and our youngest so far? At present many in the media were giving the latter honour to David Lange, currently the hero of everyone opposed to nuclear ships and American foreign policy, and world famous in New Zealand for his eloquence in an Oxford Union debate.

I never warmed to Lange, even when some years later he delivered a favourable though oddly muddled radio review of my Stafford biography, and I had not been impressed by my first sight of him a few years before on a British TV programme about Lord Soper. His

Oxford Union heroics and famous quip about nuclear breath (not original but an Australian joke given to him by Gerald Hensley) had bypassed me completely; perhaps because I was not a *Guardian* reader.

Along with cricket and rugby, British politics had been my favourite spectator sport. Now New Zealand politics in all its sometimes quite frightening absurdity joined them. I sometimes felt like a visiting Martian as I watched the Labour government metamorphose into an economically right-wing Thatcherite oligarchy while its traditional base floundered and split. I was also bemused by New Zealanders' almost universal denigration of Margaret Thatcher; then I realised that most of New Zealanders' perceptions about British politics were influenced by this country's media's reliance on the *Guardian* or, as second best, the *Independent*. In short, there was little balance – just as there had been little balance in New Zealand's historiography since William Pember Reeves.

I certainly had a lot of catching up to do in recent New Zealand history. I had a vivid experience of the emotions generated during the Muldoon years when I attended an all-day seminar at Victoria University's Stout Centre on biographies of New Zealand prime ministers, a few months before the Stafford biography came out in 1994. The seminar room was packed and the atmosphere was friendly and relaxed as I spoke about Stafford and Michael Bassett discoursed on Gordon Coates. Then, after an excellent lunch, Barry Gustafson took to the lectern to discuss progress on his Muldoon biography. Uproar ensued. Tempers flared among some former politicians and academics and, during a lull, Bill Oliver asked me if I might contemplate writing on modern politics too. I raised the easiest of laughs by vowing to stay in the 19th century (I was already thinking about a biography of James Edward FitzGerald) and concern myself only with the dead.

Ray Richards had not had an easy time finding a publisher for Stafford. The major New Zealand publishers of history were not interested: Stafford didn't seem relevant and they didn't think the time right for readers to be interested in him or his period, it seemed.

Then at last a triumphant Ray rang from Christchurch airport: he had found my publisher, not only for Stafford but also for the historical mystery novel I had written partly to amuse myself (and Gillian) while I worked on Stafford. Quentin Wilson of Hazard Press was the man, and Ray forecast great things for him and his rapidly expanding publishing house. That was a huge relief, and in Quentin – full of ideas and an even more compulsive workaholic than I was – I found a kindred spirit and friend who shared my own literary tastes and interests. Quentin's Hazard Press published seven of the 12 books I wrote during the next 25 years.

Our Wellington friends, old and new, had made us very welcome. Jan and Brick Lynch had shared their Christmas dinner with us, Mike Murtagh and I watched test cricket at the Basin Reserve (and far less happily we bade farewell to Tony Cooper before he died in Wellington Hospital), and there was a busy social life with the Zwartz family and other musical friends such as Margaret Nielsen and John Mansfield Thomson. And every time I walked along Lambton Quay to the Turnbull Library I seemed to run into more and more people I had known. There were good concerts aplenty too, especially during the International Festival.

Our cat Paws, at the centre of our family life for 12 years, finally arrived in his reinforced box on a flight from London via Los Angeles, predictably and typically furious. His affronted howls reverberated through the airport freight terminal, but though he was jet-lagged and apt to stagger for a day or two as he rushed about acquainting himself with his new home, he settled in well and became as much master of our little bit of Karori hillside as he had previously dominated our parts of Wimbledon and Folkestone. We took Sarah down to Christchurch to enrol at Canterbury University and settle into the University Halls, and back in Karori we began to develop another singing teaching practice. We liked Karori, in spite of the weather extremes and the gales from Makara.

Then in March our landlord, a friendly young man who worked at the Treasury, appeared unexpectedly at our door and Gillian read the ominous signs at once: in spite of our lease arrangement he needed the house back. His marriage had collapsed, his girlfriend was pregnant, and he had lost all his savings in the Goldcorp disaster; he was, in brief, quietly and apologetically distraught. So we released him from part of his misery and decided to move down to Christchurch after all, where, as we now knew, property prices were lower than Wellington's and where Sarah and the wider family were anyway.

TWELVE

Back Home in Christchurch

Settling back in Christchurch was certainly no hardship. In many ways it was as though I hadn't ever left, though the city itself had expanded far and wide and there were hundreds of restaurants – whereas in 1962 George Malando's had really been the only one. Every time we went into the city centre and library I encountered old acquaintances from school or university, and personalities long remembered like John and Connie Summers, the old Marxist economist Wolfgang Rosenberg, waving a greeting as he slowly cycled past on the same bike that had seemed ancient in 1954, and John Garrett, who had aged in appearance so much more obviously yet who retained all his charm and friendliness. So had Jim Gardner, John Ritchie and Maurice Till. As always, there were the Shirley Boys' High staffers of 1960–62, the Leggats, Mullins, Gordon Ogilvie, as well as returned expatriates like Elric Hooper, for many years all-powerful ruler of the dynamic Court Theatre and with whom Gillian had so many British theatrical friends in common.

We rented a house in Avonhead, fortuitously over the road from John and Jean Goodliffe, who had been among that remarkable group of young English academics who had so revitalised Canterbury

University in the 1960s, and through whom we were drawn into another very congenial community. When Sebastian arrived on holiday he was so delighted with his first experience of Christchurch, and especially with the golf courses, the Southern Alps and the southern lakes, that for a mad few days he even considered leaving the Foreign Office and settling here. We quickly dissuaded him; his career as a Chinese and South-east Asian specialist was going far too well for him to abandon it for golf and walking the Routeburn and Milford tracks. In return he urged us to take our desultory house-hunting more seriously, and so did the estate agent Barbara Geddes. During dinner with Elric and her one evening we lamented our lack of success in finding what we wanted and she took us over. For weeks she showed us houses all over Christchurch, though we must have driven her to distraction by spurning the lot. Then, just after we decided to take a break from house hunting, she rang on a Friday, announced that she had found our house and insisted on taking us to see it at once.

It was 5 Vincent Place, Opawa, a handsome 1882 villa with a large garden and two doors from St Mark's Church. The entire area to its north and east was being demolished or removed to make way for the Brougham Street motorway extension but we didn't mind about that. Queen's Road Wimbledon carried more traffic every day than any Christchurch motorway and that had never bothered us, or the foxes that used to run along the footpaths and through the front gardens every afternoon, as heedless of buses and cars as we were. We were hooked on this house even before we opened the front door and stepped onto its polished kauri floors. It was a bargain at the price being asked and we had the ready cash. Half an hour later everything was decided, and to our amazement after our English experiences of buying and selling houses when nothing was achieved in under six months, all was sealed and settled by the following Tuesday. When we moved in we acquired another cat from departing neighbours, or rather, black and domineering Ulli acquired us and our house and garden. He filled the void left by the loss of old Paws, who had finally succumbed to cancer, and of all the cats I have loved so fondly throughout my life Ulli became, perhaps, my favourite in spite of his temper, wilfulness and habit of sitting draped across my shoulders and resting his front paws on my head as I laboured over Stafford and the novel that became *The Opawa Affair*.

One aspect of Christchurch that had not – unfortunately – altered over the years was its internecine musical rivalries, common enough in music worldwide but virulent in my beloved home city. I immediately made it known that I had no intention of joining in either the ancient or the more recently generated feuds, or of allying myself with any of the rival personality-driven cliques. I intended to work with everyone and anyone if they wanted to work with me. That was by no means a given, though Chris Doig, then Arts Centre director, welcomed me back with characteristic heartiness and gave me what became a succession of recitals with Iola Shelley at the Great Hall. Chris and I had much in common, having both had so much singing experience abroad, and having both been Clifton's pupils at Boys' High (though he and that other old boy professional tenor, Richard Greager, were a dozen years or so younger). We talked the same language as far as singing went. And through him and the opera company's chairman, Lew Brown (whom I had taught at Shirley Boys' High), I began to mend fences with Canterbury Opera, at least on a personal and social level, though I was far from impressed with its standard and, especially, much of its casting.

The strength of most London operatic performances has always been in the excellent casting of minor roles. The plain fact is that even the greatest stars must be supported by singers of the highest possible quality in order to perform at their best, and Gillian and I had already found that Wellington Opera had fallen very short in its casting policy. We weren't the only ones to identify such a weakness. A number of other former expatriate singers were returning home at the same time as me, notably Peter Baillie, who had been in Vienna almost as long as I had been in London. Our opinions on the state of operatic standards and casting, as we later discovered, coincided exactly.

Through John Pattinson, whose Jubilate Singers were now by far the city's best and most professional choir, I started giving lectures for the university's Continuing Education programme, and for the next decade or more lectured on opera, song and related topics. And I was soon broadcasting again, largely through the initiatives of Dorothy Hitch, Radio New Zealand's chief Christchurch producer: a series of 10 programmes on operetta that I scripted, sang and presented for National Radio. For the next decade there were also regular *Sunday Opera Hour* talks for Concert FM, before the series ended after they made cuts to their Christchurch department. I also contributed to a series of Victorian ballads for National Radio with Peter Zwartz and his Onslow Brass Band, and adjudicated some of the annual aria contests in Napier, Nelson, Dunedin and Invercargill. I am no fan of singing competitions and in my youth entered three only – including the first Mobil Song Contest in 1958. That was merely a radio ballad competition: there were hundreds of entries and I was a semi-finalist. I never cease to be surprised at the enormous celebrity that competition has attracted since then, though at least nowadays it is more professionally run and comprehensive in its requirements than it was when trifles like 'The Song of the Flea' and 'Come to the Fair' were winners. The fact remains that often the very qualities that can produce competition winners are not necessarily those that are needed for sustained survival in the harsh professional world. Judging is never easy and, with some international panels, can be affected by rival national and political considerations; and the sheer difficulty, and sometimes unfairness, of comparing sopranos with basses, tenors, mezzos and baritones can reduce decision making to a lottery. Sopranos tend to do best.

It did not take long before I was doing as much oratorio work as I now cared to do – from Invercargill to Napier and many places in between – though the Royal Christchurch Musical Society comprehensively ignored my presence. Not long before he died, Bob Field-Dodgson apologised for that, but I did not press him about the reasons or the identities of those who made the decisions.

I had a fair idea of who they were anyway, for as Gillian and I set about developing another singing teaching practice, those who did not wish us well became easily identifiable, and it was made clear that quite a number of people inside the city's musical community saw us as threats to their own empires. Their fears were based on misunderstandings about us and very much rooted in the rivalries generated inside amateur organisations. The last thing Gillian and I wanted was to take over anything; in as musically active a place as Christchurch there was room for everyone. But a thick skin was an absolute necessity and tact would be a useful quality too. However, tactfulness, I admit, was not a gift with which I was generously endowed.

By the end of our first year back in Christchurch we had more than 30 pupils, all adults whom we thought had talent and potential (we did not take schoolchildren). During the next few years the number steadily rose to average out at between 40 and 50. From the start of 1990 we also became vocal tutors for the University of Canterbury's School of Music, though that did not turn out to be satisfactory. It was certainly good and satisfying to work closely again with Maurice Till during our weekly Friday master-classes, and in both my own and the students' regular in-house recitals, but not all the permanent music staff were co-operative or supportive. Relationships between performers and academic musicians are seldom easy, but we were dismayed by some curious staff attitudes to the students themselves, and even an apparent distrust (by one or two lecturers) of their motives in seeking entry to performance courses. It did not seem to be, I fear, an especially happy department at that time, though Sarah, majoring in music, did enjoy her three years in it. Gillian and I were pleased to end our association with the School of Music when they finally decided to put all their meagre enough resources into instrumental teaching.

By then we were busier than ever: my writing and now regular opera seasons increasingly occupied my time, and Gillian took over the bulk of the teaching, with quite spectacular success, for she had the gifts of an analytical ear and an exceptional ability – far beyond mine – to explain complicated technical matters. While we had both been instinctive singers, she had a better understanding of technique and could articulate the intanglible. By 1995 she had assumed all the teaching.

I gave my last (and depressingly ill-attended) recital in the Great Hall, with Maurice and Iola sharing the accompaniment, on the 40th anniversary of my very first recital there. Then I happily withdrew to my study and all but retired from concert work.

But not yet from opera. Chris Doig's decision to stage Wagner's *Die Meistersinger von Nürnberg* as the centrepiece of Wellington's 1990 International Festival of the Arts was brave, inspired and a piece of imaginative madness that could have turned out to be an artistic disaster of massive and (for New Zealand) unprecedented proportions. Instead, it was a triumph, a unique achievement and the greatest event so far in New Zealand's operatic history. Getting Australian Opera's huge sets erected inside the Michael Fowler Centre was a minor engineering marvel: to put together the enormous cast of 17 principal singers, a dozen young and aspiring singers for the lively ensemble of Apprentices, a chorus of nearly 100 and the New Zealand Symphony Orchestra was another exercise in people management; and to have a conductor of Heinz Wallberg's eminence and the brilliant young Hungarian director Andreas Homoki to recreate Michael Hampe's splendid Australian Opera production was the crowning administrative achievement. During our month-long rehearsal period, Bill Southgate (more knowledgeable than most about Wagner's complexities) was the ideal assistant conductor, and Rosemary Barnes, formerly a repetiteur with English National Opera and with whom I had worked in London at a New Zealand House concert, was an indispensable pianist and coach.

The cast of principals was an interesting mix and was headed by Donald McIntyre, certainly New Zealand's greatest Wagnerian and, arguably, our greatest operatic singer of any voice. He had made his reputation as the *Ring Cycle*'s Wotan, as the Flying Dutchman and *Parsifal*'s Gurnemanz, but Sachs suited him perfectly. In every respect his was a towering performance, and it was matched by the brilliant

Beckmesser of the veteran German baritone Georg Voelker, son of one of pre-war Germany's most admired Wagnerian tenors but, unlike my late bête noir, John Heddle Nash, a delightfully easy-going and friendly man. His scenes with McIntyre were unforgettable and I doubt if they have ever been bettered on any New Zealand stage.

New Zealand, Australian and German-based American singers filled all the other roles, and for several of us returned expatriates it doubled as a reunion. Peter Baillie and I, youthful competing tenors in the late 1950s, had not actually met before; now, as the oldest of the masters, we worked happily in partnership (I was Ulrich Eislinger, grocer) and, during the frenetic riot scene in Act Two, executed a cunningly choreographed wrestling match that involved very little strenuous activity but much artful resting. It was one of the most enjoyable operatic seasons I've taken part in, though the friendly atmosphere seemed to come as a surprise to the younger singers making up the Apprentices. On the first day of rehearsal one, recently returned from England, brought me greetings from former colleagues in Kent Opera and she added that all the Apprentices were amazed at how friendly we were with one another – and how old most of us were too!

The *Meistersinger* season was a grand occasion, underwritten by Petrocorp, the Federal Republic of Germany and the New Zealand 1990 Commission. The great and the good attended and even Wolfgang Wagner (the composer's grandson) came from Bayreuth to meet and be photographed with us at a dress rehearsal. Opera buffs flocked to Wellington from every part of the country and even Australia. But our most enthusiastic and perceptive audience was the packed mass of schoolchildren at our final dress rehearsal who, in spite of having to endure a seemingly interminable delay when the scenery mechanism jammed, took McIntyre and Voelker, Sachs and Beckmesser, to their hearts.

Not all performances went without a hitch. The riot scene on opening night became a shambles when an electrician accidentally disconnected the backstage tannoy system, indispensable for keeping the conductor in touch with the huge forces on stage, and not all the major principals were ideally cast. But Wahlberg, unflappable and endlessly patient, presided over a very remarkable achievement, and the choral singing was glorious.

TVNZ's refusal to film this operatic milestone in its entirety was deplorable, and the documentary they did agree to produce was a facile and utterly inadequate record of one of the most momentous artistic and theatrical events in our cultural history.

For his 1992 International Festival (his last as director) Chris Doig presented another operatic masterpiece in collaboration with Australian Opera: Richard Strauss's *Salome*, conducted again by Heinz Wallberg. Now, though, following another steady influx of returning expatriates headed by Richard Greager, Rodney McCann and Patricia Payne, and the temporary return of our greatest operatic mezzo, Heather Begg, the cast was almost entirely a New Zealand one, apart from the Australian tenor Thomas Edmonds and the huge-voiced but tiresomely temperamental American dramatic soprano Marilyn Zschau. There were no weaknesses this time and the season was another operatic triumph.

I have to admit that I do not like *Salome*, but I was number three of five argumentative Jews, on stage thankfully for a limited time, and their very difficult but spectacular argument is satisfyingly brief. So during that season I was able to get in a large amount of historical research at the Turnbull Library (far more than I had been able to manage during *Meistersinger*) and I was able to more or less finish the Stafford biography. Two years later, a week or two after that book was launched in Christchurch by Bill Oliver, I enjoyed what was really a pleasant well-paid holiday for six weeks at the Adelaide Festival when the State Opera of South Australia mounted the same production of *Salome*, imported Chris Doig, Rodney McCann, Peter Baillie and me, and summoned Heather Begg from Sydney. I found Australian attitudes towards New Zealand singers were now very different from what they had been in 1962; they cheerfully acknowledged that they couldn't do without us.

By now too I was very much part of Canterbury Opera, happy

at this stage of my career to sing the character roles when asked (if they appealed to me), although, as always in the past, sometimes irked by long rehearsal periods. But when I was also appointed to the newly constituted Artistic Panel to advise on choice of operas and casting, along with conductor Brian Law and Dorothy Hitch (who had had a successful career with Australian Opera and the old New Zealand Opera Company), joined by Chris Doig a few years later, there were cries of outrage from some local teachers that I might favour my own and Gillian's pupils. How little they understood our attitudes! If anything, our pupils had a far lower chance than others of being cast. I had strong views about what was necessary to raise our operatic standards and there was absolutely no way I would rush any pupil into a role for which they were not ready; after all, my own and Gillian's reputation as teachers of singing were at stake too, and the surest way of damaging that was to cast someone who was unsuited or not ready. I am as unashamedly elitist about operatic casting as every All Black or Black Caps supporter is about selector choices: only the very best talent available is acceptable.

Gradually the message got through to everyone, and after a year or two those complaints ceased, though some still cherished dark suspicions about the panel's casting of me, Dorothy Hitch and Chris Doig in roles. In fact, we always left meetings when that risk occurred and we were, after all, among the country's most experienced singers. I think my performances justified my inclusion. Over 11 years I appeared in 13 productions, most of which I enjoyed and some of which were memorable, and Canterbury Opera was outstandingly successful during these years, the only one of the country's opera companies remaining financially viable (just), and continually being assured by Creative New Zealand that we were 'the jewel in their operatic crown'. During those years we were lucky enough to attract some outstanding singers from Canada, the USA, Britain and Australia as well as a host of superb and experienced New Zealand artists and a succession of very good directors. I'm especially proud that we helped launch the careers of Jared Holt (Gillian's pupil), Teddy Tahu Rhodes and Jud Arthur.

Unlike Wellington's City Opera, we resisted the amalgamation with Auckland's opera company or, as it effectively would have been, its takeover, and we resisted some powerful pressures. Helen Clark, for instance, was very keen to have one central opera company, and much Auckland and Wellington criticism was heaped on our unyielding shoulders, with some unkind northern souls even muttering darkly about our company being too much under the influence of 'geriatric' singers like Dorothy and me. It fell to my lot to explain our reasons to our prime minister and her husband during the first-night intervals of a season of *Faust*. I don't think she was especially happy but our conversations were friendly, she and her husband listened, and by the end of the evening they at least understood our determination to be the South Island's major operatic centre and accepted our reasons for wanting to remain independent of Auckland.

The company's administrative structure changed in 2000, and the Artistic Panel was made redundant when the colourful and imaginative Australian conductor Brian Castles-Onion was appointed as sole artistic director. He then cast me in *The Tales of Hoffmann*'s four comic roles and it was in their congenial skins that I happily made my farewell to Christchurch operatic audiences. That was certainly my own favourite season and I considered it a privilege to work with such remarkable and much younger singers as Paul Whelan (playing the four villains) and the Russian soprano Viktorya Dodoka as Antonia and the doll Olympia. Her subsequent roles for Canterbury Opera included the best Violetta in Verdi's *La Traviata* that I have seen outside Covent Garden. As for Paul Whelan, I'm confident that sometime in the not too distant future he should rightfully be recognised as one of our country's greatest singers – and in particular a world-class Wagnerian.

Eugene Onegin was another hugely satisfying season, and I think the role of Monsieur Triquet (the heroine Tatiana's old French tutor) has to be another of my favourites. It is also about the shortest role in the repertoire, but Tchaikovsky lavished all his genius on it and gave him one of the best tunes in the opera. We were lucky to have the outstanding Russian-American Alexander Gelman as our stage director. His later production for us of *The Barber of Seville* was as good as I've ever seen anywhere. For *Onegin* we had managed to assemble a very good cast headed by the Canada-based Auckland baritone Mark Pedrotti (also superb in a succession of other roles for our company), Malvina Major in quite her finest role as Tatiana (though her Lucia ran it close), and the very fine Canadian tenor Benjamin Butterfield as Lensky. Ben returned for our *Barber* too (the last opera our Artistic Panel cast) and, as an old and retired Almaviva, his performance in that role thrilled me greatly.

Malvina and I were also in Wellington City Opera's very different but almost equally good production of *Onegin*, where it was pleasant to work with my former Kent Opera colleague Sarah Walker, visiting from England, and with Rodney Macann, so often an operatic colleague in these years. His singing of Prince Gremin's aria must rank as one of his finest roles – closely approached by his Sharpless, the American Consul, in Phillip Mann's excellent production of *Madame Butterfly* for Wellington City Opera. That was their last production before they were absorbed into the expanding Auckland-based Opera New Zealand and it was a resounding triumph. Brian Law conducted it, as he had when Phillip directed the same production for Canterbury Opera some time before. Malvina (Butterfly) and I (as Goro) were in this too.

Goro the rascally marriage broker is a very good role and some people seemed to regard it as one of my better character parts. It was certainly one I performed frequently, but I have to confess (with profound apologies to all those who regard *Butterfly* as one of their all-time favourites) that I'm more or less immune to that opera's charms.

I achieved much more satisfaction from playing St Brioche in *Merry Widow*, another operetta of which I am very fond and which was yet another production with Malvina – as was *Lucia*. We have always been friends in everyday life and our operatic relationships have been many and varied and have always amused us: I was one of her most ardent and annoying suitors in *The Widow*; as Arturo, whom she is forced to wed in *Lucia*, she killed me (offstage); in *Butterfly* I sold her into a disastrous and ultimately fatal marriage; in *Onegin* I delivered a birthday tribute, though in Alex Gelman's production I also rather bullied her; in *Tosca*, as the police spy Spoletta I hounded her to her suicide; and as the insane and grotesque dwarf Pitichinacchio in the Venetian act in *The Tales of Hoffmann* I poisoned her.

I had great fun too as the smuggler Dancaire (outside France usually sung by baritones) in Canterbury's *Carmen*, which starred another former colleague, the renowned British mezzo Sally Burgess and my celebrated Australian baritone friend Geoffrey Chard, who had been in Henze's *End of a World* with me back in my London operatic debut in 1966. And playing the lecherous Moor Monostatos in *The Magic Flute* was even better fun in Elric Hooper's splendid production – quite his best. We had been less lucky with Verdi's *Otello* a few years previously when flu had struck down more than half the cast and blighted the season.

Canterbury Opera under Brian Castles-Onion and Elizabeth Owens continued to thrive and produced some ground-breaking and high-quality seasons until the company's untimely demise in 2006. From time to time Brian and Elizabeth continued to unofficially and informally consult me on some artistic matters. The full history of this company's rise and, especially, its eventual fall needs to be written some day, but not by me. I was too closely involved. The earthquakes have disrupted the progress of its successor, Southern Opera, as disastrously as they have the rest of Christchurch's cultural life, but nothing in its brief existence has equalled Canterbury Opera's finest achievements. They do not deserve to be forgotten.

My final bows as performer were at yet another Wellington International Festival the year after *Hoffmann* in 2002, as the Marschallin's Major Domo and the Innkeeper in Strauss's *Der Rosenkavalier*. Again, I have to admit that I dislike that opera as much as I do *Salome* and *Butterfly*. Yet it was another of the festival's major triumphs, with a superb cast led by the fine Australian soprano Yvonne Kenny and crammed with so many of New Zealand's best and most successful singers: Richard Greager, Barry Mora, Rodney McCann, Patrick

Power, David Griffiths, Helen Medlyn and a host of promising younger singers. And it was a pleasure to work with such a fine stage director as Gayle Edwards.

At 66, I was the eldest of the cast by at least six years (apart from Sir Jon Trimmer, who played the non-singing role of the Hairdresser), and the five young men who accompanied me throughout this very over-long opera as my lackeys and servants were young enough to be my grandsons. The rehearsals were protracted and arduous, and long before we even got to opening night I had decided it was time to retire, much as I enjoyed working with so many valued colleagues. The main reasons, however, were that by now my writing commitments were pressing too hard to allow me the luxury of dividing my time between writing and singing any longer and, crucially, I was not enjoying singing at all. The dark cloud hovering somewhere above my head with increasing frequency on performance days was too dense and persistent to ignore, and physically I was finding performing very exhausting. It was amusing to be described by Leslie Austin in *New Zealand Opera News* as 'a national treasure' at this stage of my career (along with Barry Mora and Richard Greager), but the season had left me a rather weary one.

At this time I was working on the book that became *Climates of War*, a summation of my work on New Zealand politics and politicians of the 1860s, and I was keen to finish *A Present for the Czar*, the fifth (and I thought probably the last) O'Rorke novel. To add to all that, on the very day we started rehearsals, Ray Richards offered me a commission from the Reed Trust to write a history of the publishing house A. H. & A. W. Reed. The terms were too good to turn down.

I could no longer continue to be a singing historian; from now on I would be a singer no more, simply an historian and writer. It was a relief: no more vocal exercises and practice every day, no more having to learn new works and endure the tedious grind of memorising reams of assorted German, Italian, French, English and even Russian texts. Steadfast against Gillian's arguments that I should at least still sing at home, I have scarcely sung a note since, though it was fun to join Chris Doig and Anson Austin as one of the three Old Boy Tenors for Boys' High's 125th anniversary concert in the Christchurch Town Hall. I was sorry Richard Greager hadn't been able to join us; we four tenors are the only professional operatic singers the school has yet produced. At present our ancient rival, Christ's College, is doing better.

THIRTEEN

Historian and Historical Novelist – Again

The critical success of *Edward Stafford: New Zealand's first statesman* with academics and the reading public was immensely gratifying, and justified not only my own efforts but, even more, Ray Richards' determination to find a publisher and Quentin Wilson's bold risk in publishing the book in the first place. He had been advised not to take such a risk, but his publishing house was not named 'Hazard' for nothing. Not that the long publishing process was without its irritating delays and potentially disastrous setbacks.

The first was my own fault: I had bought a word processor that was incompatible with Hazard's computers, so the manuscript had to be transcribed by one of Quentin's assistants. But much more serious was the refusal of Internal Affairs' History Branch to give it a publishing grant on the grounds that it was too long. That was a blow. They had, after all, bestowed on me one of their first research grants and they seemed very happy with the essays commissioned for each volume of the *Dictionary of Biography*. I was prepared to trim a little, but certainly not to wreck my book by trying to reduce what I considered to be a serious study of the most dynamic man in New Zealand's formative political age into the kind of short but inadequate portrait of a major colonial figure that had been far too common in our biographical writings so far. So I rang Rosemary Wildblood at the Arts Council and she, without committing herself or her organisation to anything, gave Quentin and me enough encouragement to apply to their literary fund. That resulted in a larger publication grant than the History Branch offered anyway.

Not long after publication a member of the History Branch's advisory committee asked me why we hadn't applied to them for the grant. I explained. Astonished, he insisted that he had never been shown the manuscript. I did not try to unravel that mystery, but I have a suspicion that my last chapter, 'Stafford and the Historians', might have caused offence to someone of influence.

By the time *Stafford* came out in 1994, Keith Sinclair was dead. He had been very interested in the project and reiterated every time we met that he had got Stafford 'wrong' in his Penguin *History*. He also knew that I was not going to let him forget how wrong he had been. Our last meeting was at the Turnbull Library and Keith, full of enthusiasm even when I told him exactly what I had written in that last chapter, vowed to review the book, preferably for the *Listener*. He'd be provocative – when wasn't he? But I should then write a scorching reply and we could keep up a correspondence in their letters columns if necessary, because he was sure that sort of thing was good for sales. Sadly none of that happened. He was rather unsteady on his feet that afternoon, so I rang for his taxi to get him to the airport, helped him into it, told the driver who he was, and asked him to make sure that Sir Keith got to the right checkout. I think he probably did.

The most gratifying aspect of Stafford's success was that the man had at last been brought back into our mainstream history. Yet there was another satisfying result too: politicians took notice, especially of Stafford's ability as the supreme creator and manipulator of governing coalitions. In 1994 and 1995, with MMP a burning issue, the subject of wide debate throughout the land and looming in all its uncertainty on the horizon, there could not have been a better time for this book's appearance. In the *Sunday Star-Times*

Michael Bassett urged everyone to read it specifically because, with its account of a political age in which all governments had to be coalitions, it was a timely warning. Prime Minister Bolger urged his people to read it, and he announced in the House that he intended to be another Stafford as a creator of coalitions. This prompted Helen Clark – as she has proudly reminded me several times at post-opera receptions – to raise a laugh by reminding him that there is a chapter entitled 'He deserted his old friends'. Sir Geoffrey Palmer gave it a plug too, on radio with Kim Hill and in a short column about what he was reading for the *Evening Post*, and among the many letters I received from readers was a very kind one from Speaker Doug Kidd. I am grateful to the politicians from both sides of the House for the incidental publicity they provided – and for buying the book.

A pleasant immediate result of *Stafford*'s appearance was that a number of his numerous descendants contacted me, surprised and delighted to have at last found out about their ancestor's New Zealand career. One, from Auckland, bearded and astonishingly like Stafford himself, visited me in Wellington; another sent me from Australia Stafford's informative and amusing 1859 travel diary; and her cousin and a brother wrote from England with more interesting family information, including the family tree dating back to the early kings of Scotland. I have edited the travel diary and deposited it in the Turnbull archives. I wish I'd had it sooner. It offers so much new information that my chapter on his important 1859 travels needs to be revised. When I met members of the family during our visit to Britain in 1997 to complete my research on my biography of Governor George Grey, I was able to take more notes from family papers and go through their photo albums.

Stafford made the finals of both book awards in 1995: as one of the three non-fiction finalists in the Arts Council's New Zealand Book Awards and as one of the 10 finalists in the Montana Book Awards. (The following year the two awards merged.) *Stafford* and C. K. Stead's *Singing Whakapapa* were the only books to be included in both. It was after the announcement of the Montana list that I had my first brush with Whitcoulls when I went into Christchurch's main shop in Cashel Mall and found that every finalist except my book was on display. For the first and only time I asked a bookshop's staff why it wasn't. They were mystified. They hadn't a copy and I doubt if they'd even heard of it. I suggested they go round and get some from Hazard Press in Gloucester Street. But they couldn't do that. All orders – and books, presumably – had to come from Auckland.

The announcement of the New Zealand Book Awards winners was made at an evening reception at Premier House on Tinakori Road, where the native trees Stafford had planted in the 1860s still flourished and from which he stubbornly refused to budge after his parliamentary defeat in 1869, to the exasperation of his few remaining friends and the sustained fury of William Fox who had defeated him. Our biography did not win, though there had been whispers during the afternoon that it was a favourite. It was beaten by a memoir of an elderly Auckland publisher; and when she appeared in her wheelchair accompanied by her Auckland publisher, Brian Easton cheerfully remarked that I clearly hadn't stood a chance. I was too young. Otherwise it was a good evening.

The Montana finalists were announced at a far more lavish ceremony at the Auckland Art Gallery, where I was accompanied by Sarah, by then living in Auckland, and again I met a host of interesting people as well as several friends of my youth not seen for more than 20 years. The splendid main gallery was festooned with giant banners celebrating each book (the Stafford banner is still rolled up in a cupboard, I think), and each finalist was presented with an inscribed pen (which I use daily) and a bottle of champagne. There were lots of photographs taken (none of which I ever saw) and promises of lots of publicity, but as with most literary festivities of this kind, I suspect that the general public was indifferent to our small literary community's annual spasm of excitement. I doubt if these events generate all that many book sales either.

Stafford did not win the Montana either. I wasn't surprised. He had been rated a 'worthy roughy' but 'a long odds outsider' by one pundit with an obvious horseracing bent, but he wasn't even placed.

As a result of my work on Stafford I became the 1995 J. D. Stout Fellow at Victoria University's Stout Centre, a hectic tenure but one from which I gained much and which I enjoyed enormously, for during it I was able to research not only my next biography, of the mercurial and vastly entertaining James Edward FitzGerald, but also start on a commission from Paul Bradwell of HarperCollins to write a short illustrated history of New Zealand that might appeal to young people. They were long-term projects, though the short history did have a deadline, and a very strict word length.

Alan Thomas and everyone at the Stout Centre made me very welcome. I rented a comfortable Salamanca Road flat owned by Hugh, Beverley and Susan Price, and I found the companionship of such congenial associates as Bill Renwick, John Mansfield Thomson, Jock Phillips (Neville's son), Barry Rigby and especially Brian Easton and Brad Patterson encouraging and intellectually stimulating. The Tuesday lunches, leisurely and long, were a weekly highlight, when often extravagant and always stimulating conversation flourished and even the arguments were good-tempered and informative. The Turnbull Library's staff also made me welcome, as did many in the wider historical community attracted to the Stout seminars and conferences. David Hamer, then Professor of History, was interested in what I was writing and invited me to deliver a lecture to a crowded undergraduate seminar on our New Zealand's 19th-century political world. Not all his departmental colleagues were as welcoming, and the pervasive influence of political correctness in some departments seemed to me to produce an unpleasant intellectual fascism far removed from the kind of free exchange of thought and opinion that a university should encourage. Once again I was glad I had chosen to make a career outside academia.

The illustrated history project, masterminded by Paul Bradwell at HarperCollins, was unlike any other book project in which I had so far been involved. Paul was coming to the end of his distinguished publishing career and had long cherished the idea of a popular history of New Zealand for young readers, but as our project developed he saw its potential for a general readership and I was able to relax a little and expand my own ideas. Paul was demanding. Once I began writing, after my intensive research period, he would phone every morning without fail (we never actually met face to face), suggesting minor changes, demanding little modifications such as seven more words on such and such a page or 12 fewer words on another and so on, and discussing where the illustrations should be placed. We agreed, disagreed amicably or made compromises, and we exchanged sharp words once only: when he demanded even more photographs. That tried my patience – and my pocket – too far. According to the contract, I was responsible for buying them, and by then the libraries were demanding ever-higher fees for their illustrative material. Paul apologised profusely and gave me a small extra subsidy.

It was his last publishing project and he retired soon after I had completed the manuscript. But before he did depart the scene he rang to thank me for including him in my acknowledgements. I was astonished to learn that I was the only author who had ever done so.

New Zealand: The story so far was well received and bought by quite a number of schools and in satisfactory numbers by libraries, so its only edition was sold out comparatively soon. When I wanted to give a copy to my grandson Frederick's school, St Mark's Opawa (I had dedicated it to Freddy), it had to be my own last one. Boosted by the annual Lending Right proceeds, it has also become the best earner of all my books.

I was attracted to FitzGerald as a biographical subject by the man's extraordinary range of interests and abilities, what to his contemporaries was his all but overwhelming personality, and the fact that, like Stafford, he was an Irishman who, although personally far more popular than Stafford (whom he loathed) and socially the epitome of the Irish aristocrat, was often pilloried for being an archetypal 'stage' Irishman. Increasingly I was concerned to reveal the racial divisions inside the British communities that made up colonial Pakeha New Zealand. It had been an argument I had often with Keith Sinclair, who refused to admit that the differences between Britain's mutually antagonistic racial groups – Irish, Scots, Welsh and English – and their religious beliefs were of much historical consequence in New Zealand. But I came from a mixed Scottish Presbyterian and Irish Catholic heritage and all too often the Reevesian-influenced and almost exclusively secular New Zealand history with which I had been fed did not reflect my own or my family's experiences and observations. Twenty-five years in Britain had left me in no doubt about the intense mutual dislikes and prejudices that existed not only between the four main races, but inside those racial communities too: between North and South Welsh, Lowlander and Highland Scot, Protestant Ulsterman and Catholic Ulsterman and between the various regional English. I'd discovered that regional conflict in no uncertain terms even inside the ISM: the northern dislike and suspicion of London and the home counties was just the most obvious. And the Celtic South West bred a very different people from the Norse-influenced fenlands of Lincolnshire.

The emergence of powerful and radical nationalist political parties in the 1970s was a manifestation (sometimes violent) of these ancient rivalries, and by then the serious newspapers were debating the issues and already lamenting the eventual fragmentation of the British Isles. Similarly, colonial New Zealand was not a place inhabited merely by Maori and a blandly homogeneous race of British Pakeha. Old prejudices and historical grudges came on the immigrant ships, and even though in time they mellowed they were still alive and sometimes kicking during my formative years.

FitzGerald was a true renaissance man, as a mere list of his accomplishments and achievements shows: would-be poet (a poor one), all-round intellectual, journalist, essayist, artist and woodcarver, architect, singer, civil servant, politician, farmer, and always controversialist. He was the first secretary of the Colonial Reform Society; friend of Gladstone, John Robert Godley, Lord Lyttelton and Edward Gibbon Wakefield (before becoming his unforgiving enemy); he was the first Canterbury pilgrim ashore; first editor of the *Lyttelton Times*; Canterbury's first superintendent; arguably our first premier in the disastrous first parliament of 1854; founder of the *Press*; New Zealand's first Comptroller General of Finance; a founder of the Public Service Association and first president of the Incorporated Society of Accountants. He was also the beloved husband of Fanny Erskine Draper, one of the most accomplished, witty and interesting of colonial wives, and the adored father of a very large family – as far removed from being an archetypal grim Victorian pater familias as anyone could imagine. And in spite of his reputation as the greatest orator in an age of political oratory never subsequently equalled in our history, he failed as abysmally in politics as he did in farming and business.

I couldn't resist a subject as colourful as that. I wasn't the first to attempt a biography: at least three others had begun but given up the struggle, and their notes added mightily to the already vast archival hoard of FitzGerald material and other collections spread between Canterbury Museum, the Canterbury Public Library, the Turnbull and Victoria University Library. This time Canterbury University Press was the publisher, and I now had the happy and always rewarding experience of working with Mike Bradstock and Richard King. When Mark Stocker gathered a series of essays for his book *Remembering Godley*, I provided one on the close friendship FitzGerald and Godley shared. I fear I do not have as high an opinion of John Robert Godley as do some of his more enthusiastic and uncritical admirers.

'Blest Madman': FitzGerald of Canterbury came out in 1998, and in some ways was overshadowed by appearing at the same time as my third major historical biography of yet another renaissance man, Sir George Grey.

To Be a Hero was another commission from HarperCollins, but this time from Ian Watt, who had taken over from Paul Bradwell. Some time before publication of *New Zealand: The story so far*, Ian took me out for a very good lunch, and over an even better bottle of wine remarked that 1998 marked the centenary of Grey's death. Would I care to produce a biography of no more than 120,000 words to celebrate it? I would have about 18 months to do it. I considered the offer deeply for at least half a minute and committed myself. Grey had fascinated and also repelled me since I'd met him, as it were, back in 1958 when I was writing my thesis and decided he was more or less mad, and I had turned him into a comic character in *The Opawa Affair*. By now I had a mass of research material left over from my old thesis, the Stafford and FitzGerald books and the copious notes I had made from the *Hansard*s of the 1850s to the 1880s. I started work later that same day and drafted the chapters on the Grey government (1877–79) and the 1879 election.

They were the easy parts. After that I went up to Auckland and, under the eagle and friendly yet critical eye of Grey's doughty champion, Donald Kerr, plunged into the goldmine that is the Grey manuscript collection. I emerged with a much more balanced view of the most extraordinary of all our extraordinary 19th-century personalities. After that I worked longer hours even than usual, and Creative New Zealand generously gave me a grant to finish it and travel to London to complete research. We stayed with Sebastian (at that time seconded from the Foreign Office to be personal secretary to the Cabinet Secretary in Downing Street) and his growing family in Sevenoaks. Years before, he had provided the photographs of Stafford's long-neglected grave in Kensal Green Cemetery, which he, his wife Sirinat (Nok) and Gillian had literally stumbled across. Now he photographed Grey's grave in St Paul's Crypt, and when the generous tourist guides learnt that I was writing his biography they not only escorted us past the long slow-moving tourist queues, but waived the entry fees too.

To Be a Hero is, I am proud to say, a balanced portrait of Grey. His detractors considered me far too kind; his devotees – and there are still those – considered me too censorious. I concluded I must have got him nearly right, and for once could agree wholeheartedly with Keith Sinclair's opinion that Grey was arguably the most remarkable man who has ever lived here.

Once again the reviews were mainly good. There were academic quibbles: it was too short and not as 'scholarly' as Rutherford's very long biography published 35 years before, and I suspect that at least two or three distinguished academic historians were miffed because I had actually got around to writing it while they had merely been considering doing so in some future leisurely retirement. Interestingly, after my research grant was announced, Geoff Walker of Penguin had written to ask if I had a publisher and, if not, whether they might consider it. He said he had for some years pondered a new Grey biography but had not been able to interest several academics in his project.

As for length, it was relatively short because that's what a very commercially minded publishing house demanded. Rutherford had laboured over his massive volume for more than a dozen years; I had 18 months. I'm glad it wasn't like Rutherford's book, though I do give Rutherford credit for having a better prose style than so many of his successors. As a book reviewer I am continually appalled by how badly so many academics write.

The book sold well and has been widely read. Some years later I was commissioned to write a shorter version (*Hero to an Age*) specifically for South Africa, where the schools Grey and his wife founded during his momentous and dramatic governorship have flourished mightily. That was published in South Africa in 2009.

To Be a Hero also made the 1999 Montana finals, one of the three non-fiction choices, joining Gordon Ogilvie's superb *Denis Glover: His Life* and Kevin Ireland's memoir *Under the Bridge and Over the Moon*. I had enjoyed meeting Kevin at various book launches. This time Montana hosted no elaborate pre-match festivities on the 1995 scale, but I enjoyed the evening when the winners were announced in Wellington, though to start with I thought I wouldn't. Before I got there I had visited Te Papa for the first time and came away from it in a far from happy frame of mind; Bill Oliver said ruefully that he fully understood why I was slightly grumpy. He had been too when he first went there. I'm told our capital's cultural icon has improved greatly; I hope so.

Meeting him, Gordon Ogilvie, and a large number of other friends at the reception helped me recover my good spirits soon enough, and I was not surprised or cast down when I didn't win; after all, the Auckland chief judge had referred to me rather dismissively on National Radio as 'scribbling away down in Christchurch'. However, I was amazed and disappointed when Gordon didn't win.

Subsequently, I was pleased to be able to discuss Grey in two television series: TVNZ's *Frontier of Dreams*, and Prime's *New Zealand's Top 100 History Makers*.

Throughout these years I was also writing the O'Rorke novels, the origin of which lay far back in my researches for my 1958 thesis. *The Opawa Affair* came out in 1996 and was generally well reviewed, sold steadily enough and it is still in demand by library borrowers. Some critical minds agonised about exactly what genre it belonged to, but I hadn't really been bothered about that. It was an historical novel with a mystery or two at its centre. It was not simply a crime novel, even though its central character happened to be a colonial police detective, but an ironical Victorian melodrama and a comedy of manners concerned with hypocrisy, obsessions and the class and racial bigotries that dominated our colonial world. It was the kind of novel appearing frequently in Britain and America, and as Lawrence Jones described it in his chapter on the novel in the 1998 edition of *The Oxford History of New Zealand Literature in English,* it was 'a sophisticated contemporary version of the Victorian sensation novel'. Others got the point too, and I especially liked Nelson Wattie's summation in *New Zealand Studies* when he observed how its cover – George Leslie's fascinating late Victorian painting *The Wizard's Garden* – 'suggests much of what is inside: elegance, mystery, autumnal sadness, careful design and a pre-Raphaelite sensuality. Although short, it is a book of several dimensions.'

The book's original title had been *Turn on Old Time*, the opening lines of a trio from Vincent Wallace's opera *Maritana*, whose performance by a visiting opera company lies at the heart of the story, and a fine piece that I had, incidentally, recorded on London Concert Artists' first commercial recording, *When Song is Sweet* in the late 1970s. In many ways it was a more apt title because another underlying theme is how the past returns to haunt and accuse even as time pushes on relentlessly, but Quentin and others thought a more specific identification with part of Victorian Christchurch (in which I happened to live) was more appropriate. Probably they were right. The Allens' house, in which so many dark deeds occur, was inspired by that fine 1879 villa on Opawa Road that one sees so clearly from the Shell Service Station on Brougham Street.

'Turn on Old Time', however, is very much the overriding theme of the O'Rorke series as a whole. Even before *The Opawa Affair* came out we had decided that the character of O'Rorke himself was worth persevering with and developing further. So I started on *The Dancing Man*, which was published in 1997.

The Dancing Man is not a murder mystery. It is simply an historical novel, the darkest toned of the series and in many ways the first specifically O'Rorke book. I like to think of *The Opawa Affair* as a prologue to his saga. *The Dancing Man* also has the most complex plot, with much shifting of times and places as O'Rorke's Fenian past, the horrors of his Crimean experiences and incidents of his Civil War years are laid bare and return to threaten him. It is also the story of Catherine Martin. She is O'Rorke's great love, though a powerful rival for that honour, Rebecca Rothstein, was to appear in the next story, *The Matter of Parihaka*. Kate and Rebecca are my favourite characters, rivalled only by O'Rorke himself.

Again, the themes of this story are obvious: the rigid codes of Victorian military honour, inexorable retribution, sexuality and society's hypocrisy, religious bigotry and the abrasive relationship between colonial Christchurch's English and Irish communities.

The Dancing Man has been the least popular O'Rorke novel and it is not a particularly easy read, yet in so many ways, perversely perhaps, it is my favourite. And writing it introduced me to Anna Rogers, who not only edited it but, with infinite and friendly patience and tact, has guided me safely through several subsequent books as well.

The third O'Rorke, *The Matter of Parihaka*, appeared in 2000 and, in contrast to *The Dancing Man*, has been quite the most popular of the series. It has been the most widely and generously reviewed of all five books, its initial print run sold out, and it seems to be the most frequently discussed by book clubs and borrowed from libraries. Its scheduled and imminent reprint was one of the many casualties when the receivers finally ended Hazard Press's 21-year existence.

The story is reasonably straightforward. In 1882 O'Rorke is appointed by the government to investigate allegations of police brutality perpetrated during John Bryce's notorious invasion of Parihaka in November 1881, and is, in brief, a political thriller, though like the others also a comedy of colonial manners. It includes other characters I like very much: the irrepressible Janet Robertson, Taylor, his ex-Irish Constabulary father-in-law Old Tom Smith, and two who appeared in *The Opawa Affair* – Henare Greaves and George White. One of the delights of creating a series is that there is time and space to develop its characters.

Number four, *The Irish Yankee*, runner-up in the 2001 Richard Webster Popular Fiction Award and published in 2002, is different again from its predecessors, and that was a conscious decision. I was never interested in establishing a formulaic pattern. I leave that to those who are purely practitioners of crime fiction and murder mysteries and whose work I enjoy reading for pleasure. O'Rorke is certainly called on to solve some murders, but not many, and for most that do occur the perpetrator is obvious enough but simply needs to be caught. O'Rorke is essentially a political detective and a complex man haunted by his past. There are no murders in *The Dancing Man*, and those in *The Irish Yankee* are incidental to the attempts of his old enemies from the American Civil War to exact their revenge on O'Rorke himself.

A Present for the Czar, originally to be the last O'Rorke novel, appeared in 2003 and is set during the real and extraordinary period of the Russian scare of 1885, when a world war between the British and Russian empires seemed inevitable. Near hysteria had been whipped up by sensationalist newspaper editors and influential pressure groups of Polish refugees from their failed revolutions of 1848 and 1866, for it was believed that Russian naval vessels might threaten the large gold deposits held in Dunedin, Auckland

and Melbourne banks. New Zealand and the Australian colonies reorganised their volunteer militias, imported Armstrong guns and erected gun batteries to defend their ports. It was also a period when Maori taonga were being acquired or stolen and sold to an eager European market. The Austrian collector, taxidermist and explorer Andreas Reischek, Dr Julius von Haast's companion during their expeditions in the Southern Alps and later in Fiordland, was the most notorious.

All that was my historical background, and a new character, the colourful Colonel Jamieson, is modelled loosely on the real and remarkable Colonel James de Renzie Brett. At last O'Rorke has to choose between his lovers. And for the first time he is faced with a true villain, a man of many names and appearances but known to Southern Ngai Tahu, Henare Greaves' people, as Boyland the Collector. I wished I'd invented him sooner.

Some reviewers and some of O'Rorke's fans (yes, he has a sturdy faithful band of those here and in England) rated this the best of the series, and its edition also seems to have been sold out by the time Hazard folded. Certainly the receivers could find no copies, and as I've only one left myself I scour the second-hand bookshops for more. I've only one of *Parihaka*, too, so I search for that as well. I find the good second-hand copies advertised by British and American online bookshops too expensive!

And of course it wasn't the last of the series. I did write a sequel to the *Czar* – *Taonga*. It was set and ready for the printer when first a shocked Ray Richards and then a devastated Quentin rang within minutes of one another to break the news that the receivers were on the premises and had taken over.

Whitcoulls' book buyers had what Quentin and I thought a rather peculiar attitude to the O'Rorke novels: a policy of stocking very few copies and not reordering them when they were sold, but then claiming that they did not sell in large enough numbers to warrant stocking the later books. It was no wonder that during the years when the former Whitcoulls management reigned so undeservingly supreme within our book trade, New Zealand books generally sold in comparatively small numbers.

While I was writing the O'Rorke books I was continuing with non-fiction endeavours. *The House of Reed: Great days in New Zealand publishing* was another massive research project, for there was the huge Reed archive in the Turnbull Library, containing not simply all the firm's papers but also the remarkable correspondence between A. H. Reed and A. W. (Clif) Reed, who from 1932 until A. H.'s death in January 1975 wrote to one another almost every day with detailed, frank and very revealing information on the firm's progress, its authors and its staff. In addition I received an enormous amount of material and help from Ray Richards, so crucial to the company's expansion and dominance; David Elworthy, another who had a major impact; other company ex-employees; and the Reed family. John Reed in Australia gave me all his papers, with carte blanche to do with them whatever I wished. He never wanted to see them again, he said. I took him at his word and have since deposited them in the Turnbull to join the rest of this treasure trove of New Zealand publishing history.

The last decade of this truly iconic firm was dramatic and rent with internal dissension as the accountant Malcolm Mason gradually assumed control before his own eventual dismissal by Clif Reed, followed a few years later by John Reed's sale of the company. As I soon discovered, the emotions generated then still ran deep and many scars were far from being healed. Having never been a Reed author I considered that my narrative of those events was impartial and my conclusions measured.

Not everyone thought so. Malcolm Mason's sons were incensed by what they regarded as my unfair treatment of a man they both admitted could be difficult and controversial, and Andrew Mason assailed me with furious letters accusing me of not having consulted him but only his father's enemies. I reminded him that I was not writing a biography of his father but of a company that had changed the face of New Zealand publishing; had even more or less invented it. Of all the many people I consulted, not one had actually had a good word to say about his father – not even generous and mild Hugh Price.

Otherwise the three years this commission consumed were pleasant ones and I was always amused when writers with whom I was sharing the Turnbull would enquire, sometimes with an all too obvious air of indifference, whether there was any mention of them in the Reed Papers. Michael King, though, never pretended indifference: he was eager to know if I'd come across any reasons why Reed had turned down his first book; he was still offended. I pleaded ignorance, but I had found the editor's report. He'd simply thought it rather poor. And I was amused when another of our eminent literary men assured me firmly that of course he'd never had any dealings with Reed. I knew he had: they had turned down his early poems two or three times.

About the time I was finishing *The House of Reed*, Quentin offered me the choice of two commissions: one was a biography of a well-known local lady renowned for her sponsorship of the arts and all manner of good works and who, apparently, favoured me as her biographer; the other was a biography of Philip Burdon. The latter had already been contracted, but neither the Burdons nor Richard Griffin, who was driving the project, were happy with the arrangement.

There was no competition as far as I was concerned: I had met Ros Burdon often while she was on Canterbury Opera's Board but had only a nodding acquaintance with Philip. Yet I had followed his career with interest and I was attracted by the challenge of writing about recent New Zealand affairs. Always the pragmatist, I abandoned my vow made at the Stout seminar eight years before and accepted his commission, transferred his papers and personal archive from Hazard's office to my study, and plunged into a political world far stranger to me than my familiar 19th-century one.

My long absence from New Zealand and my hitherto very sketchy knowledge of the Muldoon years was a great advantage, for little of its storms and controversies had caused more than an occasional and barely discernable ripple in the wider British media. My ideological and emotional detachment from any New Zealand political party was an even greater benefit. The project proved to be an absorbing one, for Philip is a very interesting man who is in so many ways a paradox: far from being the Anglocentric conservative his family background might suggest, I discovered a nationalist republican, a self-made millionaire with a powerful social conscience, a liberal who fought hard against his party's right-wing ideologues, a dynamic Trade Minister during the protracted GATT negotiations of the Uruguay Round, a founder of the Asia 2000 Foundation and a champion of multicultural harmony.

Richard Griffin did the honours at the largest-ever book launch held in Christchurch's Great Hall; Winston Peters starred at the lively and companionable one at Turnbull House in Wellington; and Don Brash, perhaps not quite sure why he had been invited, launched it at a lunch at Auckland's handsome and historic Northern Club, where long ago the elderly and eccentric Sir George Grey was cold-shouldered by disapproving fellow members. The book's reception followed predictable lines: those who didn't like Burdon's politics sneered, and one or two former politicians of eminence felt unaccountably insulted. Most of those expressing opinions, however, liked it.

Climates of War (2005) was the summation of my 15 years' work on the politics and politicians of the 1860s: the Stafford, FitzGerald and Grey biographies, and the numerous articles, essays and lectures I had written and delivered on them and their contemporaries. It is not, however, merely about the wars fought over that period between Maori and British, Maori and settler and Maori against Maori. Perhaps I should have given it another title: *Biography of a Decade* or something like that, because it is about the constitutional warfare for self-determination between settlers and the British government, and between New Zealand's central and provincial governments – political conflicts culminating in the abolition of the provinces, the emergence of a Maori nationalism and the entry of Maori into parliament. I also tried to place New Zealand's various struggles in a world context: that decade's momentous events, wars and civil wars worldwide shaped not only much of our modern world, but quite a number of New Zealand's concurrent civil debates and problems also.

Its initial printing seems to have been all but sold out: Hazard's receivers found few copies, and librarians tell me it is borrowed frequently. I was also gratified by most of the reviews, especially those that praised my objectivity and 'dispassionate eye'. But what I liked best was to be described as 'mercilessly detached'. As an historian I'd be quite happy to have that as my epitaph.

Climates of War was not meant to be my last foray into New Zealand's 19th-century political maelstrom. While I was working on it in the Turnbull, Ray Fargher told me that after nearly 60 years intermittent labour he had finally given up ever completing his biography of Sir Donald McLean, Grey's and Governor Gore Browne's controversial Land Purchase Commissioner and Native Secretary, Fox and Vogel's Native Minister and one of Hawke's Bay's early settlers and major landowners. Some time later, and at the suggestion of several other historians, I decided to write one myself. Not that I liked McLean: he had been Stafford's political nemesis, a grim and largely humourless Presbyterian bigot who had none of the wide intellectual interests Stafford, FitzGerald and Grey shared. And he was a poor parliamentary performer. But because of his importance in his time, and the disastrous consequences of so many of his land purchases that have, in effect, given the Waitangi Tribunal reason to exist, a new biography was needed. So I drafted a book proposal, received a large grant from Creative New Zealand, undertook extensive research during the next year, and got as far as writing 15,000 words of text. I presented a paper – 'Te Makarini: Turbulent Highlandman: Towards a new biography of Donald McLean, 1820–1877' – to the 2007 conference 'Scots Abroad: The New Zealand Scots in International Perspective', which Brad Patterson so ably organised for the Stout Centre.

I was more than a little surprised at the end of that presentation when Ray Fargher told me that he had, after all, resumed his book and it would be published at long last in another year. But it would clearly be very different from mine, he added, because I was concentrating on McLean as politician. Ray was being far too sanguine on my behalf, though there was no doubt that my book would have been radically different. There was little chance of any publisher issuing two books on McLean within a few years of one another, so I abandoned my effort forthwith, wrote a long report to Creative New Zealand, put my finished chapters into a file box, and deposited that in the vast hall cupboard that houses my own personal archive.

The Brad Patterson-inspired conferences on Irish and Scottish Studies, under the auspices originally of the Stout Centre but latterly Massey University, have all been great events at which it has been my huge pleasure to meet, exchange ideas, talk endlessly and drink Guinness with so many fellow historians and writers whose companionship I value and whose company I have enjoyed. As well as that on McLean, I have given papers at these events on the Irish in New Zealand politics 1860–80, on the journalist politicians Crosbie Ward and John Williamson, and on Colonel James de Renzie Brett, hero of the East India Company wars, deputy commander of the ferocious irregular Arab and Albanian Bashi Bazouks in the Crimea, outspoken legislative councillor and champion of Canterbury small farmers against the run-holders. Apart from the essay on McLean, they have been subsequently published in the books Brad has edited after each conference: *The Irish in New Zealand: Historical contexts & perspectives* (2002); *Ulster–New Zealand Migration and Cultural Transfers* (2006); and *Ireland and the Irish Antipodes: One world or worlds apart?* (2010).

Other presentations I have given to conferences such as those organised by the New Zealand Society of Genealogists have also been published over the years.

FOURTEEN

CULTIVATING AN OPAWA GARDEN – BUT NOT RETIRING

VOLTAIRE'S CANDIDE, STILL CONVINCED in spite of his appalling experiences that all was for the best in the best of all possible worlds, retired to cultivate his garden. I, never accepting that it is the best of all possible worlds but being, above all, a pragmatist without illusions, certainly do enjoy cultivating my garden, though I do not intend to retire from the world.

The slow onset but remorseless progress of Gillian's Parkinson's has circumscribed our social activities in many different ways but not dampened our predominantly cheerful natures or the strong sense of humour we've always shared. Travel has become a casualty. With Sebastian serving as the British ambassador to China we would have hugely enjoyed exploring Beijing, the Great Wall of China, the Ming Tombs and all the other fascinating sights and sounds, but Skype is a wonderful invention and we make do with face-to-screen encounters. Sebastian Skypes every week – largely, I suspect, to make sure that our minds are not being adversely affected by our addiction to watching *Midsomer Murders*, *Poirot* and *Lewis* – and he visits us whenever he can manage to. Sarah, her partner John and the three children, Freddy, George and Vanessa, are only a few blocks away and we see them daily so are comfortably but firmly kept in proper order. I think I enjoy being a grandfather more than anything else I've been. Life is never dull.

Nor is it ever without lots to do, the major problem often being too few hours in the day or days in the week to do it all.

I have enjoyed gardening all my life, even as a child 'helping' Father whose meticulously tended vegetable gardens and roses were always his pride and joy. The worst trouble I ever got into during my childhood was when he got home from work one evening to find the garden littered with the seed potatoes whose sowing he'd been looking forward to all day. My friends and I had emptied an entire sea chest of them and had a glorious battle. Father's shouts shook the street and I fled across the back fence and stayed up at the top of a large blue gum until Mum had calmed him enough for me to creep back home in safety. Father never hit me, either then or on any other occasion; he had a mighty voice and his shouting alone was always sufficient to bring me back to civilised behaviour.

Luckily none of my gardens have ever suffered such damage from children and grandchildren. The worst our long narrow vegetable garden at 124 Faraday Road in Wimbledon had to endure was a raid by a huge and ferocious escaped pet rabbit that decimated my cabbages, broccoli, peas, runner beans and courgettes while the neighbourhood's cats (including our Paws) watched from a safe distance. A large and angry rabbit can do terrible damage to a careless cat. I cultivated no vegetables at Queen's Road or Bournemouth Road in Folkestone. Instead I lavished much care on roses, bulbs and all kinds of perennials, and I do the same here in Opawa with, additionally, a wide variety of bushes and trees, camellias, azaleas and rhododendrons. I wage unceasing war against weeds, and although one can never hope to defeat the enemy, it provides wonderful exercise. So do laying down new brick paths, re-routing old ones and carrying out some new scheme of minor landscaping. The bricks salvaged from our four chimneys – toppled by the September 2010 earthquake that so changed everyone's lives here and reawakened us to the things in life that really matter – have been of inestimable use in my path making and I walk on them every day as I do my garden rounds. I know of no more soothing activity than tending one's garden to help banish – even if only temporarily – the cares and frustrations that affect the lives of both singers and writers.

Reading comes closest. My reading tastes (not taking into account what I am called on to review) haven't really changed in essence since I was a child: predominantly non-fiction, and especially history and biography, though I do also read a lot of fiction. That in recent years has come to include much crime writing and, as ever, historical fiction in all its tremendous variety – increasingly including the vast range of historical crime. I still enjoy Sherlock Holmes and I still get occasional pleasure rereading the traditional or 'classic' whodunit of Agatha Christie, Dorothy Sayers, Margery Allingham and their ilk, though I confess to finding our Ngaio Marsh unreadable. I think her autobiographical writing is by far her most interesting and best; I have always been far more repelled by her snobbery and intellectual arrogance than that of her much greater English contemporaries.

And while I admire Ian Rankin's skill and characterisation I don't really care for the contemporary obsessions with the minutiae of forensics of a Kathy Reich. For an entertaining read give me any day (among a great many others) that remarkable Russian Boris Akunin (very much a favourite), Iain Pears, Frank Tallis and so many others. And I can always happily reread Bernard Cornwell's *Sharpe* historical novels with pleasure, though so far Sebastian has failed to convert me to Patrick O'Brian's Napoleonic sea sagas.

My 19th-century literary loves remain constant: Wilkie Collins' *Woman in White, The Moonstone, No Name* and *Armadale*; George Eliot's *Middlemarch*; Trollope's Palliser and Phineus Finn political novels (but the Barsetshires only occasionally); the Charles Dickens of *Bleak House, Hard Times, Little Dorritt* and *Our Mutual Friend*; and Leo Totstoy's *War and Peace*. I can never understand why that latter is so often quoted as a great 'unreadable', any more than I can fathom the inclusion of James Joyce's *Ulysses* in such a list. Clearly the people who seem to derive peculiar pleasure in deriding them as over-long or boring haven't actually read them. I couldn't be without them, any more than I could dispense with the music of Bach and Haydn, Schubert, Brahms, Mendelssohn, Berlioz, Chopin or Dvorak. *Ulysses* is a great book for dipping into, and for an old singer with a taste for the 19th-century operas and songs that Joyce himself (an aspiring, even fanatical, tenor) loved, sang, quoted or referred to so often, a perennial delight.

As I grow older I read fewer and fewer purely 'literary' or 'serious' novels. Life is simply too short. Nor do I listen to singers or opera very much nowadays either, though Gillian does, for she retains her professional interest. But I can always still be uplifted and find new inspiration in Bach's *St Matthew Passion*, in spite of having sung in it so often for over 40 years, and I could never tire of Gilbert and Sullivan. Mostly, though, we listen to chamber, orchestral and piano music. And if it weren't for Sky TV we wouldn't watch television at all. New Zealand's free-to-air TV companies clearly lost, many years ago, any slight interest they might ever have had in people of our age group and with our tastes and interests.

Speaking engagements continue to keep me as busy as I want to be and I enjoy them fully as much as I once did giving concerts. They invariably double as very agreeable social events too, as do book launches and similar kinds of functions, though I seem to attend far too many funerals. There are still possible new books to think about, or unpublished manuscripts to reconsider and maybe tinker with, and one day I really must knuckle down to sorting and putting in order the bulging file boxes of letters, newspaper cuttings, diaries, concert and opera programmes and assorted papers (well over 100 boxes of them) that fill my hall cupboard, invade my study and have been so indispensable to the writing of these memoirs, for unaided memory alone can sometimes play tricks with the chronology of one's life.

I have always been sceptical of the real value of oral history as a reliable guide to the past rather than a sometime colourful embellishment of established fact, and writing this memoir reinforced that scepticism as I repeatedly delved into my archives to make sure I'd got things right and that my memory had not misled me. I experienced a quite remarkable instance of how plain wrong oral history can be years ago in the late 1960s when I was doing a concert in Tonypandy, south Wales, one of the Rhondda's most famous mining towns, and was walking slowly to the concert venue with the local conductor's aged father. He was a dear old man, a frail little ex-miner wracked by explosive coughing fits, every one of which threatened to send him tottering into a wall. So he clung tightly to my arm until he stopped suddenly and pointed a trembling hand at a particular spot in the main street. That, he then assured me solemnly, was the very place where Winston Churchill had stood in 1910 when he gave orders for the troops to fire on the striking miners and rioting citizens. He, a young striking miner himself at the time, had seen Churchill with his own eyes. The troops had killed many miners and it was Churchill's fault. He had hated the miners. The Welsh had never forgiven him.

At least that last statement was true, but not the rest. There had been only one death on 8 November 1910 – from a police baton – and Churchill, then Liberal Home Secretary, hadn't left London and was actually supportive of the miners in their dispute with their employers. But our walk to the concert was neither the time nor the place to lecture this gentle but dying old man on historical truth and fallible memory reinforced by steadfastly held political and ideological opinion. Even in the 1960s and 1970s most south Welshmen still blamed Churchill for Tonypandy.

That incident brought home to me again the sheer power of myth, and New Zealand history, I fear, is still as permeated and afflicted by myth and new myth-making as it was in the 1950s when I began waging my own war against its falsities. I fear I'll never really win that war – just as I'll never really win my war against garden weeds – but I'll go on fighting all the same. I think old writers are like old soldiers are supposed to be, and I've no intention yet of fading away.

ACKNOWLEDGMENTS

My thanks to Rachel Scott, Publisher at CUP, for encouraging and agreeing to publish this memoir, and to her staff, headed by Kaye Godfrey. I am also grateful to Antoinette Wilson, my editor, for her insight, expertise and the suggestions that have, I believe, made this a better book than it might have been, and to my good friend Quentin Wilson for his design. Working again with this group of longstanding friends, all of whom have been involved with so many of my previous books, has made it one of my most enjoyable publishing experiences.

And, as always, my heartfelt thanks go to Gillian for her love, companionship, encouragement and ever-vigilant critical eye over the last 45 years.